D0398080

The Maltese Falcon

Rutgers Films in Print

Charles Affron, Mirella Jona Affron, and Robert Lyons, editors

My Darling Clementine, John Ford, director
edited by Robert Lyons

The Last Metro, François Truffaut, director
edited by Mirella Jona Affron and E. Rubinstein

Touch of Evil, Orson Welles, director
edited by Terry Comito

The Marriage of Maria Braun, Rainer Werner Fassbinder, director
edited by Joyce Rheuban

Letter from an Unknown Woman, Max Ophuls, director
edited by Virginia Wright Wexman with Karen Hollinger

Rashomon, Akira Kurosawa, director
edited by Donald Richie

8½, Federico Fellini, director
edited by Charles Affron

La Strada, Federico Fellini, director
edited by Peter Bondanella and Manuela Gieri

Breathless, Jean-Luc Godard, director
edited by Dudley Andrew

Bringing Up Baby, Howard Hawks, director
edited by Gerald Mast

Chimes at Midnight, Orson Welles, director
edited by Bridget Gellert Lyons

L'avventura, Michelangelo Antonioni, director
edited by Seymour Chatman and Guido Fink

Meet John Doe, Frank Capra, director
edited by Charles Wolfe

Invasion of the Body Snatchers, Don Siegel, director
edited by Al LaValley

Memories of Underdevelopment, Tomás Guitérrez Alea, director
introduction by Michael Chanan

Imitation of Life, Douglas Sirk, director
edited by Lucy Fischer

Ugetsu, Kenji Mizoguchi, director
edited by Keiko I. McDonald

Shoot the Piano Player, François Truffaut, director
edited by Peter Brunette

My Night at Maud's, Eric Rohmer, director
edited by English Showalter

North by Northwest, Alfred Hitchcock, director
edited by James Naremore

The Birth of a Nation, D. W. Griffith, director
edited by Robert Lang

The Maltese Falcon, John Huston, director
edited by William Luhr

The Maltese Falcon

John Huston, director

William Luhr, editor

Rutgers University Press
New Brunswick, New Jersey

The Maltese Falcon is volume 22 in the Rutgers Films in Print series

This collection copyright © 1995 by Rutgers, The State University

Library of Congress Cataloging-in-Publication Data

The Maltese falcon : John Huston, director / William Luhr, editor.

    p.   cm.—(Rutgers films in print; v. 22)

    Filmography: p.

    Includes bibliographical references.

    ISBN 0-8135-2236-6 (cloth) : alk. paper).

    —ISBN 0-8135-2237-4 (pbk. : alk. paper)

    1. Maltese falcon (Motion picture) 2. Huston, John, 1906– —Criticism and interpretation.

I. Luhr, William. II. Series.

PN1997.M256743M36   1996

791.433072—dc20   95-15172

                          CIP

British Cataloging-in-Publication information available

For Helen and Grace Luhr:
Who Have Always Been There for Me, and
Who Have Always Been Wonderful

Acknowledgments

The assistance of many people and institutions made this book possible. My thanks first go to the contributors and their estates who not only have let me use their work but have also often pointed me in helpful research directions.

Peter Lehman suggested that I write on *The Maltese Falcon* and spurred my interest in the film. Leslie Mitchner and Marilyn Campbell, my editors at Rutgers, have been a pleasure to work with. Krin Gabbard and Fina Bathrick kindly read sections of the manuscript and improved it. Connor Hartnett has generously translated not only materials reprinted here but also research. William Kenney and Don Staples shared unpublished materials with me. Michel Ciment, Hubert Niogret, and Jean-Loup Bourget of *Positif* helped me to explore the European reception of *The Maltese Falcon* and *film noir*. The late Chris Steinbrunner of the Mystery Writers of America was unfailingly generous with his knowledge of and resources in detective fiction and film and I am one of many who mourn his loss.

The New York University Faculty Resources Network, especially Sidney Borowitz and Leslie Berlowitz, along with Robert Sklar and Bill Simon of the Department of Cinema Studies, have been invaluable in providing me with research help and facilities.

I should also like to thank the staff of the Film Study Center at the Museum of Modern Art, particularly Charles Silver and Steve Higgins; the staff of the Margaret Herrick Library of the Academy of Motion Picture Arts and Sciences and Academy Foundation, especially Sam Gill; the Cinema-Television Library and Archives of Performing Arts at the University of Southern California; the Bibliothèque de l'Arsenal et Department des Arts du Spectacle of the Bibliothèque Nationale in Paris; the Library of the Writers Guild of America, West; the Center for Film and Theater Research at the Wisconsin State Historical Society; the Department of Special Collections at the library of the University of California at Los Angeles; and Joanna Ney of the Film Society of Lincoln Center.

At Saint Peter's College, I am grateful for support from members of my department, particularly Connor Hartnett, Steve Rosen, and Victoria Sullivan; from members of the administration, particularly Vice President George Martin and Dean Peter Alexander for support with research; at the O'Toole Library, Mary George, Karen Romanko, and Grace Schut have aided my research; Bill Knapp and the staff of the Instructional Resources Center has, as always, been indispensable; as have Professor Alexander Calianese and Lazar V. Mustur of the Computer Science Department. The Committee for the Professional Development of the Faculty has supported my requests for research assistance. Maureen Polera and Peggy Greenwood have given expert secretarial aid. Oscar Magnan, S.J., has also helped with translations. Leonor I. Lega has been of great help with research, support, and translations.

As always, I am deeply indebted to my father, Walter C. Luhr, to my aunts, Helen and Grace (cited in the dedication), to Walter and Richie, and Bob and Carole and Jim and Randy and Roger and, most particularly, to Judy and David.

Contents

 # Introduction

The Maltese Falcon, the Detective Genre, and *Film Noir*

William Luhr

T *he Maltese Falcon* is an extraordinarily entertaining and well-crafted film. Immensely popular since its release more than half a century ago, it is still frequently shown in revival houses and on television, and is widely available in videotape and laserdisk formats. It may, however, be too popular for its own critical good: Scholars have paid little attention to it. I hope that the perspectives presented in this book will help to change that situation.

The movie is remarkable not only for its long-term popularity but also for its significance in either inaugurating or changing crucial aspects of film history. These include the careers of individuals like John Huston and Humphrey Bogart; genres like the detective film; styles like *film noir;* and cultural trends such as redefinitions of American masculinity and femininity, the influence of psychoanalysis on popular culture, and isolationist America's perception of the international scene.

The Movie's Initial Reception

The Maltese Falcon appeared in the fall of 1941 with little fanfare and few expectations. A modestly budgeted ($381,000) genre movie that was shot in less than six weeks (from June 9 to July 18, 1941), it had a first-time director and no major stars. The project offered so little promise that, before production began, at least two stars (George Raft and Geraldine Fitzgerald) had turned down the lead roles. It was based upon the popular Dashiell Hammett novel that had already been used as the basis for two films by the same studio (*The Maltese Falcon,* 1931, also known as *Dangerous Female,* and *Satan Met a Lady,* 1936), neither of which had been particularly successful. In fact, most of the reviewers seemed to be aware only of the 1931 film, and many, like Bosley Crowther of the *New York Times* (October 4, 1941), had not even seen that.

Unexpectedly, the film became a major success. Crowther remarks upon his pleasurable surprise in the first paragraph of his review:

The Warners have been strangely bashful about their new mystery film, *The Maltese Falcon,* and about the young man, John Huston, whose first directorial job it is. Maybe they thought it best to bring both along under wraps, seeing as how the picture is a remake of an old Dashiell Hammett yarn done ten years ago, and Mr. Huston is a fledgling whose previous efforts have been devoted to writing scripts. And maybe—which is somehow more likely—they wanted to give everyone a nice surprise. For *The Maltese Falcon . . .* only turns out to be the best mystery thriller of the year, and young Mr. Huston gives promise of becoming one of the smartest directors in the field.

Many critics agreed with Crowther in characterizing the movie as a revelation. Leo Mishkin of the *Telegraph* (October 4, 1941) compared Huston with Alfred Hitchcock and Orson Welles and closed his review with, "Suffice it to say that *The Maltese Falcon* is the finest mystery picture to have come this way this year, suffice it to say that John Huston is a man to be reckoned with in naming the great directors of our time, suffice it to say that in the end, you'll have a tough time finding a better movie. What did they say about *Kane*? It's terrific! So is *The Maltese Falcon.*"

Most of the credit went to the writer/director, John Huston, who, like Orson Welles that same year, emerged as a major talent with his first film. The praise came not only from critics in major cities upon the movie's initial release but also in December of 1941 when the film opened in a second tier of cities, like Baltimore and Dallas.[1] The positive reception continued internationally, most notably when the film first appeared in Paris in the summer of 1946 and was admiringly characterized as part of a major new style in American film dubbed *film noir*.

The enthusiastic French response to the film stressed somewhat different issues than the American response, such as the international literary prestige of Dashiell Hammett. In fact, Nino Frank opened his review of the film in *L'Ecran Français* (August 7, 1946) in this way: "I will not insult my reader by telling him who Dashiell Hammett is: a private detective become writer." But even beyond Hammett's prestige, the movie was singled out with others that appeared in France after World War II for ushering in "a new type of detective story." This phrase was used as the title of a related article by Frank in the same journal (August 28, 1946) in which, referring to the traditional type of detective film, he simply says, "We are witnesses to the death of this formula" and "Thus these 'black' films have nothing in common with detective films of the usual type." Like American reviews, but with a different focus, the French reviews celebrate something new and important being born.

While the film was an immediate success, the people associated with it took some time to achieve the prominence in film history they now have. After *The Maltese Falcon,* Warner Bros. gave Huston a prestigious Bette Davis film, *In This Our Life* (1942), that turned out to be one of his least-known works. He did not enjoy another major Hollywood success until *The Treasure of the Sierra Madre* in 1948. Comparably, Humphrey Bogart was making the transition from featured character roles to star roles; although he had a distinguishing success with *High Sierra* (1941), he did not become a major star until *Casablanca* in 1943. However, *The Maltese Falcon* would forever be seen as the turning point in both Huston's and Bogart's careers: Before it, they were minor figures in Hollywood; after it, they became industry legends.

The movie's star-making potential was immediately recognized. This is evident in a bevy of jokes in gossip columns when the film appeared in late 1941. The *L.A. Herald* reported that since Bogart "clicked" in three roles turned down by George Raft (*High Sierra, All Through the Night,* and *The Maltese Falcon*), "he says he won't take another role unless Raft turns it down." Raft, in turn, when asked to comment on Bogart's success in the role, retorted, "There, but for the grace of me, go I" (*New York Post,* October 10, 1941). These jokes continued into the next year. Sidney Skolsky quoted Bogart in *The Citizen News* (March 16, 1942) as saying, "That Mark Twain is a great part. I hope they give it to George Raft, because I'd love to play it." Underlying the playful banter was the widespread assumption that *The Maltese Falcon* had done something of major significance for Bogart.

Although this was the only time he played Sam Spade in films, he has become indelibly linked with the character, and "Sam Spade" has become a generic term for hard-boiled private detective, recognized even by those who have neither seen the movie nor read Hammett's novel.

Dashiell Hammett and Detective Fiction

The Maltese Falcon did more than transform individual careers; it helped change the detective genre and paved the way for *film noir*. Indeed, Huston's film represents a change in film detectives somewhat comparable with the influence of Dashiell Hammett's work on detectives in literature. The literary genre was itself a relatively new one when Hammett's work first appeared in the 1920s. The genre had its origins in the mid-nineteenth century in the works of Edgar Allen Poe, Charles Dickens, and Wilkie Collins, but did not hit its stride until the wildfire popularity of Sir Arthur Conan Doyle's Sherlock Holmes stories at the end of the century. These, followed by the work of writers like Dorothy L. Sayers and Agatha Christie, set the tone for what has become known as the British school of detective fiction. These stories and novels generally involved a very bright detective, a very bright criminal, and an extremely clever crime in a comfortable, highly mannered, and largely benign society. When the crime is solved, that society returns to a peaceful "normality."

Hammett's work, which first appeared in the popular "pulp" magazine *Black Mask* in 1923, was characterized as part of the "hard-boiled" school of detective writing, which was a reaction against the more genteel British tradition. The detectives were proletarians rather than aristocrats (Sam Spade as opposed to Lord Peter Wimsey), and the crimes tended to be brutal and often senseless. The criminal acts and the moral decay they revealed were representative of rather than aberrations from the workings of the society in which they occurred. Social problems such as organized crime and urban corruption that were largely irrelevant to the British stories were central to the American ones. The language was not polite discourse but street slang and, even though the individual crime might be cleared up at the end, the social and personal evils it revealed tended to be endemic. This fiction offered little in the way of a return to a polite "normality," even when the mystery was solved. Hard-boiled writers like Hammett, James M. Cain, Cornell Woolrich, Raymond Chandler, and Jim Thompson were less interested in the complex orchestration and clear-cut resolution of the crime than they were in the dark motivations of the criminals and their relationships to the society in which they functioned.

Hammett was not the first of the hard-boiled detective writers, but he quickly became one of the most admired and remains a standard by which others are judged. *The Maltese Falcon,* his third novel, appeared in serial form in 1929 and in book form in 1930. It was an immediate success and the film rights were quickly purchased for $8,500 by Warner Bros. Although Hammett's fiction won him an international reputation, he only completed two more novels. His work had helped create a genuine revolution in detective fiction, but by the time John Huston's film would help create a revolution in detective films, Hammett's star was beginning to set. In fact, although the film was shot using the title of Hammett's novel, the probable release title in the summer of 1941 was *The Gent from Frisco;* it was only returned to *The Maltese Falcon* on September 8, less then a month before general release. (The 1936 version had been called *Satan Met a Lady.*) This indicates that the studio did not presume the film's relation to Hammett's novel to be a major selling point. By 1941, all of Hammett's major creative work was behind him, and the remaining two decades of his life (he died on January 10, 1961) were plagued with ill health and political and personal problems.

The Detective Film and *Film Noir*

Detective movies had existed at least since *Sherlock Holmes Baffled* in 1903 but did not become a significant genre until the sound era. This was partly due to the fact that many of the literary detectives that frequently appeared in films were not created until after 1925 (such as Hercule Poirot, Philo Vance, Charlie Chan, Ellery Queen, the "Saint," Philip Marlowe, Nick and Nora Charles, and Sam Spade). Furthermore, the major role that elaborate verbal reasoning plays in the form was difficult to present in silent cinema.

When sound came to dominate Hollywood around 1930, however, detective films flourished, but they employed thematic norms quite different from the "hard-boiled" fiction popular at the time, even when they used that fiction as their source. Most 1930s detective movies tended to leaven the gruesome aspects of their mystery with light comedy and many appeared in series formats that focussed largely upon the charm of the detective. Examples include the "Thin Man" series (based upon the Dashiell Hammett novel), and the Sherlock Holmes, Charlie Chan, Bulldog Drummond, Ellery Queen, Mike Shayne, and Saint series.

This pattern is evident in the first two versions of *The Maltese Falcon.* In each, the detective (called Sam Spade in the 1931 and 1941 films, as well as in Hammett's novel, and Ted Shane in the 1936 film) is a happy-go-lucky, wisecracking, two-fisted ladies' man. The films give as much attention to comedy and seduction as to the mystery and, in many ways, the mystery is really an excuse for the comedy and seduction.

Huston's film is altogether different in tone and points to a major trend for detective films to follow. Except for dark and cynical wisecracks, there is little comedy and hardly any seduction. Spade does not happily juggle a plethora of women but is bitterly involved with only two—his partner's wife, whom he has grown to loathe, and Brigid O'Shaughnessy, whom he knows to be duplicitous and deadly. For him, sexuality is not carefree but dangerous and guilt-ridden. The mystery and the evil world it reveals dominate the mood of the movie, and this sinister atmosphere does not entirely disappear at the end.

Such an atmosphere presages *film noir*. The term means "black film" and indicates a darker view of life than previously common and a concentration upon human depravity, failure, and despair. The term also implies a cinematic style—a way of lighting, of positioning and moving the camera, the use of an introspective voice-over narration, often heavily reliant on flashbacks—and a choice of setting, generally a seedy, urban landscape, a world gone wrong. *Film noir* has stylistic antecedents in German expressionist films of the 1920s, as well as in American horror films and radio dramas of the 1930s, and thematic antecedents in the hard-boiled fiction of the 1920s and 1930s.

The style did not fully develop until a few years later with films such as *Double Indemnity* (1944) and *Murder, My Sweet* (1944). However, substantial foundations were laid in 1941 with films such as *The Maltese Falcon* with its themes of widespread evil and deviant as well as manipulative sexuality, and *Citizen Kane* with its dark, expressionist look and fragmented narration. Even earlier, in 1940, *Stranger on the Third Floor*, with its sinister look, nightmare sequence, and atmosphere of perverse and unstable masculinity, provided a precedent.

As has often been noted, *The Maltese Falcon* does not have the murky, chiaroscuro look of *film noir* but rather a well-lit "studio" look fairly typical for its time. It also does not stress the confusions, ambivalence, sexual degradation, and weakness of its central male character, and does not use a fragmented and/or voice-over narration. It does, however, share a number of themes important to the style, such as the "black widow," sexual deviance, and dark, tormented obsessions, many of which were drawn specifically from Hammett's novel and hardboiled fiction in general.

John Huston admired Hammett's work and considered the novel ideal for his first directorial project. He was well aware that *The Maltese Falcon* had been adapted for film twice before but, contrary to common industry logic, did not consider this a disadvantage.

> Only successful pictures are made over again; I've never understood why. I've never known of an instance where the remake was as good as the original. There is no formula that enables one to re-create the unique chemistry that went into making a particular picture a success. It should be the other way around. Unsuccessful pictures—those based on good material—which for reasons of time, place or circumstance just don't come off the first time around, are the ones that should be given a second chance.[2]

Huston realized that the earlier film versions of Hammett's novel had not substantially explored the darker components of the novel, partly due to norms for detective films of the 1930s, but also because of censorship. He chose to develop

2. John Huston, *An Open Book* (New York: Knopf, 1980), 218–282.

those darker implications in his film and had little trouble with the censors. "Despite the fact that I have a poor opinion of censorship in any form, I must admit that no picture of mine was ever really damaged by the censors. There was usually a way around them."[3]

The "way around them" would ultimately give much of *film noir* its unsettling and evocative flavor. Sexual activity, such as Spade's affair with O'Shaughnessy, or hers with Thursby, or sexual deviance, such as Cairo's probable homosexuality, is hinted at in a number of ways but never overtly shown or stated. The excess of the hints combined with the avoidance of explicit declaration gives the style its overdetermined and unsettling atmosphere; the viewer often feels poised at the borders of the forbidden without verification.

The borders of the forbidden, of what was allowed to be shown, were also shifting in the 1940s. As *film noir* developed as a style, it incorporated many things earlier censored, or untouched due to fear of censorship. Hollywood's approach to much of hard-boiled fiction provides an example. Some novels with dark implications, such as *The Maltese Falcon,* had earlier been made into light-hearted films; others remained untouched until the cultural climate changed. James M. Cain's scandalous *The Postman Always Rings Twice* was purchased by Hollywood soon after its publication in 1934 but was not filmed there until 1946. A French version and an unauthorized Italian version (*Ossessione* by Luchino Visconti) were made, but the material was considered too depraved for American audiences in the 1930s and early 1940s. With the development of *film noir,* however, such material suddenly became not only acceptable but also part of a popular new style sought out by the major studios. By 1947, only a year after the M-G-M *The Postman Always Rings Twice* starring Lana Turner and John Garfield, *film noir* had become so widely known that much of its style and themes were parodied by Bob Hope in *My Favorite Brunette.*

Film Noir, Gender, Psychoanalysis, and Xenophobia

One of the most culturally resonant characteristics of *film noir* is its critique of masculinity and femininity. It tends to drastically upset the traditional power balance between the sexes and construct women as powerful and men as weak and threatened. An important character type of the style is the "black widow," a woman who seduces, exploits, and then destroys her sexual partners. These characters, like Brigid O'Shaughnessy (Mary Astor) in *The Maltese Falcon,* Phyllis Dietrichson (Barbara Stanwyck) in *Double Indemnity,* Helen Grayle (Claire Trevor) in *Murder, My Sweet,* or Kathie (Jane Greer) in *Out of the Past,* were evil and homicidal, but they were also smart and ambitious. They were not adjuncts of their men but competitors who often succeeded, at least to a point.

3. Ibid., 83.

They tended to be destroyed in the end, but their very independence and skill at power politics has been seen by some feminist scholars as a positive step in developing representations of women. The flip side of this new empowerment of female characters was the emasculation of many of the male ones, an aspect of the genre that plays itself out repeatedly.

Out of the Past (1947) provides an ideal example. In it, Robert Mitchum plays Jeff, a private detective hired by a gangster, Whit (Kirk Douglas), to find his girlfriend, Kathie (Jane Greer), who has shot him and stolen his money. Although Jeff finds her, she seduces him and they run off together. When Jeff's partner tracks them down, she kills the partner and returns to Whit. Later, they conspire to frame Jeff for murder. In the end, she kills Whit and, when Jeff tries to turn her in to the police, she kills him by shooting him in the groin, making his emasculation literal.

Kathie repeatedly exploits and betrays the men. Although they seem intelligent and resourceful, they are repeatedly degraded by her, and they come back for more. She shoots and robs Whit, yet he wants her back; she gets Jeff to betray his employer, his partner, and his hopes for a new life, yet he also constantly returns to her. Both men are killed by her after repeatedly demonstrating their inability, while fully aware of her treachery, to resist her spell.

In *The Maltese Falcon,* Brigid O'Shaughnessy plays a comparable role. Near the end, when Spade hands her over to the police after telling her that he is not going to walk in the shoes of the dead men who preceded him in her life, he, unlike many men in *film noir,* reveals his awareness of her manipulations of men and his ability to resist her.

While Brigid's type of character quickly became a stereotype, it was so new to films when it appeared that some critics hardly knew what to do with it. Otis Ferguson's review in *The New Republic* (October 20, 1941) provides an example:

> The story is one of the few cases where they have their cake and eat it too, for the detective *is* in love with the mystery woman, and she *might* turn out in the end to be another case of (a) innocence wronged, (b) the most trusted agent of the United States Government. But she doesn't, and he sends her up for twenty years. There is bound to be a little confusion in this, for an audience likes to know where it stands, and neither Mary Astor's lines nor her abilities above them quite get over the difficulty of seeming black and then seeming white, and being both all along.

The character did not conform to traditional patterns and this new type of woman was, to some extent, unsettling.

The recurring invocation of the importance of past events, of doomed obsessions, of tormented and degrading sexual compulsions, of sexual deviation, of dreams and hallucinatory states, all point to the influence of psychoanalysis in forming the motives of the characters in *film noir.* Since the second decade of the twentieth century, psychoanalysis had influenced more elitist art works (such as

German expressionist drama and film as well as such plays of Eugene O'Neill as *Mourning Becomes Electra* and *Strange Interlude*) but by the 1940s its assumptions and discourse were appearing in popular films, particularly, but not exclusively, *films noir.* This goes beyond the overt inclusion of therapists as characters in the films, whether the quack psychic Jules Amthor and the evil Dr. Sonderborg of *Murder, My Sweet* or the sympathetic analysts in *Now, Voyager* (1942) and *Lady in the Dark* (1944); it can be seen in new elements of character motivation as well as imagery.

An example of this can be seen in some films starring James Cagney, who was famous for playing sociopathic gangsters. In the 1930s, films such as *The Public Enemy, The Roaring Twenties,* and *Angels with Dirty Faces* tended to associate the roots of his characters' criminal behavior with social problems such as urban poverty, Prohibition, and the Depression. In the late 1940s, however, he played a psychopathic gangster with an Oedipal complex in *White Heat*. The roots of this character's criminality had little to do with social problems but rather with a profound psychosis that manifested itself in debilitating headaches and an obsessive and unhealthy relationship with his criminal mother. At one point, this middle-aged man sits on her lap to have his headaches soothed; when he learns of her death he erupts into a psychotic explosion of violence and winds up in a straitjacket. Such overt employment of psychoanalytic notions in character construction had become fairly common by the late 1940s but had seldom appeared in popular genres in the 1930s.

The Maltese Falcon joins with many films of its era from different genres in demonstrating a distrust of things foreign. Non-U.S. characters, places, and things tend to be exotic at best, and often perverse, sexually overcharged, and dangerous. The Falcon itself is foreign—Maltese. Gutman, Cairo, and O'Shaughnessy have tracked it in their evil and murderous travels through foreign lands before winding up in San Francisco and encountering Spade. The very overlay of foreign cities and countries, given the cultural climate of the 1940s, compounds the evil of their murderous deeds.

Spade himself is no saint. He is having an affair with his partner's wife and has a reputation for balancing on the borders of the law, and perhaps crossing over to the outlaw's domain. He is clearly comfortable with criminals and maneuvers well among them in ways they respect. At the same time, he is not gleefully sociopathic as Gutman, Cairo, and O'Shaughnessy appear. He is developed as having his own moral calculus that separates him from them even while he is involved with them. Huston repeatedly photographs him in ways that suggest a dark, inner turbulence over the implications of the activities in which he is involved, and he behaves morally, with clearly stated reasons, at the conclusion while the others prepare to continue their life of crime. The film establishes Spade's Americanism, while flawed, as the desirable norm, sharing widespread isolationist American prejudices on the eve of World War II.

That same year, Huston worked on the screenplay of the Academy Award–winning *Sergeant York*. That film, about the most decorated soldier of World

War I, also reveals a strong pro-U.S. bias. As Huston's career progressed, he would move away from these assumptions, shooting more and more of his films in foreign countries, using foreign themes, and even renouncing his U.S. citizenship to reside in Ireland and Mexico. *The Maltese Falcon* serves as a kind of baseline against which to measure Huston's later critique of American xenophobia; it also reflects widespread American cultural presumptions less than a month before its entry into World War II: In it, things from foreign lands are associated with evil, perversity, and death.

The Film's Critical Reputation

On December 6, 1994, one of the Maltese Falcon statuettes used in the film was auctioned off at Christie's East for $398,500, an astounding sum, particularly since it had been expected to raise only $30,000 to $50,000 by the auction house. The feverish bidding, and the publicity the sale garnered, testifies to the ongoing popularity of the film. Why, then, has it not received comparable scholarly attention?

Any reasons must be speculative. It is hard to say why people do *not* do something, but a number of explanations are likely that incorporate both the film's initial and enduring popularity as well as historical shifts in the critical discourse surrounding it.

Other films of its era, such as *Double Indemnity* and *The Big Sleep* (1946), have not been neglected but have accreted a substantial body of critical literature around them. Is *The Maltese Falcon* an inferior film, or are other explanations likely?

One possible explanation lies in the vagaries of Huston's critical reputation. When the auteur theory was developing in France in the 1950s and in the U.S. in the 1960s, Huston often served as a whipping boy. He was considered a director, unlike Alfred Hitchcock or Welles, without a discernible visual style or obvious thematic continuities. The sorts of rich, career-wide extrapolations that were easily made when analyzing films by Charlie Chaplin or John Ford did not seem as readily available with Huston's work, and very possibly influenced choices in film analysis, causing *The Maltese Falcon* to be overlooked.

Furthermore, by the late 1950s and through the 1960s, Huston's career was widely seen as having peaked and in severe decline. This sort of perception may have had a ripple effect upon critics' willingness to explore earlier works that had initially been praised.

The decline in Huston's reputation also occurred when serious critical enthusiasm for *film noir* was building, beginning perhaps in 1955 with Raymonde Borde and Etienne Chaumeton's *Panorama du film noir américain (1941–1953).*[4] Huston did not make many films associated with the style and *The Maltese Falcon*

4. (Paris: Editions du Minuit, 1955).

holds a transitional place in the style's development, so the building enthusiasm for *film noir* did not help his, or *The Maltese Falcon*'s reputation substantially.

Both the auteur theory and the development of interest in *film noir* are part of the historical urge for the young discipline of serious film discourse to justify itself. Eager to differentiate their work from the gushings of fan magazines and ephemeral journalism, film theorists used the auteur theory, with its presumption of authorial vision and stylistic continuity over an oeuvre, implicitly to equate their discourse with those of serious scholars of literature, music, and painting. Such a self-validating imperative may also be associated with the growing critical enthusiasm for *film noir*. Not authorial at all, work on the style traces stylistic and thematic continuities over diverse works by different authors. Both the auteur theory and the study of *film noir* made claims for the exploration of film as a serious and not merely a popular pursuit.

Within this context, the Bogart cult in France and the U.S. in the late 1950s and 1960s, which categorized *The Maltese Falcon* as preeminently a "Bogart" movie, may have reflected the film's popularity but worked against its critical reputation. The cult fell into an area, star and personality fandom, from which serious film discourse was endeavoring to distance itself. Only recently has film scholarship taken on the area of stars.

Presuming these speculations to have some validity in explaining the critical neglect of *The Maltese Falcon,* the climate may very possibly be changing. Not only did John Huston's career undergo a major upswing in the late 1970s but Andrew Sarris, the major U.S. champion of auteurism, wrote a famous and positive reappraisal of his work. Interest in *film noir* remains strong and *The Maltese Falcon*'s place in it is a critical "given" too longstanding not to provoke further exploration. Furthermore, the recent serious work on star careers has so established itself as substantial that appraisals of films often considered star vehicles has proven not only respectable but capable of producing profound new insights.

The Format of This Book

The materials in this book provide critical and historical perspectives upon *The Maltese Falcon* and expand upon the issues raised in this introduction.

"Contexts" provides a brief segment from Chapter Seven of the film's source, Dashiell Hammett's novel: Samuel Spade's story of Mr. Flitcraft and the falling beam. Although this story was not used in the film, it is a justly famous piece that reads like a short story. It gives a good sense of Hammett's prose style as well as what has been termed his existentialist perspective upon experience. It also reveals a good deal about Hammett's Sam Spade. Rudy Behlmer's "'The Stuff That Dreams Are Made Of': *The Maltese Falcon*" gives a detailed account of the origins and production of the movie. It draws heavily upon Warner Bros. archives to give fascinating information about Hammett's sources for characters in the novel, the 1931 and 1936 film versions of the novel, censorship problems encountered during the making of Huston's film, difficulties in casting, the relatively easy time with shooting and retakes, and the film's effect upon Bogart's career.

"Reviews" consists of significant critical responses to the film during the first decade after its release, showing how its reputation began and then shifted over time. Bosley Crowther's review in the *New York Times* is fairly typical of the initial American response in its wholesale enthusiasm for the film and for Huston's debut as well as in its perception of the film as unusually tough, unsentimental, and violent.

Otis Ferguson's review in *The New Republic* shares Crowther's praise for the film as well as for Huston's work, while also making special note of Bogart's contribution. His somewhat bewildered description of Mary Astor's "black widow" character points to the newness of this character type at the time, a newness that is particularly interesting since similar characters so quickly became so central to *film noir.*

Following this early review are two important French responses to the film by Nino Frank. *Film noir* is arguably the most influential American film style. First identified by the French in the postwar era, their term for it has defined it ever since, but because little of the actual response has ever appeared in English, these two important essays fill a major gap. The first is Frank's review of *The Maltese Falcon* for *L'Écran Français.* It is a positive review but, unlike many American reviews which tended to focus upon Huston's debut or the brutality of the film, Frank treats the film as springing almost entirely from Dashiell Hammett's novel and, by extension, the distinctively American hard-boiled detective story.

Three weeks after the appearance of his review, Frank published another essay that places *The Maltese Falcon* within a much larger context, that of "a new kind of detective story" or, as he termed it, "*film noir.*" Citing half a dozen films that had just appeared in France (including *Double Indemnity, Laura* [1944] and *Murder, My Sweet*) he sees the detective film as moving in entirely new directions, away from the elaborate but arid puzzles in films based upon the novels of S. S. Van Dine and Sir Arthur Conan Doyle and toward the enigmatic psychological complexity, violence, misogyny, and narrational density of *film noir.* The term then carried with it associations of "black" French films of the 1930s (such as Marcel Carne's *Hôtel du Nord,* 1938, or *Le Jour se lève,* 1939) as well as Marcel Duhamel's *Serie Noire* books. As in the earlier essay, Frank gives dominating importance to the literary sources of the films, particularly the novels of Hammett and Raymond Chandler. These two essays in many ways mark the beginning of the cottage industry of film discourse that has sprung up around *film noir.*

Almost taking their cue from the expanded range of Frank's second essay, the essays in the "Commentaries" section present significant cultural and historical perspectives upon the film. James Agee, who termed *The Maltese Falcon* "the best private-eye melodrama ever made," was an important early champion of Huston's career. His essay, "Undirectable Director," is a watershed work comparable in importance to his essay on silent comedy in providing a nodal point for major critical revaluation. It appeared nearly ten years after *The Maltese Falcon* and gives a good sense of the cult of personality that was beginning to form around the director. Agee calls Huston "the most inventive director of his generation" and describes him as doing more than anyone since D. W. Griffith to invigorate American films. His essay is an enthusiastic and perceptive appraisal of Huston at what was probably the high point of his career. Agee and Huston later became friends and worked together on *The African Queen*. The essay is historically interesting because it places *The Maltese Falcon* not as much within the context of the detective film or *film noir* but within the context of Huston's diverse and important career.

Academic film studies first became a widespread discipline in American universities in the 1970s. James Naremore's article, "John Huston and *The Maltese Falcon*," is one of the first and still one of the most impressive appraisals of the film from within the field. Writing more than twenty years after Agee, Naremore charts the critical decline of Huston's reputation and presents his analysis of *The Maltese Falcon* as a corrective. He calls *The Maltese Falcon* "typical of Huston's themes" and "the finest achievement of his visual style." He is careful to distinguish Huston's achievement from that of Hammett's novel as well as from that of the 1931 film based upon it, and he makes a strong case for Huston as a visual stylist.

The Maltese Falcon was very much a product of the Hollywood studio system at its peak. My essay, "Tracking *The Maltese Falcon:* Classical Hollywood Narration and Sam Spade," discusses the film as an example of classical Hollywood narration, taking a close look at its narrative strategies and formal motifs. It also examines a number of its thematic strategies, such as its xenophobia, its presentation of sexual deviation, its construction of masculinity and femininity, the ways in which major characters deceptively assume different roles and contrive different narratives for themselves and the relationship of this to the film's sense of diverse ways to see history.

Jean-Loup Bourget, writing in France in 1975, reveals a disposition similar to that of Nino Frank thirty years earlier to link the film's value with that of its literary source in the very title of his "On the Trail of Dashiell Hammett (The Three Versions of *The Maltese Falcon*)." Bourget's article compares the three adaptations of Hammett's novel on the grounds that "it would be wrong to give the impression (false, in my opinion) that the Huston version is practically the only one and in any case the best." Defying traditional evaluations, Bourget makes a case for the 1936 *Satan Met a Lady* as the best of the three films. He discusses a number of narrative, stylistic, character, and thematic transmutations among the novel and three films, and considers the films representative of cinematic trends of the decades in which they were made—the first two reflecting the buoyancy and spirit of the 1930s and Huston's film the more somber tone of the 1940s.

Ilsa J. Bick's article, "The Beam That Fell and Other Crises in *The Maltese Falcon*," also discusses the novel and the three film adaptations but from the perspective of contemporary film theory. She uses as her jumping-off point the most oft-cited passage in Hammett's novel, Spade's story of Mr. Flitcraft and the falling beam, a story that, interestingly, has never been used in any of the film adaptations of the novel. She develops the story's fatalistic notion of the repetitive circularity of characters' destinies as central to Hammett's novel but largely absent from Huston's film. To discuss the significance of this deviation from Hammett's fatalism, she contextualizes Huston's film within a discussion of the two earlier films, centering upon the emphasis in all four works upon seduction. She then differentiates the unrestrained and ebullient sexuality of the Spade characters in the 1930s films from the constrained and dangerous sexuality of Spade in Huston's film. She places these shifts within developments in American film and culture, such as the influence of psychoanalysis, of war trauma, and of genre shifts like that from the gangster films of the early 1930s to the screwball comedies of the late 1930s. A central focus throughout is the ways in which the films reveal shifting constructions of femininity and masculinity.

These are rich approaches to *The Maltese Falcon* intended to enhance the pleasure of viewing the film and of reflecting upon the multiplicity of contexts for understanding it. More are certainly possible. With luck, this volume will provoke them.

John Huston:
A Biographical
Sketch

William Luhr

When The Film Society of Lincoln Center honored John Huston in 1980, Andrew Sarris wrote, "As he sat in patriarchal splendor in his box on the evening of the gala, I could not help wondering whether he was the god of light or the god of darkness" (Desser and Studlar, 276). Sarris's suggestions of grandeur as well as the ambivalence of his characterization represent a widespread critical response to Huston, one which he himself shared. In his autobiography, *An Open Book,* he characterized his life, marriages, and films as having no discernible consistency. His life was one of grand enthusiasms and remarkable diversity of experience. Unusual for most directors, popular interest in his life has often matched that in his films. His career is frequently described as uneven in quality but, from his first film as a director, *The Maltese Falcon* (1941), to his last, *The Dead* (1987), he was a highly visible Hollywood icon who never lacked work.

As an individual, Huston was wildly enthusiastic and charismatic. He had passions for filmmaking, painting, horsemanship, boxing, literature, gambling, and alcohol, as well as women. He possessed many creative talents; successful in Hollywood as a writer, a director, and, late in life, as an actor, he was also a serious painter, he wrote and directed Broadway plays, he published fiction, and he even directed an opera at La Scala, among other endeavors.

His film projects cover broad territory. He made films in a great variety of genres and under different production circumstances. He was successful under Hollywood's studio system but had little trouble breaking free of that system to make films all over the world. He has even been accused of making films for reasons having nothing to do with filmmaking, of going to Africa to shoot *The African Queen* (1951) because he wanted to shoot an elephant and of going to Mexico to shoot *The Unforgiven* (1960) in order to collect pre-Colombian art. He was often honored as a screenwriter and had widespread literary interests. Many of his films are literary adaptations as diverse in scope and ambition as *The Maltese Falcon, The Dead, Wise Blood, Moby Dick,* and *The Bible.* His career and life have been characterized as focusing dominantly on masculine issues, which is largely true, but they also systematically critique those issues in complex ways.

John Huston was born on August 5, 1906, in Nevada, Missouri, a town that, according to Huston family legend, his adventurous grandfather, John Gore, won a large part of in a poker game. Huston's parents had been married eighteen months at the time of his birth; they would separate three years later and divorce in 1912. Much of his youth was nomadic and shadowed by disease. A revealing incident occurred when he was ten and diagnosed as having an enlarged heart. He felt his youth ended there since he was placed on a restricted diet and was forbidden to engage in youthful activities. About two years later, two things brought him out of it—a doctor who told him to return to a normal diet and a decision to sneak out of his rooms to swim in a canal. It was an activity, according to his elders, likely to kill him. When it did not, he returned to a normal life with a robust and adventurous attitude that characterized the rest of his life. As a teen he developed passions for boxing and painting. He also developed an abiding interest in theater. A formative and magical experience for him was watching his father, Walter Huston (then a rising actor), and Eugene O'Neill rehearse for the premiere of O'Neill's *Desire under the Elms* in 1924.

He spent much of the 1920s and 1930s making false starts in a variety of endeavors—boxing, stage acting, short story writing, screenwriting, painting, and newspaper reporting. He also married twice, to Dorothy Harvey and Lesley Black. These and his subsequent three marriages all ended in divorce. He followed his father to Hollywood in the early 1930s and received dialogue writing credit on two films in which his father starred (*A House Divided,* 1931, and *Law and Order,* 1932) as well as *Murders in the Rue Morgue* (1932).

Law and Order points to major aspects of his career. It stars his father as Frame Johnson, a Western peace officer based upon Wyatt Earp. Johnson does not jubilate in his manly skills but realizes his way of life costs as much as it gains. The script is based upon a novel by W. R. Burnett, a writer Huston admired. A decade later, Huston would adapt another Burnett novel, *High Sierra,* this time about a modern-day gangster, loosely based upon John Dillinger. The film (1941) starred Humphrey Bogart whose sympathetic stoicism resembled that of Johnson in *Law and Order.* A decade later, Huston would direct another adaptation of a Burnett novel, *The Asphalt Jungle* (1950), about the ill-fated enterprise of a gang of jaded thieves. These three works point to a lifelong interest not only in literary adaptations but also in the underside of largely doomed male endeavors.

By the late 1930s, Huston began to achieve some success as a screenwriter in Hollywood, with credits on films like *The Amazing Dr. Clitterhouse* (1938), *Juarez* (1939), and *Dr. Erlich's Magic Bullet* (1940). Nineteen forty-one was the turnaround year for his career. He co-authored the script for *Sergeant York* (1941) and wrote and directed his first feature, *The Maltese Falcon.* Both films received Academy Award nominations for Best Picture of that year and Huston received nominations for Best Screenplay (*The Maltese Falcon*) and for Best Original

John Huston at around the time of the filming of *The Maltese Falcon*

Screenplay (*Sergeant York*). Perceived by the studio as a minor, "B" feature without major stars and made largely to accommodate Huston as a writer, *The Maltese Falcon* was an unexpected critical and popular success. It launched Huston as a major director, Humphrey Bogart as a star, and, with *Citizen Kane* that same year and *Stranger on the Third Floor* the year before, helped provide a seedbed for *film noir.*

Huston made two more studio films, *In This Our Life* (1942) and *Across the Pacific* (1942), before enlisting in the Signal Corps in World War II where he made three highly acclaimed documentaries. These are revealing of number of aspects of his life and career. After success in Hollywood studio filmmaking, he was able, with little difficulty, to shift gears and move into entirely different production circumstances—documentary filmmaking for the U.S. government. In his personal life, he spent some of the time living in high style at the St. Regis Hotel in New York and drinking at "21" and some of the time bunking in Quonset huts in the Aleutian Islands or under fire in wartime Italy.

His reputation as a filmmaking rebel really begins with these wartime documentaries since *The Battle of San Pietro* (1945) was considered too gruesome by the army hierarchy and almost suppressed. Only the intervention of General George C. Marshall got it released, although in a shortened version. *Let There Be Light* (1946), dealing with battle fatigue victims at a Veterans Administration mental hospital on Long Island, was suppressed by the War Department and not publicly shown until 1980.

In both films Huston deals with obsessively masculine issues in complex ways. On the one hand, both support the U.S. military and focus on concerns of men in battle and its effects; on the other, the films are not simple glorifications but explore profound contradictions in terms of the human costs of these endeavors. Huston felt that it was important in these films to counter what he termed the warrior myth, the sense that combat was universally ennobling. The films leave the viewer with a great sense of loss. Throughout his career, Huston was known as a "man's man" and he probably used more male action stars than any other major director. They include Robert Mitchum, Humphrey Bogart, Clark Gable, John Wayne, Sean Connery, Paul Newman, Walter Huston, Richard Burton, Burt Lancaster, Errol Flynn, Gregory Peck, Marlon Brando, Montgomery Clift, Audie Murphy, Michael Caine, and Sylvester Stallone, among others. But, interestingly, his films have very few action scenes and tend to be more about masculine failure than triumph.

This is evident in his first postwar studio film, *The Treasure of Sierra Madre* (1948), a powerful tale of doomed prospectors in Mexico. The film was important for two somewhat opposed reasons. On the one hand, it signified his arrival as a major Hollywood director, proving that *The Maltese Falcon* was no flash in the pan. An "A" film, it starred Bogart, now a major star although cast against type as a degraded, seedy coward, and Huston's father, Walter Huston. While the film, typically for Huston, has no romance, no happy ending, and tells a grim, downbeat story of failure, it was a great critical success and earned both Huston and his father Academy Awards (Huston for Best Director and Best Screenplay and his father for Best Actor). But this very Hollywood success also marked the beginning of his detachment from Hollywood. It was one of the first major studio films to be shot entirely on location (in Mexico) and fueled his desire to leave Hollywood. He would soon make nearly all of his films outside of Hollywood and largely outside of the U.S.

For much of his life, Huston mastered things only to soon tire of them. He had great affection for and success in the Hollywood studio system of making films but, after the success of *The Treasure of the Sierra Madre* for Warner Bros., he formed his own production company, Horizon Pictures, with Sam Spiegel, and, for the rest of his life, generally made films under independent financing. An enthusiastic enlistee in World War II, he became disaffected with the U.S. during the McCarthy era and eventually made most of his films out of the country. He helped found the Committee for the First Amendment in 1947 as a counter to the prevailing rightist atmosphere but the attempt was politically naive, soon fizzling out, and leaving Huston with a bitter taste for politics and the U.S. He moved to Ireland in the 1970s and renounced his citizenship. His marriages also tended to be short lived, he married again in 1946, to Evelyn Keyes; in 1950, to Ricki Soma; and in 1972, to Celeste (Cici) Shane.

His critiquing of heroic men continued in the 1950s. Where *The Maltese Falcon* and *Key Largo* (1948) had been crime films with heroic central characters, both played by Humphrey Bogart, *The Asphalt Jungle* was a crime film without a central hero; a film in which all prove inadequate and all lose. He cast Audie Murphy, the most decorated soldier of World War II, in *The Red Badge of Courage* (1951) as an undistinguished soldier who runs from battle. Huston's last two films with Bogart, *The African Queen* and *Beat the Devil* (1954), cast him as a goofy, comic figure.

Walter Huston died in 1950, an enormous loss to his son (John Huston's mother had died in 1938) and Bogart died in 1957. Starting in the mid-1950s, Huston's career was widely perceived as suffering an artistic decline while becoming grander in its thematic ambitions, as evidenced by films such as *Moby Dick* (1956), *The Unforgiven, The Misfits* (1961), *Freud* (1962), and *The Bible* (1966). He did become concerned with experimenting with color in films like *Moulin Rouge* (1952), *Moby Dick, The Barbarian and the Geisha* (1958), and *Reflections in a Golden Eye* (1967) but, aside from little gems like *Heaven Knows, Mr. Allison* (1957) and *Night of the Iguana* (1964), he was perceived from the mid-1950s through the 1960s as embarking on ambitious but insufficiently realized projects like *The Roots of Heaven* (1958).

In the early 1970s, with *Fat City* (1972), his career turned around and began its final ascent. A small, tight film without major stars, *Fat City* was seen as evidence that Huston was still capable of intense, controlled filmmaking. He enjoyed both critical and popular success with *The Man Who Would Be King* (1975) and had another critical success with *Wiseblood* (1979). The 1980s brought him a number of industry awards such as the 1983 American Film Institute Life Achievement Award and a 1984 tribute at the Cannes Film Festival. The 1980s also brought him respectful reviews for his last three films—*Under the Volcano* (1984), *Prizzi's Honor* (1985), and *The Dead. Prizzi's Honor* was particularly satisfying for him since it garnered an Academy Award as Best Supporting Actress for his daughter Anjelica, and a Best Director nomination for him, making him the oldest director to be so nominated.

Throughout much of the 1960s, he lived in baronial splendor on his Irish estate, St. Clerans. By the late 1970s he had moved into an almost antithetical life, living at Las Caletas near Puerto Vallarta in Mexico with his final companion, Maricela Hernandez (Cici's former maid). Where his Irish life had been royal and complex in flavor, his Mexican life was primitive and simple. He died on August 28, 1987, shortly before the critically praised release of his final film, *The Dead.*

Sources

Grobel, Lawrence. *The Hustons.* New York: Avon Books, 1989.

Huston, John. *An Open Book.* New York: Alfred A. Knopf, 1980

Studlar, Gaylyn, and David Desser, eds. *Reflections in a Male Eye: John Huston and the American Experience.* Washington, D.C.: Smithsonian Institution Press, 1993.

The Maltese Falcon

The Maltese Falcon

I have based this continuity upon the 100-minute release print of *The Maltese Falcon,* now widely available in 16mm, videotape, and laserdisk formats. It records in greatest detail the film's dialogue; the placement, behavior, and movement of the characters; the camera movement; the lighting; and the continuity between the shots. It presumes all transitions between shots to be cuts unless specifically noted (such as in the case of dissolves, fades, wipes, and the like). It gives little detail about the sets, props, and wardrobe beyond general descriptions ("Spade's office") and discusses music and background sound primarily when they motivate the plot.

I have used the following standard abbreviations to describe the placement of the camera with relation to the main focus of the shot:

CS	close shot
MCS	medium close shot
MS	medium shot
LS	long shot
ELS	extreme long shot

Credits

Director
John Huston

Executive Producer
Hal B. Wallis

Associate Producer
Henry Blanke

Production Company
Warner Brothers–First National

Screenplay
John Huston, based upon the novel by
    Dashiell Hammett

Director of Photography
Arthur Edeson, A.S.C.

Art Director
Robert Haas

Gowns by
Orry-Kelly

Editor
Thomas Richards

Dialogue Director
Robert Foulk

Makeup Artist
Perc Westmore

Music
Adolph Deutsch

Musical Director
Leo F. Forbstein

Release Date
October 3, 1941 (New York City)

Length
100 minutes

Cast

Samuel Spade
Humphrey Bogart

Brigid O'Shaughnessy
Mary Astor

Iva Archer
Gladys George

Joel Cairo
Peter Lorre

Lt. of Detectives Dundy
Barton MacLane

Effie Perine
Lee Patrick

Kasper Gutman
Sydney Greenstreet

Detective Tom Polhaus
Ward Bond

Miles Archer
Jerome Cowan

Wilmer Cook
Elisha Cook, Jr.

Frank Richman
Murray Alper

Bryan
John Hamilton

[Captain Jacoby]
[Walter Huston]

The Continuity Script

The film opens, after the "Warner Bros." logo, in the middle of a camera pullback from a medium shot to a long shot of the Maltese Falcon statuette. It is darkly lit with a harsh shadow to screen right. The credits appear in a series of vaseline dissolves against this shot. The lighting, the wavy, uneven dissolves, and the ponderous music give a sinister effect. At the end of the credits the following words are scrolled up against a closer shot of the Falcon.

In 1539 the Knight Templars of Malta, paid tribute to Charles V of Spain, by sending him a Golden Falcon encrusted from beak to claw with rarest jewels——but pirates seized the galley carrying this priceless token and the fate of the Maltese Falcon remains a mystery to this day——

San Francisco, exterior, day

1. ELS: *San Francisco Bay, framed by part of the Golden Gate Bridge, with title "SAN FRANCISCO" superimposed.*
   Dissolve.
2. ELS: *San Francisco, different view, seen from the Bay, with "Golden Gate Bridge" in large letters on top of a structure.*
   Dissolve.
3. ELS: *Golden Gate Bridge.*
   Dissolve.
4. ELS: *San Francisco. Camera pans right from bridge.*
   Dissolve.

Spade's office, interior, day

5. CS: *Spade's office window, with "SPADE AND ARCHER" in mirror image on it, the Golden Gate Bridge in the background. Camera tilts down to a MCS of Spade rolling a cigarette. A door is heard opening.*
   SPADE (*without looking up*): Yes, sweetheart?
6. LS: *Effie standing by office door. The back of Spade's head and shoulders is in the foreground of the frame.*
   EFFIE: There's a girl who wants to see you. Her name's Wonderly.
   SPADE: Customer?
7. CS: *Effie, low angle.*
   EFFIE: I guess so. You'll want to see her, anyway. She's a knockout.
8. MCS: *Spade, still rolling the cigarette.*
   SPADE: Shoo her in, Effie darling, shoo her in.
9. LS: *Effie and Spade, as in 6. Effie turns and opens office door, letting Brigid in, who walks toward Spade as Effie leaves. Spade rises to greet her.*
   EFFIE: Will you come in, Miss Wonderly?

BRIGID: Thank you.

10. MS: *Spade on right behind desk, Brigid on left, reverse angle of 9.*

SPADE: Won't you sit down, Miss Wonderly?

She moves to left side of desk and sits down. Spade sits also.

BRIGID: Thank you. I inquired at the hotel for the name of a reliable private detective. They mentioned yours.

SPADE: Suppose you tell me about it from the very beginning.

11. MCS: *Brigid on left, facing camera; Spade on right, from side.*

BRIGID: I'm from New York.

SPADE: Uh-huh.

BRIGID: I'm trying to find my sister. I have reason to believe that she's here in San Francisco with a man by the name of Thursby, Floyd Thursby. (*Spade lights cigarette. Brigid is nervously avoiding eye contact.*) I don't know where she met him. We've never been as close as sisters ought to be. If we had, perhaps Corinne would have told me that she was planning on running away with him. Mother and Father are in Honolulu. It would kill them. I've got to find her before they get back home.

12. MCS: *reverse angle of 11.*

BRIGID: They're coming home the first of the month.

SPADE: You've had word of your sister?

13. CS: *Brigid, still nervous.*

BRIGID: A letter from her about two weeks ago. It said nothing except that she was all right. I sent her a telegram begging her to come home. I sent it to the general delivery here. That was the only address she gave me. I waited a week and no answer came so I decided to come here myself. I wrote her that I was coming.

14. MCS: *as in 12.*

BRIGID: I shouldn't have done that, should I?

SPADE: Oh, it's not always easy to know what to do. You haven't found her?

15. CS: *Brigid, as in 13.*

BRIGID: No. I told her in my letter that I'd be at the St. Mark and for her to meet me there. I waited three whole days. She didn't come, didn't even send a message.

16. MCS: *Spade.*

BRIGID (*off*): It was horrible. Waiting.

17. CS: *Brigid, as in 13.*

BRIGID: I sent her another letter to general delivery. Yesterday afternoon I went to the post office. Corinne didn't call for her mail but Floyd Thursby did. He wouldn't tell me where Corinne was. He said she didn't want to see me. I can't believe that. He promised to bring her to the hotel if she'd come this evening. He said he knew she wouldn't. He promised to come himself if she didn't. He would . . .

18. MS: *Miles, from side angle, entering office. He sees Brigid and removes his hat.*

MILES: Oh, excuse me.

19. MCS: *Brigid and Spade, as in 11.*

SPADE: Oh, it's all right, Miles. Come in.

20. MS: *Miles, as in 18. Camera follows him into office where he stands, screen left, behind Brigid. Spade stands, screen right. Brigid remains seated.*

SPADE: Miss Wonderly, my partner, Miles Archer. (*Addresses Archer.*) Miss Wonderly's sister ran away from New York with a fellow named Floyd Thursby. They're here in San Francisco. Miss Wonderly has seen Thursby and has a date to meet him tonight. Maybe he'll bring the sister with him; the chances are he won't. Miss Wonderly wants us to find the sister, get her away from him, and back home. Right?

BRIGID: Yes.

Miles, who has been ogling Brigid from behind, lasciviously rolls his eyes and purses his lips for Spade to see. He then walks over and sits on the

opposite side of the desk, facing Brigid, with Spade now in the center of the composition. The camera repositions slightly.

SPADE: Now it's, uh, a simple matter of having a man at the hotel this evening to shadow him when he leads us to your sister. If, after we've found her, she still doesn't want to leave him, well, we have ways of managing that.

MILES: Yeah.

BRIGID: Oh, but you must be careful. I'm deathly afraid of him, what he might do. She's so young. And his bringing her here from New York is such a serious . . .

21. MS: *Brigid, Spade, and Miles, reverse angle of 20.*

BRIGID: Mightn't he, mightn't he do something to her?

SPADE: Now just leave that to us. We'll know how to handle him.

22. CS: *Brigid, as in 13.*

BRIGID: Oh, but I want you to know he's a dangerous man. I honestly don't think he'd stop at anything. I don't think he'd hesitate to . . . to kill Corinne if he thought it would save him.

23. MS: *Brigid, Spade, and Miles, as in 21.*

MILES: Could he cover up by marrying her?

BRIGID: He has a wife and three children in England.

SPADE: Yes, they usually do, though not always in England. (*He leans forward and starts taking notes.*) What does he look like?

24. CS: *Brigid, as in 13.*

BRIGID: He has dark hair and thick, bushy eyebrows. He talks in a loud, blustery manner. He gives the impression of being a violent person.

25. MS: *Brigid and Spade, closer view of 21.*

BRIGID: He was wearing a light gray suit and a, a gray hat when I saw him this morning.

SPADE: What does he do for a living?

26. CS: *Brigid, as in 13.*

BRIGID: Why, I haven't the faintest idea.

27. MS: *Spade and Miles.*

SPADE: What time's he coming to see you?

BRIGID (*off*): After eight o'clock.

SPADE: All right, Miss Wonderly. We'll have a man there.

MILES (*leaning forward, eager to please*): I'll look after it myself.

28. CS: *Brigid, as in 13.*

BRIGID: Oh, thank you.

29. MS: *Brigid and Spade, as in 25.*

BRIGID: Uh, oh yes. (*Opens her handbag and searches for money. Spade watches attentively. Camera pans to show Miles, also impressed by the money in her bag.*)

30. CS: *Brigid, as in 13. She knows they are watching her bag.*

31. MS: *Brigid, Spade, and Miles, as in 21.*

BRIGID: Will that be enough?

Spade nods "Yes."

32. LS: *Brigid, Spade, and Miles. All three stand up and the camera moves with Spade and Brigid as he escorts her to the door and she leaves.*

BRIGID: Thank you.

SPADE: Not at all. Oh, it'll help some if you meet Thursby in the lobby.

BRIGID: I will.

MILES: Hey, you don't have to look for me. I'll see you all right.

BRIGID (*to Miles, as she shakes his hand*): Thank you. (*She then goes to the door and, as she leaves, shakes Spade's hand.*) Thank you so much.

SPADE: Good-bye.

33. CS: *Miles, examining the money. Spade enters frame and camera pulls back to* MS.

MILES: They're right enough. They have brothers in her bag.

Camera continues to pull back as both move into the frame and sit at their desks on opposite sides of the frame.

SPADE: What do you think of her?

MILES: Oh she's sweet. Ah ha-ha, maybe you saw her first, Sam, but I spoke first.

SPADE: You've got brains. (*Camera moves down to shadow image of the* "SPADE AND ARCHER" *window lettering in the floor.*) Yes you have.

Dissolve.

Exterior, night

34. CS: *Street sign—*"BUSH ST."

35. MS: *camera shows Miles's feet enter the frame, then it tilts up to show him looking slightly to camera right. A revolver appears in the lower right corner of the frame, pointed at him. Miles is confused. It fires and he falls backwards.*

36. LS: *a dark hillside as Miles's body tumbles down, away from the camera.*

Spade's bedroom, interior, night

37. CS: *a telephone on a night table, with fluttering curtains behind it. It rings and Spade's hand pulls it out of frame. His voice is heard offscreen.*

SPADE: Hello. . . . Yeah, speaking. . . . Miles Archer dead? . . . Where? . . . Bush and Stockton? . . . Yeah. . . . Fifteen minutes. Thanks. (*As he replaces the phone on the table, the camera pulls back and pans slightly to the right. His head enters the frame. He turns on the light and dials a number.*) Hello, Effie, it's me. Now listen, precious. Miles has been shot. . . . Yeah, dead. . . . Now don't get excited. Yeah, uh-huh. Now you'll have to break the news to Iva. I'd fry first. . . . And keep her away from me. . . . That's a good girl. Get right over there. You're an angel. 'Bye.

Dissolve.

Exterior, night

38. MS: *a crowded street near the crime scene. A taxi pulls up and Spade gets out and the camera follows as he walks left to a policeman.*

POLICEMAN: What do you want here?

SPADE: Oh, I'm Sam Spade. Tom Polhaus phoned.

POLICEMAN: Oh, I didn't know you at first. They're back there.

39. LS: *a low angle, frontal view of Spade as he stands behind the railing through which Miles fell and looks down.*

40. MS: *a high-angle shot of Miles's body being photographed by a police photographer.*

41. LS: *a high-angle shot of Spade, reverse of 39, as he surveys the railing through which Miles fell and the hillside beneath. Polhaus is climbing the hill toward him.*

42. LS: *Spade, as in 39. Polhaus approaches him.*

POLHAUS: Hello, Sam.

43. MS: *Spade and Polhaus.*

POLHAUS: I figured you'd want to see it before we took him away.

SPADE: Well, thanks, Tom. What happened?

POLHAUS: Got him right through the pump with this. It's a Webley.
44. CS: *a revolver in a handkerchief.*
POLHAUS'S VOICE: English, ain't it?
45. MS: *Spade and Polhaus, as in 43.*
SPADE: Yeah. A Webley-Forsby forty-five automatic, eight-shot. They don't make 'em anymore. How many gone out of it?
POLHAUS: Just one.
SPADE: Let's see, uh . . .
46. LS: *Spade and Polhaus, as in 41.*
SPADE: . . . shot up here, huh? Standing like you are, with his back to the fence. The man who shot him stood here. Went over backwards, taking the back of the fence with him, and went on down the hill and got caught on that rock. That's it?
47. MS: *Spade and Polhaus, as in 43. Spade paces back and forth, looking all around.*
POLHAUS: That's it. The blast burned his coat.
SPADE: Who found him?
POLHAUS: Man on the beat.
SPADE: Anybody hear the shot?

POLHAUS: Well, somebody must've. We just got here. You want to go down and have a look at him before we take him away?

SPADE: No. You've seen everything I could.

POLHAUS: His gun was still tucked away on his hip. Hadn't been fired. His overcoat was buttoned. I found a hundred-dollar bill in his vest pocket and thirty-some bucks in his pants. Was he working, Sam? Well?

SPADE: Yeah, he was tailing a guy named Thursby.

POLHAUS: What for? What *for?*

SPADE: He wanted to find out where he lived. Don't crowd me, Tom. I'm going on down and break the news to Miles's wife.

POLHAUS: Gee, it's tough him getting it like that, ain't it? Miles had his faults, just like any of the rest of us, but I guess he must have had some good points too, huh?

SPADE: I guess so.

Side wipe.

Interior, night

48. CS :   *Spade in telephone booth.*

SPADE: Miss Wonderly, please. . . . Huh, checked out? What time? . . . Oh, any forwarding address? . . . Thanks. *Camera pulls back and pans left to follow Spade as he walks out of a drugstore.*

Side wipe.

Interior, night

49. MS :   *Spade enters his apartment and turns on a light switch. Camera pans right as he walks over to bed while taking overcoat, hat, and jacket off. He sits on the bed and, as he pours himself a drink, the doorbuzzer sounds.*

50. LS :   *Spade's apartment door. Spade walks into frame to answer it.*

SPADE: Oh, hello, Tom. Hello, Lieutenant. Come in.

Camera follows as he walks with Polhaus and Dundy into his apartment. They sit facing camera in MS, he sits on bed with back to camera. All look guarded and suspicious.

SPADE: Sit down. Sit down. Drink?

They shake their heads.

POLHAUS: Did you, uh, break the news to Miles's wife, Sam?

SPADE (*repositioning himself so that he now sits at right angle to the camera*): Uh huh.

POLHAUS: How'd she take it?

SPADE: I don't know anything about women.

POLHAUS: Since when?

DUNDY: What kind of gun do you carry?

SPADE: None. I don't like then. 'Course there are some at the office.

DUNDY: You don't happen to have one here? You sure about that?

SPADE: Look around. Turn the dump upside down if you want to. I won't squawk, *if* you've got a search warrant.

POLHAUS: Now, we don't want to make any trouble.

SPADE (*becoming antagonistic*): I don't like this. What're you birds sucking around here for? Tell me or get out.

51. CS: *Dundy and Polhaus, side angle.*

POLHAUS: Well, you can't treat us like that, Sam. It ain't right. We got our work to do.

DUNDY: Why were you tailing Thursby?

52. MS: *Spade. The back of Dundy's head is visible in the foreground.*

SPADE: I wasn't. Miles was. And for the simple reason we had a client.

DUNDY: Who's your client?

SPADE: Sorry, I can't tell you that.

53. CS: *Dundy and Polhaus, as in 51.*

POLHAUS: Be reasonable, Sam. Give us a break, will you? How we going to turn up anything on Miles's killing if you don't tell us what you got?

DUNDY: Tom says you were in too much of a hurry to even stop and take a look at your dead partner. And you didn't go to Archer's house to tell his wife. We called your office and the girl there said you told her to do it.

54. MS: *Dundy, Polhaus, and Spade, as in 50. Dundy leans forward and Spade sits facing them again. The camera moves in, emphasizing Spade's back.*

DUNDY: I'll give you ten minutes to get to a phone and do your talking to the girl. I'll give you ten minutes to get to Thursby's joint, Geary and Leavenworth. You could do it easily in that time.

55. MS: *Polhaus, Spade, and Dundy, reverse of 54.*

SPADE: What's your boyfriend getting at, Tom?

56. CS: *Dundy.*

DUNDY: Just this. Thursby was shot down in front of his hotel about a half an hour after you left Bush Street.

57. MS: *Polhaus, Spade, and Dundy, as in 55.*

SPADE: Keep your paws off me!

DUNDY: What time did you get home?

SPADE: Just a few minutes ahead of you. I was walking around thinking things over.

DUNDY: We knew you weren't here. We tried to get you on the phone. Where did you walk to?

SPADE: Out Bush Street.

58. MS: *Dundy, Polhaus, and Spade, as in 50. Spade gets up while talking and walks to the back of the room, then turns to face them. They face him and Dundy stands up.*

DUNDY: Did you see anybody?

SPADE: No, no witnesses. Well, I know where I stand now. Sorry I got up on my hind legs, boys, but you fellows trying to rope me made me nervous. Miles getting bumped off upset me and then you birds cracking foxy. But it's all right now, now that I know what it's all about.

POLHAUS: Oh, forget it, Sam.

SPADE: Thursby die?

POLHAUS: Yup.

SPADE: How'd I kill him? I forget.

59. CS: *high-angle shot of Polhaus.*

POLHAUS: He was shot in the back four times with a forty-four or forty-five from across the street. Nobody saw it, but that's how it figures.

60. MS: *Dundy, Spade, and Polhaus, as in 58, but a tighter shot.*

SPADE: Hotel people know anything about him?

POLHAUS: Nothing except that he lived there a week.

SPADE: Alone?

POLHAUS: Yeah, alone.

SPADE: Did you find out who he was? What his game was? Well, did you?

DUNDY: We thought you could tell us that.

SPADE: I've never seen Thursby, dead or alive.

61. CS: *low-angle shot of Dundy; rear angle of Spade, facing him.*

DUNDY: Well, you know me, Spade. If you did it or if you didn't, you'll get a square deal from me, and most of the breaks. Don't know if I'd blame you much; a man that killed your partner, but that won't stop me from nailing you.

62. MS: *Dundy, Spade, and Polhaus, as in 60.*

SPADE: Fair enough.

63. CS: *Dundy, Spade, and Polhaus, as in 58.*

SPADE: But I'd feel better about it if you'd have a drink with me. (*He hands them glasses, then walks between them, toward the camera. He picks up a bottle and pours the drinks; his back now faces the camera.*)

64. CS: *Dundy, Polhaus, and Spade, high-angle shot.*

SPADE (*toasting*): Success to crime.

65. CS: *Newspaper headline*—"THURSBY, ARCHER MURDERS LINKED." *Camera moves in on sub-headline*—"*Private Detective Was Shadowing Thursby.*"

Spade's office, interior, day

66. MS: *Spade's outer office. Spade opens door and enters.*

EFFIE (*off*): She's in there.

SPADE: I told you to keep her away from me.

Camera pulls to include Effie, seated at her desk.

EFFIE: Yes, but you didn't tell me how. Oh, don't be cranky with me, Sam. I've had her all night.

SPADE: Sorry, angel. I didn't mean . . .

Offscreen sound of a door opening. Spade and Effie look offscreen right.

67. LS: *Spade and Effie seen from behind Iva's back. Iva stands to the right of the doorway in Spade's inner office*

SPADE: Hello, Iva. (*Spade walks toward her and closes the door. They are now in close shot.*)

IVA: Oh, Sam.

They embrace and kiss.

SPADE: Darling, Effie take care of everything?

They disengage. Iva looks into Spade's eyes.

IVA: I think so. Sam, did you kill him?

SPADE: Who put that bright idea into your head?

IVA: Well, I thought you said if it wasn't for Miles you'd . . . Be kind to me, Sam.

Camera follows Spade as he walks over to his desk and sits on the edge, his back to it, facing Iva. His facial expression changes from concerned to a sarcastic grin and he claps his hands together.

SPADE: Ha! (*sarcastically*) "You killed my husband, Sam, be kind to me." (*Iva moves into the frame and bursts into tears, then turns her back to Spade. Touched, he removes his hat and walks up behind her, tenderly holding her shoulders.)* Don't, Iva, don't. You shouldn't have come here today, darling. You ought to be home.

IVA: You'll come soon?

Spade's expression changes from one of tenderness to one of repressed annoyance; he wants to get rid of her.

SPADE: Soon as I can. Good-bye, Iva. *The camera follows her as she walks to the door, stares longingly back at Spade, places the black veil from her hat over her face, and leaves.*

68. MS: *Spade looking out of the window behind his desk. Camera moves in for a CS, side angle of him as he sits down at his desk, begins rolling a cigarette, and stares solemnly across the room.*

69. CS: *Miles's empty desk.*

70. CS: *Spade staring, same as end of 68.*

71. LS: *Effie walking across the office toward Spade's desk.*

EFFIE: Well, how did you and the widow make out?

72. MS: *Spade at his desk. Effie walks into the frame and sits on Spade's desk, taking his cigarette makings and rolling them as they speak.*

SPADE: She thinks I shot Miles.

EFFIE: So you could marry her?

SPADE: The cops think I killed Thursby, the guy Miles was tailing for that Wonderly dame. Who do you think I shot?

EFFIE: Are you going to marry Iva?

SPADE: Aw, don't be silly. I wish I'd never laid eyes on her.

Effie leans over and has Spade lick the cigarette paper. He pats her knee.

IVA: You suppose she could have killed him?

SPADE (*laughing*):   You're an angel, a nice rattle-brained little angel.

73. MS: *low-angle view of Effie; the rear of Spade's head is in the bottom right of the frame. Effie places the cigarette in Spade's mouth and lights it.*

EFFIE: Oh, am I?

SPADE: Thanks, honey.

EFFIE: Suppose I told you that your Iva hadn't been home many minutes when I arrived to break the news at three o'clock this morning?

SPADE: *Are* you telling me?

EFFIE: She kept me waiting at the door while she undressed. Her clothes were on a chair where she'd dumped them, hat and coat underneath. Her slip, on top, was still warm.

74. CS: *high angle of Spade, with the back of Effie's head in the left of the frame, reverse of 73.*

EFFIE: She'd wrinkled up the bed, but the wrinkles weren't mashed down.

SPADE: You're a detective, darling, but she didn't kill him.

75. MS: *Effie, same as 73.*

EFFIE: Do the police really think you shot this what's-his-name? Do
they? . . .
76. CS: *Effie and Spade, same as 74.*
EFFIE: . . . Look at me, Sam.
He looks up at her.
77. MS: *Effie, same as 75.*
EFFIE: You worry me. You always think you know what you're doing,
but you're too slick for your own good. Some day you're going to find it
out. (*She answers the ringing telephone.*) Spade and Archer.
78. CS: *Spade, same as 74.*
EFFIE: Oh yes, Miss Wonderly. (*She hands the phone to Spade.*)
SPADE: Hello. Yeah, this is Sam Spade. Where?
79. MS: *Effie, similar to 73. She writes down what Spade says.*
SPADE: Coronet Apartments, California Avenue, Apartment 1001.
80. MS: *Effie and Spade, side angle, with the window with* "SPADE AND
ARCHER" *on it behind them.*
SPADE: What's the name? Miss Le Blanc. OK, I'll be right over.
*The camera follows him as he rises and walks around his desk, taking the
note from Effie. After looking at it, he sets it aflame and places it in his
ashtray. At the end of the shot, the camera moves in for a close shot of the
flaming note. While Spade is doing this, he gives Effie these orders, but
does not look her in the eye. She stares at him.*
SPADE: Oh, have Miles's desk moved out of the office and have "SPADE
AND ARCHER" taken off all the doors and windows and, er, have "SAMUEL
SPADE" put on.
Dissolve.

Coronet Apartments, interior, day

81. LS: *Spade exits an elevator, walks down a corridor and rings the buzzer
on room 1001.*

Brigid's rooms, interior, day

82. LS: *Brigid opens door and lets Spade in.*
BRIGID: Oh, come in, Mr. Spade. (*The camera follows as she escorts
Spade into the room, taking his hat and clearing a chair for him. He sits
with his back to the camera and she stands, facing him and talking in an
agitated manner.*) Oh, everything's upside down. I haven't finished un-
packing. Sit down. Mr. Spade, I, I have a terrible, terrible confession to
make. That story I told you yesterday was just a story.
SPADE: Oh, that. Well, we, we didn't exactly believe your story, Miss,
uh, what is your name, Wonderly or Le Blanc?
BRIGID: It's really O'Shaughnessy, Brigid O'Shaughnessy.
83. CS: *Spade, shot from above.*
SPADE: We didn't exactly believe your story, Miss O'Shaughnessy. We
believed your two hundred dollars.

84. MS: *Brigid, shot from below. The camera moves back as she sits down to include the back of Spade's head.*

BRIGID: You mean that . . .

SPADE: I mean you paid us more than if you'd been telling us the truth and enough more to make it all right.

BRIGID: Tell me, Mr. Spade, am I to blame for last night?

85. MS: *Spade and Brigid, reverse angle of 84.*

SPADE: Well, you warned us that Thursby was dangerous. Of course, you lied to us about your sister and all that, but that didn't count, we didn't believe you.

86. MS: *Brigid and Spade, reverse angle of 85.*

SPADE: No, I wouldn't say that you were at fault.

BRIGID: Thank you. Mr. Archer was so alive yesterday, so solid and hearty, and . . .

SPADE: Stop it. He knew what he was doing. Those are the chances we take.

BRIGID: Was he married?

87. MS: *Spade and Brigid, as in 85.*

SPADE: Yeah, with ten thousand insurance, no children, and a wife that didn't like him.

88. MS: *Spade and Brigid, side angle.*

BRIGID: Please don't.

SPADE: Well, that's the way it was. (*He rises and walks to the far side of the fireplace, turning to face Brigid. He is now in* LS.) Anyway, there's no time for worrying about that now. Out there's a flock of policemen and assistant district attorneys running around with their noses to the ground.

Brigid rises and nervously walks around to the back of her chair, now facing Spade again. An alcove of four windows is behind and, visually, between them.

BRIGID: Mr. Spade, do they know about me?

SPADE: Not yet. I've been stalling them until I could see you.

BRIGID: Do they have to know about me? I mean, can't you shield me so that I won't have to answer their questions?

SPADE: Maybe, but I gotta know what it's all about.

89. CS: *Brigid.*

BRIGID: I can't tell you. I can't tell you now. I will later, when I can. (*The camera follows her as she paces nervously around the room. She briefly comes into a two-shot with Spade.*) You've got to trust me, Mr. Spade. (*She then sits down and the camera follows into a high-angle* CS.) Oh, I'm so alone and afraid. I've got nobody to help me if you won't help me. Be generous, Mr. Spade. You're brave, you're strong. You can spare me some of that courage and strength, surely. Help me,

Mr. Spade, I need help so badly. I've no right to ask you, I know I
haven't, but I do ask you. (*Pleading.*) Help me.

90. M S : *Spade, condescendingly amused by her performance.*

   S P A D E :   You won't need much of anybody's help. You're good. (*Brigid
rises into the frame, her back to the camera.*) It's chiefly your eyes, I
think, and that throb you get in your voice when you say things like, "Be
generous, Mr. Spade."

91. C S :   *Brigid and Spade, reverse angle of end of 90.*

   B R I G I D :   I deserved that. But the lie was in the way I said it, not at all in
what I said. (*Self-righteously.*) It's my own fault if you can't believe me
now.

92. M S :   *Spade, same as 90. Brigid's back is visible. She sits, disappearing
below the frame.*

   S P A D E :   Ah, now you *are* dangerous.

93. M S :   *Spade and Brigid. Spade walks over and sits next to her as he
speaks. The camera follows and moves into a C S of them. She is leaning
back and her eyes are closed.*

   S P A D E :   Well, I'm afraid I'm, I'm not going to be able to be of much help
to you unless I've got some idea of what it's all about. For instance, I've

got to have some sort of a line on your Floyd Thursby. (*The back of his head is to the camera. Her eyes slowly open.*)

BRIGID: I met him in the Orient. We came here from Hong Kong last week. He promised to help me. He took advantage of my dependence on him to betray me.

SPADE: Betray you? How? Why did you want him shadowed?

BRIGID: I wanted to find out how far he'd gone, whom he was meeting, things like that.

SPADE: Did he kill Archer?

BRIGID: Certainly.

SPADE: He had a Luger in his shoulder holster. Archer wasn't shot with a Luger.

BRIGID (*turning her head to look directly at Spade*): Mr. Spade, you don't think I had anything to do with the death of Mr. Archer?

94. CS: *Brigid and Spade, reverse angle of the end of 93.*

SPADE: Did you?

BRIGID: No.

SPADE: That's good.

BRIGID (*turning her eyes away from Spade to stare in front of her*): Floyd always carried an extra revolver in his overcoat pocket.

SPADE: Well, why all the guns?

BRIGID: He lived by them. The story in Hong Kong is that he first came to the Orient as bodyguard to a gambler who'd had to leave the States. The gambler had since disappeared and Floyd knew about the disappearance; I don't know. I do know he always went heavily armed, and that he never went to sleep without covering the floor around his bed with crumpled newspapers, so that nobody could come silently into his room.

SPADE: You picked a nice sort of a playmate.

BRIGID: Only that sort could have helped me, if he'd been loyal.

SPADE: How bad a spot are you actually in?

95. CS: *Spade and Brigid, reverse angle of 94.*

BRIGID: Bad as could be.

SPADE: Physical danger?

BRIGID (*turning again to look at Spade*): I'm not heroic. I don't think there's anything worse than death.

SPADE: Then it's that?

BRIGID: It's that, as surely as we're sitting here, unless you help me.

96. CS: *Brigid and Spade, reverse angle of 95.*

SPADE: Who killed Thursby, your enemies or his?

97. CS: *Spade and Brigid, as in 95.*

BRIGID: I don't know. His, I suppose. I'm afraid, I, I don't know.

SPADE: Ah, this is hopeless. (*He stands up, exasperated.*)

98. LS : *Spade and Brigid. Camera pulls back as Spade walks over to get his hat. Brigid also stands in response.*

   SPADE : I don't know what you want done. I don't even know if you know what you want done.

   BRIGID : You won't go to the police?

   SPADE : Go to them? All I've got to do is stand still and they'll be swarming all over me.

99. MS : *Spade, about to leave.*

   SPADE : All right, I'll tell 'em all I know, and you'll have to take your chances.

100. CS : *Brigid.*

   BRIGID : You've been patient with me. You've tried to help me. It's useless and hopeless, I suppose. I do thank you for what you've done. I'll have to take my chances. (*She turns her head away.*)

101. MS : *Spade, touching his hat brim and reconsidering, then turning back toward her, no longer annoyed. As he walks toward her, the camera moves back to include the back of her head and shoulder.*

   SPADE : How much money have you got?

102. LS : *Brigid and Spade.*

   BRIGID : I've got about five hundred dollars left.

   SPADE : Give it to me.

   She walks through the doorway to the right. Spade walks to a table to the right of the doorway and the camera moves with him. He picks up a hat from the table.

103. CS : *label: "Lucille Shop, Queen's Road C, Hong Kong."*

104. MS : *Brigid and Spade, same as end of 102. Brigid comes into view from the interior room and hands Spade money. He counts it.*

   SPADE : There's only four hundred here.

   BRIGID : Why, I had to keep some to live on.

   SPADE : Well, can't you get some more?

   BRIGID : No.

   SPADE : Haven't you got anything you can raise some money on?

   BRIGID : I've got some furs and a little jewelry.

   SPADE : You'll have to hock 'em. (*He puts his hand out. She reaches into her robe and gives him the remaining money. He hands her a bill back.*) There you are. I'll be back as soon as I can with the best news I can manage. I'll ring four times: long, short, long, short. No (*showing her a key*), you needn't bother to come to the door. I'll let myself in.

   He leaves as the camera moves in for a CS of her, tensely watching him go. Dissolve.

   Corridor outside of Spade's office, interior, day

105. LS : *Spade walks toward the camera from the elevator, past a painter who is changing the name on his office door, and into his office.*

Spade's outer office, interior, night

106. L S : *Spade and Effie. The camera pans right with Spade as he walks quickly through his outer office to his inner office and talks to Effie, who is seated at her desk.*

    S P A D E : Anything stirring? Did you send the flowers? You're invaluable, darling. Say, get my lawyer on the phone, will you?

Spade's inner office, interior, night

107. M S : *Spade closes door, walks over to his desk, sits down, and begins to roll a cigarette. The camera moves in to* C S. *The telephone rings and he answers.*

    S P A D E : Hello, Sid? . . . I think I'm going to have to tell a coroner to go to blazes, Sid. . . . Say, can I hide behind the sanctity of my client's identity, secrets and what-nots, all the same, priest or lawyer? . . . Yeah, I know, but Dundy's getting a little rambunctious, and maybe it is a bit thick this time.

108. L S : *Effie and Spade, reverse angle of 107. Effie walks toward Spade's desk and hands a business card to him.*

    S P A D E (*into telephone*): Yeah, what'll it cost to be on the safe side? . . . Well, maybe it's worth it.

109. C S : *Spade, as in 107. He smells the card, raises his eyebrows, and looks in an amused way at Effie after saying:*

    S P A D E (*into telephone*): OK, go ahead.

110. M S : *Effie and Spade, as in the end of 108. Effie has an amused look on her face.*

    E F F I E : Gardenia.

    S P A D E (*in an affected voice*): Quick, darling, in with him.

    Effie walks back toward the door and opens it.

    E F F I E : Will you come in, Mr. Cairo?

111. C S : *Spade. Camera moves in as he looks up and registers mild shock.*

112. L S : *Cairo and Spade's back. Cairo comes from the office door toward Spade's desk. Spade removes his hat and rises.*

    S P A D E : Will you sit down, Mr. Cairo?

113. M S : *Cairo.*

    C A I R O : Thank you, sir. (*The camera follows as he moves to screen right, near a chair by the side of Spade's desk, bringing Spade into view.*)

    S P A D E : Now what can I do for you, Mr. Cairo?

    C A I R O : May a stranger offer condolences for your partner's unfortunate death? (*Cairo has a dandified appearance and manner. He carefully places his hat and gloves on Spade's desk and sits in the chair. When he speaks to Spade he carefully toys with and studies his walking stick.*)

    S P A D E : Thanks.

    C A I R O : Is there, Mr. Spade, as the newspapers imply, a certain relationship between that, er, unfortunate happening and, er, the death a little later of the man Thursby?

114. M S : *Spade and side, rear angle of Cairo.*
     C A I R O : I beg your pardon. No.
115. C S : *Cairo from a low angle.*
     C A I R O : More than idle curiosity prompted my question. See, Mr. Spade,
     I'm trying to recover an ornament that, shall we say, has been mislaid.
     (*He places the top of his walking stick to his lips as he looks at Spade.*)
116. M S : *Spade and Cairo, as in 114.*
     S P A D E : Un-huh.
     C A I R O : I thought and hoped you could assist me.
117. C S : *Cairo, as in 115.*
     C A I R O : The ornament, er, is a statuette, black figure of a bird.
118. C S : *Spade, smoking and listening intently.*
     C A I R O (*off*): I am prepared to pay on behalf of the . . .
119. C S : *Cairo, as in 115.*
     C A I R O : . . . figure's rightful owner, the sum of five thousand dollars for
     its recovery. I am prepared to promise that, what is the phrase, "No ques-
     tions will be asked." (*He smiles in an unctuous manner.*)
120. M S : *Spade and Cairo, as in 116.*
     S P A D E : Five thousand dollars is a lot of money. (*His intercom buzzer
     rings and he answers it.*) Yes, Effie?
     E F F I E ' S V O I C E : Is there anything else?
     *The camera has panned right with Spade. Cairo is out of frame but we see
     his walking stick in front of Spade as he speaks.*
     S P A D E : No, that'll be all. Just be sure to lock the door behind you on
     your way out.
121. C S : *Spade, as he puts phone down. His head almost conceals Cairo.*
     S P A D E : Good night. (*He turns toward Cairo again.*) Five thousand dol-
     lars is a . . .
     Cairo rises and holds a gun on Spade.
     C A I R O : You will clasp your hands together at the back of your neck?
122. C S : *Spade. He places his hands behind his neck.*
123. M S : *Cairo and Spade, as in the end of 121.*
     C A I R O : I intend to search your offices, Mr. Spade. I warn you, if you at-
     tempt to prevent me, I shall certainly shoot you.
     S P A D E : Go ahead and search.
     C A I R O : You will please come to the center of the room?
     *Spade rises and follows as Cairo backs into the center of the room. The
     camera pans left with them.*
124. M S : *Cairo and Spade from a low angle. Cairo makes Spade turn around
     and begins to search his pockets.*
     C A I R O : I have to make certain that you are not armed.
     *Spade abruptly turns around and punches him, forcing him to drop his
     pistol.*

125. CS: *the pistol dropping onto the rug.*
126. MS: *Cairo and Spade, same as end of 124. Spade punches Cairo again and, with a sadistic grin, forces him to back across the room. He then punches Cairo hard, knocking him out. Cairo falls unconscious onto a couch. The camera pans left with them throughout the shot. Spade sits on the couch and goes through Cairo's pockets.*
127. MS: *Spade, Cairo's head visible in the lower left of the frame. Spade empties Cairo's pockets and places the contents on a nearby table.*
128. CS: *Cairo, as Spade pulls a passport from his vest pocket.*
129. CS: *a Greek passport of Cairo's, then a French one, then a British one.*
130. MS: *Spade and Cairo, as in 127. Spade places Cairo's passports on the table.*
131. CS: *Spade's hands open the wallet from the table and pull out a theater ticket.*
132. CS: *theater ticket to the Geary Theater for Wednesday the eighteenth.*
133. CS: *Spade's hands taking money from the wallet as the camera pulls back to show his face. He then takes a handkerchief from the wallet, smells it, and looks back in Cairo's direction.*

134. CS: *Cairo, waking up.*
135. MS: *Cairo and Spade, as in 130. Spade watches Cairo stirring, then
      stands up and walks to the center of the room to pick up Cairo's pistol. The
      camera pans to the right to follow him and then pans back to the left as he
      walks back to the table and watches Cairo awaken. Cairo arises and the
      camera pans again right with him as he walks in front of Spade and across
      the room to a mirror in which we see Spade watching.*
      CAIRO: Look what you did to my shirt.
136. MS: *Spade.*
      SPADE: Sorry, but imagine my embarrassment when I found out that five-
      thousand dollar offer was just hooey.
137. MS: *Cairo at mirror, reverse angle from 135. He is cleaning his shirt and
      adjusting his tie.*
      CAIRO: Mr. Spade, my offer is genuine. I am prepared to pay five thou-
      sand dollars for the figure's return.
138. MS: *Cairo, as in end of 135. He turns and walks toward Spade, bringing
      Spade into the shot.*
      CAIRO: You have it?
      SPADE: No.
      CAIRO: But if it isn't here, why did you risk serious injury to prevent my
      searching for it?
      SPADE: Why, I should sit around here and let people come in and stick
      me up?
139. CS: *Spade and Cairo.*
      CAIRO: Certainly it is only natural that I try to save the owner such a con-
      siderable expense, if possible.
      SPADE: Who is he?
      CAIRO (*smiling*): Mr. Spade, you'll forgive my not answering that question.
140. MS: *Spade and Cairo, as in 138.*
      SPADE: Yeah, well, I think we'd be better off all around if we'd put our
      cards on the table.
141. CS: *Spade and Cairo, as in 139.*
      CAIRO: No, I do not think it would be better. You see, Mr. Spade, if you
      know more than I do, then I shall profit by your knowledge. So will you,
      to the extent of five thousand dollars.
142. MS: *Spade and Cairo, as in 140.*
      SPADE (*referring to the contents of Cairo's pockets on the table*): Oh,
      there's nothing like five thousand dollars here.
143. CS: *Spade and Cairo, as in 141.*
      CAIRO: Oh, you want some assurance of my sincerity?
144. MS: *Spade and Cairo, as in 142.*
      CAIRO: A retainer, would that do?
      SPADE: It might.

CAIRO: You will take, say, one hundred dollars?

SPADE: No, I will take, say, two hundred dollars. (*He takes the money from Cairo's things on the table, then walks between Cairo and the camera and Cairo moves closer to the table, so that both have changed positions. Cairo takes and swallows a pill from a case.*) Now, let's see. Your first guess was that I had the bird. There's nothing to that. What's your second guess?

CAIRO: That you know where it is or, at least, you know it is where you can get it.

145. MS: *Cairo and Spade, reverse positions of 143.*

SPADE: You're not hiring me to do any murders or burglaries, but simply to get it back, if possible, in an honest, lawful way?

CAIRO: If possible, but, in any case, with discretion. When you wish to contact me, sir, I'm staying at the Hotel Belvedere, room 635.

146. MS: *Cairo and Spade, as in 144.*

CAIRO (*taking his things from the table*): I sincerely expect the greatest mutual benefit from our association, Mr. Spade. Oh, may I please have my gun now?

147. MS: *Cairo and Spade, as in 145.*

SPADE: Oh, sure, I'd forgotten all about it. (*He hands Cairo the gun.*)

148. MS: *Cairo and Spade, as in 146. Cairo points the gun at Spade.*

CAIRO: You will please clasp your hands together at the back of your neck. I intend to search your offices.

Spade places his hands up and, as Cairo advances, he backs across the office and sits on the edge of his desk. The camera pans right to follow. Spade is laughing at Cairo's nerve.

SPADE: Well, I'll be . . . Why, sure. Go ahead. I won't stop you.

Fade to black.

Busy street, exterior, night

149. LS: *Spade walking along a crowded sidewalk as camera precedes him. He passes out of frame and we see Wilmer standing in a building entrance watching him. The camera moves with Wilmer as he furtively follows Spade.*

150. LS: *Spade and Wilmer. Spade walks toward the camera, which tracks backwards before him, as Wilmer follows with his hat pulled low over his eyes. Spade seems oblivious to Wilmer's presence. Spade moves out of frame and we see Wilmer bumping into people as he follows.*

151. LS: *Spade ducks into the entrance of a theater playing "The Girl from Albany" and positions himself to see who is following him.*

152. CS: *Spade looking. His hat now casts a sinister shadow over his eyes. He begins to move.*

153. LS: *Spade walking across the sidewalk to a taxi.*

154. LS: *Wilmer. Camera moves back and right as, watching Spade offscreen, he tags a taxi driver and climbs into a cab.*

Interior, taxicab, night

155. MS: *Spade and taxi driver. Spade looks out of the rear window, then turns to the driver.*

SPADE: Turn to the right and go up the hill, driver.

DRIVER: OK.

Wipe.

Exterior, deserted street, night

156. LS: *taxi pulls up and Spade climbs out and walks into the entrance of an apartment building.*

157. CS: *Spade pressing all of the buzzers in the apartment directory.*

158. LS: *Spade, as in 156, walks into the building. Wilmer's taxi pulls up.*

Interior, apartment building, night

159. LS: *Spade walking toward the camera in the ground floor hallway of the apartment building. He turns to screen right and descends a stairway. Behind him, through opaque glass doors, we see Wilmer's shadow coming up to the apartment directory.*

Exterior, apartment building, night

160. MS: *Wilmer staring at the apartment directory.*

161. LS: *Spade coming out of a dark alley to the side of the apartment building and walking toward the camera, which moves back and to the left to show Wilmer still staring in confusion at the apartment directory. Spade smiles to himself and walks out of frame.*

Wipe.

Interior, Brigid's rooms, night

162. CS: *Spade's hand giving the prearranged signal on Brigid's door buzzer. The camera moves back to show him use a key to open the door and let himself in.*

163. LS: *Spade and Brigid. Spade enters Brigid's rooms and she comes into frame to greet him. He removes his hat and coat.*

BRIGID: Mr. Spade, do you bring me any news? I mean, did you manage it so that the police won't have to know about me?

SPADE: Well, they won't for a while, anyway.

BRIGID: Oh, you are wonderful. You won't get into any trouble, will you?

SPADE: I don't mind a reasonable amount of trouble.

The camera follows as they move around the room to the chair and couch near the window. Spade watches her with evident amusement in his face.

BRIGID: Do sit down.

They sit.

164. MS: *Spade and Brigid. He is on the chair facing the camera; she is on the couch with her left side facing the camera.*

SPADE: You, you aren't exactly the sort of person you pretend to be, are you? (*He looks directly at her; she tends to avoid eye contact.*)

BRIGID: Why I, I'm not sure I know exactly what you mean.

SPADE: The schoolgirl manner, you know, blushing, stammering, and all that.

BRIGID: I haven't lived a good life. I've been bad, worse than you could know.

SPADE (*leaning back in the chair*): Yeah, well that's good, because if you actually were as innocent as you pretend to be, we'd never get anywhere.

165. CS: *Spade and Brigid, reverse angle of 164. Brigid now looks directly into his eyes.*

BRIGID: I won't be innocent.

SPADE: Good. Oh, by the way, I saw Joel Cairo tonight.

BRIGID: Do you know him?

166. MS: *Spade and Brigid, same angle, but farther back, as 163.*

SPADE: Only slightly.

Brigid stands up and walks in front of Spade to the fireplace. She takes a poker and, her back to Spade, begins stoking the fire. He takes the poker from her hand and replaces it. She looks for something on top of the mantel, then on top of the coffee table as she walks in front of Spade again. She stops at a table to screen right, selects and lights a cigarette, and walks in front of Spade again to sit facing the camera and with her back to him at screen left. During all of this nervous movement, Spade is watching intently and smiling broadly.

SPADE: You're good; you're very good.

BRIGID: What did he say?

SPADE: About what?

BRIGID: About me.

SPADE: Nothing.

BRIGID: What did you talk about, then?

SPADE: He offered me five thousand dollars for the black bird. (*She stands up.*) Er, you're not going to go around the room straightening things and poking the fire again, are you?

BRIGID (*smiling and turning to face him*) No, I'm not. What did you say?

SPADE: I said five thousand dollars was a lot of money.

BRIGID: It is. It's more than I can ever offer you if I have to *bid* for your loyalty.

Spade stands up and walks toward her so that they are soon in a tight close shot.

SPADE: That's good, coming from you. What have you ever given me besides money? Have you ever given me any of your confidence, any of the truth? Haven't you tried to buy my loyalty with money and nothing else?

BRIGID: What else is there I can buy you with?

He takes her face in his hands and kisses her, then pulls back and walks frame right and across the room to stop at the door to her bedroom. The camera pans with him.

SPADE: I don't care what your secrets are, but I can't go ahead without more confidence in you than I've got now. (*He becomes more agitated and angry as he speaks.*) You've got to convince me that you know what this is all about, that you aren't just fiddling around, hoping it'll come out all right in the end.

Brigid comes into the frame from the left and he turns to face her as she speaks.

BRIGID: Can't you trust me a little longer?

SPADE: Well, how much is a little longer? What are you waiting for?

BRIGID: I, I've got to talk to Joel Cairo.

SPADE: You can see him tonight. He's at the theater. It'll be out soon. (*He dials the telephone.*) I'll leave a message at his hotel.

BRIGID: But he can't come here. I can't let him know where I am. I'm afraid.

SPADE: My place then. (*He speaks into the telephone.*) Hello. I want to leave a message for Joel Cairo.

BRIGID: All right.

Side wipe.

Street outside of Spade's apartment building, exterior, night

167. MS: *Spade and Brigid pull up in a taxicab, climb out, and walk toward the building entrance. Spade glances briefly toward a car parked in front of the building. The camera pans left with them as they move.*

168. CS: *Iva in the parked car watching Spade and Brigid.*

Side wipe.

Hallway outside of Spade's apartment, interior, night

169. MS: *Spade and Brigid. The camera pans right with them as they walk from the elevator to the door of Spade's apartment. He opens it.*

BRIGID (*coyly*): You know I never would have placed myself in this position if I didn't trust you completely.

SPADE (*laughing smugly*): Huh? That again?

Spade's apartment, interior, night

170. LS: *Spade and Brigid. They enter the apartment and the camera pans right with them as he turns the lights on and they remove their hats and coats.*

BRIGID: You know that's true, though.

SPADE: You don't have to trust me as long as you can persuade me to trust you. But don't worry about that now, he'll be along any minute. You get your business with Cairo over with and then we'll see how we stand. (*He looks out of the window.*)

BRIGID: And you'll let me go about it with him . . .

171. LS: *Spade's point of view as he looks out of the window. Wilmer is across the street looking up at the camera.*

BRIGID (*off*): . . . in my own way?

SPADE'S VOICE: Oh, sure.

172. CS: *Brigid and Spade. She walks into frame as he looks out of the window.*

BRIGID: You are a godsend.

He turns to face her with an amused look on his face.

SPADE: Oh, now, don't overdo it.

The doorbuzzer rings.

173. MS: *Spade and Brigid. The camera pans left with Spade as he walks over to answer the door. Cairo enters, nervously.*

CAIRO: Mr. Spade, there is a boy outside. He seems to be watching the house.

SPADE: Yeah, I know. I spotted him.

BRIGID (*entering anxiously from frame right*): What? What's that? What boy?

SPADE: I don't know, a kid. He's been tailing me all evening.

BRIGID: Did he follow you to my apartment?

SPADE: No, I shook him long before that. Come in, Mr. Cairo.
The camera pans right with all three as they walk to the center of the room. Cairo places his coat, gloves, and cane on a table near the window.
CAIRO: I'm delighted to see you again, madame.
BRIGID: I was sure you would be, Joel. Mr. Spade told me about your offer for the Falcon. How soon can you have the money ready?
The camera has been moving in as all three sit in separate seats, facing one another in a triangle. We see the back of Spade's head in the center, Cairo to the right, and Brigid to the left.
CAIRO: The money is ready.
BRIGID: In cash?
CAIRO: Oh, yes.
BRIGID: You're ready to pay five thousand dollars if we turn over the Falcon to you?
174. MS: *Brigid, from rear, and Cairo, with the window curtains behind him.*
CAIRO: Excuse me, please. I must have expressed myself badly. I did not mean to say that I have the money in my pocket, but that I am ready to get it for you on a few minutes's notice at any time during banking hours.
175. MS: *Spade, from a low angle.*
SPADE: Yes, that's probably true. He only had a couple of hundred on him when I searched him late this afternoon in my office. (*He smirks.*)
176. MS: *Brigid, Cairo, and Spade, from a high angle over Spade's left shoulder.*
CAIRO: I shall be able to have the money for you at, say, half-past ten in the morning.
BRIGID (*Sitting back in her chair*): But I haven't got the Falcon. . . .
177. MS: *Spade, as in 175, watching.*
178. MS: *Brigid, Cairo, and Spade, as in 176.*
BRIGID: I'll have it in another week at the most, though.
CAIRO: Then where is it?
179. MS: *Brigid and Cairo.*
BRIGID: Where Floyd hid it.
CAIRO: Floyd Thursby, and you know where he hid it? (*She nods.*) Then why do we have to wait a week?
BRIGID: Oh, perhaps not a whole week.
180. CS: *Cairo.*
CAIRO: And why, if I may ask another question, are you willing to sell it to me?
181. MS: *Brigid and Cairo, as in 179.*
BRIGID: Because I'm afraid. After what happened to Floyd, I'm afraid to touch it except to turn it over to somebody else.
182. CS: *Cairo.*

CAIRO: What exactly did happen to Floyd?
183. CS: *Brigid. She darts her eyes in Spade's direction and whispers, trying to prevent Spade from hearing.*
    BRIGID: The fat man.
184. MS: *Brigid and Cairo. He stands up, fearful.*
    CAIRO: The fat man? Is he here?
185. CS: *Spade, as in 177. He leans forward, listening intently.*
    BRIGID (*off*): I don't know. I suppose so. . . .
186. CS: *Brigid, as in 183.*
    BRIGID: . . . What difference does it make?
187. CS: *Cairo, from a low angle.*
    CAIRO: It might make a world of difference.
188. CS: *Brigid, as in 186.*
    BRIGID: Or you or me.
189. LS: *Brigid, Spade's back, Cairo, as in the end of 173.*
    CAIRO: Precisely, but, shall we add, more precisely, the boy outside?
    BRIGID: Yes. But you might be able to get around him, Joel, as you did the one in Istanbul. (*Provocatively, in a manner calculated to annoy him.*) What was his name?

CAIRO: You mean the one you couldn't get to . . .

Brigid leaps from her chair and slaps him. He prepares to hit her when Spade leaps from his chair and knocks Cairo back into his chair.

190. MS: *Cairo and Spade. Cairo is pulling his pistol from his jacket when Spade yanks him up and knocks the gun from his hand. The camera shows them from a low angle.*

CAIRO (*furiously*): This is the second time that you laid hands on me!

SPADE: When you're slapped, you'll take it and like it. (*He slaps him repeatedly.*)

191. MS: *Brigid, Spade, and Cairo. The doorbuzzer rings and all three look toward the door.*

BRIGID: Who's that?

SPADE: I don't know. Keep quiet. (*He shoves Cairo away as he walks to the door. The camera pans left with him.*)

192. CS: *Spade. The camera follows as he closes the door to the small hall and opens his apartment door to find Polhaus and Dundy standing in the hallway.*

SPADE: Hello. Well, you guys pick swell hours to do your visiting in. What is it this time?

DUNDY: We want to talk to you, Spade.

SPADE: Well, go ahead and talk.

POLHAUS: We don't have to do it here in the hall, do we, Sam?

SPADE: You can't come in.

POLHAUS: Oh, come off it now, Sam. (*He places his hand on Spade's shoulder.*)

193. CS: *Dundy, Spade, and Polhaus. We now see only Spade's face.*

SPADE: You aren't trying to strong-arm me, are you, Tom?

POLHAUS: Why don't you . . .

194. CS: *Spade, seen from the rear, Dundy, and Polhaus, as in the end of 192.*

POLHAUS: . . . be reasonable?

DUNDY: It would pay you to play along with us a little, Spade. You got away with this and you got away with that, but you can't keep it up forever.

SPADE: Stop me when you can.

DUNDY: That's what I intend to do. There's talk going around about you and Archer's wife. Is there anything to it?

SPADE: Not a thing.

DUNDY: The talk is that she tried to get a divorce from him so she could put in with you and he wouldn't give it to her. Anything in that?

SPADE: No.

DUNDY: There's even talk that that's why he was put on the spot.

195. CS: *Dundy, Spade, and Polhaus, as in 193.*

SPADE: Oh, don't be a hog, Dundy. Your first idea that I killed Thursby because he killed Miles falls to pieces if you blame me for killing Miles, too.

196. CS: *Spade, Polhaus, and Dundy, as in 194.*

DUNDY: You haven't heard me say you killed anybody. You're the one that keeps bringing that up.

197. CS: *Dundy, Spade, and Polhaus, as in 195.*

SPADE: Say, haven't you got anything better to do than to keep popping in here early every morning asking a lot of fool questions?

DUNDY: Yeah, and getting a lot of lying answers.

SPADE: Take it easy.

198. CS: *Spade, Polhaus, and Dundy, as in 196.*

DUNDY: If you say there's nothing between you and Archer's wife, you're a liar and I'm telling you so.

199. CS: *Dundy, Spade, and Polhaus, as in 197.*

SPADE: Is that the hot tip that brought you up here at this ungodly hour of the night?

DUNDY: That's one of them.

SPADE: And the other?

200. CS: *Spade, Polhaus, and Dundy, as in 198.*

DUNDY: Let us in! (*Spade shakes his head.*) All right, Spade, we'll go. Maybe you're right in bucking us. Think it over.

Sounds of a struggle come from inside Spade's apartment. All look to frame right.

CAIRO'S VOICE: Help!

DUNDY: I guess we're going in.

SPADE: I guess you are.

The camera follows Dundy as he enters the apartment and opens the inner door.

201. LS: *Dundy and Polhaus, entering the apartment. They move to the middle of the room and Dundy stands between Brigid and Cairo, breaking up their fight. Cairo has blood on his forehead. The camera has followed the detectives and the characters have repositioned themselves so that we now see Spade's back on the left, Brigid sitting in a chair, Dundy, Cairo, and Polhaus standing.*

DUNDY: Here, what's going on in here?

CAIRO: Look! Look! Look what she did!

DUNDY: Did you do that?

BRIGID: I had to. I was alone in here with him. He tried to attack me. I had to keep him off. I couldn't bring myself to shoot him.

CAIRO: You dirty, filthy liar! You . . .

Dundy shoves Cairo into a chair to quiet him. Cairo stands up.

202. MS: *Dundy and Cairo.*

CAIRO: It isn't true! I came up here in good faith and then both of them attacked me. And then, when he went out to talk to you, he left her in here with a pistol and she said, as soon as you leave, they're going to kill me. So I called for help because I didn't want you to leave me and be murdered . . .

203. LS: *Spade, Brigid, Dundy, Cairo, and Polhaus, as in 201.*

CAIRO: . . . and then, then she struck me with a pistol.

BRIGID: Why don't you make him tell the truth? (*She stands up and kicks Cairo and they begin fighting again. Dundy and Polhaus separate them and return Brigid to her chair.*)

POLHAUS: Aw, behave yourself, sister. That's no way to act!

DUNDY: Well, Tom, I don't guess we'll be wrong running the lot of them in.

204. CS: *Spade.*

SPADE: Now, don't be in a hurry, boys. Everything can be explained.

205. LS: *Spade's back, Dundy, Brigid, Cairo, and Polhaus.*

DUNDY: I'll bet.

SPADE: Miss O'Shaughnessy, may I present Lieutenant Dundy and Detective Sergeant Polhaus? Miss O'Shaughnessy is an operative in my employ, uh, since yesterday.

CAIRO: That's a lie, too.

206. CS: *Spade, as in 204.*

SPADE: That is Mr. Joel Cairo.

207. CS: *Dundy and Cairo.*

SPADE'S VOICE: Cairo was an acquaintance of Thursby's. He came into my office late this afternoon . . .

208. CS: *Spade, as in 206.*

SPADE: . . . and hired me to find something that Thursby was supposed to have on him when he was bumped off. It looked funny to me the way he put it, so I wouldn't touch it.

209. LS: *Spade's back, Dundy, Brigid, Cairo, and Polhaus, as in 205.*

SPADE: Then he pulled a gun on me. Well, that's neither here nor there, unless we start preferring charges against each other.

Cairo realizes he is being threatened and sits down. Brigid's face begins to smile in admiration of Spade's cunning.

210. CS: *Spade, as in 208.*

SPADE: Well, anyway, Miss O'Shaughnessy and I discussed the matter and we decided to find out exactly how much he knew about Miles's and Thursby's killings, so we asked him to come up here.

211. LS: *Spade's back, Dundy, Brigid, Cairo, and Polhaus, as in 208.*

SPADE: Now, maybe we did put the questions to him a little roughly, you know how that is, Lieutenant . . .

212. CS: *Spade, as in 210.*

SPADE: . . . but we didn't hurt him enough to make him cry for help.

213.   MS: *Dundy, Cairo, and Polhaus.*

DUNDY: Well, what have you got to say to that?

CAIRO: I don't know what to say.

DUNDY: Try telling the facts.

CAIRO: What? (*As if the notion never occurred to him.*) Facts?

DUNDY: Aw, quit stalling! All you have to do is swear out a complaint they took a poke at you and I'll throw them in the can.

214.   CS: *Spade, as in 212.*

SPADE: Go ahead, Cairo. Tell him you'll do it. Then we'll swear out a complaint against you and . . .

215.   LS: *Spade's back, Dundy, Brigid, Cairo, and Polhaus, as in 211.*

SPADE: . . . he'll have the lot of us.

DUNDY: Get your hats.

216.   CS: *Spade, as in 214. He is laughing.*

SPADE: Well, boys and girls, we put it over nicely!

217.   MS: *Spade's back, Dundy, Cairo, and Polhaus. Dundy walks up to Spade.*

DUNDY: Go on, get your hats.

SPADE: Aw, don't you know when you're being kidded?

DUNDY: No, but that can wait till we get down to the hall.

218.   MS: *Spade, Brigid, Dundy, Cairo, and Polhaus.*

SPADE: Aw, wake up, Dundy, you're being kidded. When I heard the buzzer, I said to Miss O'Shaughnessy and Cairo here, I said, "There's the police again. They're getting to be a nuisance." (*He walks across the room and leans on a chair.*)

219.   CS: *Spade, from a low angle and to his left side.*

SPADE: . . . "When you hear them going, one of you scream and then we'll see how far along we can string them until they tumble."

220.   LS: *Dundy, Brigid, Cairo, Polhaus, and Spade, as in the end of 218.*

POLHAUS: Stop it, Sam.

DUNDY: That cut on his head, how did that get there?

SPADE: Ask him. Maybe he cut himself shaving.

CAIRO: The cut? No, when we pretended to be struggling for the gun, I fell over the carpet. I fell.

POLHAUS: Aw, horsefeathers!

DUNDY: Take him along anyway, for packing a gun.

SPADE (*walking over to face Dundy*): Naw, don't be a sap. That gun was a plant. It was one of mine.

221.   MS: *Dundy's back, Spade, and Polhaus.*

SPADE: Too bad it was only a twenty-five or maybe you could prove that was the gun that Miles and Thursby were shot with.

222. L S : *Dundy, Brigid, Spade, Cairo, and Polhaus, as at the end of 220. Dundy punches Spade in the face and Spade staggers back into Polhaus's arms. Polhaus then restrains Spade from attacking Dundy.*

POLHAUS: No, Sam, no!

SPADE: Well, then, get him out of here.

DUNDY: Get their names and addresses.

CAIRO: My name is Joel Cairo, Hotel Belvedere.

BRIGID: I . . .

SPADE: Miss O'Shaughnessy's address is my office.

DUNDY: Where do you live?

SPADE: Get him out of here! I've had enough of this!

POLHAUS: Now, now, take it easy, will you, Sam? (*To Dundy.*) Is that all you want, Lieutenant?

DUNDY: Yeah.

CAIRO: I think I'll be going now.

SPADE: Well, what's the hurry, Cairo?

CAIRO (*leaving*): There is no hurry. It's getting quite late, and . . .

SPADE (*To Polhaus, referring to Dundy.*): Tell him to leave the gun.

Dundy puts the gun on a table and leaves.

POLHAUS: I hope you know what you're doing, Sam. (*Polhaus leaves and the camera follows him to the door.*)

223. M S : *Brigid and Spade. He is laughing as he picks up her shoe and hands it to her.*

BRIGID: You're absolutely the wildest, most unpredictable person I've ever known. Do you always carry on so high-handedly?

He begins to roll a cigarette by the desk with his back to her. She buttons her sleeve buttons.

SPADE: Well, you've had your talk with Cairo. Now you can talk to me.

BRIGID: Oh, yes, of course.

SPADE: I'm listening. . . . I'm still listening.

BRIGID: Oh, look at the time! I must be going.

SPADE: Oh, no. Not till you've told me all about it.

BRIGID: Am I a prisoner?

SPADE: Maybe the boy outside hasn't gone home yet.

BRIGID (*standing up and walking over to look out of the window*): Do you suppose he's still there?

SPADE: Likely. You can start now.

BRIGID: You are the most insistent person. (*She sits down.*)

SPADE: And wild and unpredictable, huh? Say, what's this bird, this falcon, that everybody's all steamed up about?

BRIGID: Supposing I wouldn't tell you anything about it at all? What would you do? Something wild and unpredictable?

SPADE: I might.

BRIGID: It's a black figure, as you know, smooth and shiny, of a bird, a hawk or falcon, about that high.

SPADE: Oh, here. (*He takes a coat from the chair she is sitting on.*) Well, what er . . . what makes it so important?

BRIGID: I don't know. They wouldn't tell me. They offered me five hundred pounds if I'd help them get it away from the man who had it.

Spade walks into the next room, turns on the light and walks out of sight.

SPADE (*off*): That was in Istanbul?

BRIGID: Er, Marmora.

He reappears, preparing coffee in a coffeepot.

SPADE: Go ahead.

BRIGID: But that's all. They promised me five hundred pounds if I'd help them, and I did. Then we found out that Joel Cairo intended to desert us, taking the Falcon with him, and leaving Floyd and me nothing, so we did exactly that to him. (*Spade has disappeared into the kitchen again, and then returned with two coffee cups.*) But then I wasn't any better off than I was before because Floyd hadn't any intention of keeping his promise to me . . .

224. CS: *Brigid.*

BRIGID: . . . about sharing equally. I'd learned that by the time we got here.

225. MS: *Spade, walking over to Brigid, bringing her into frame.*

SPADE: What's the bird made of?

BRIGID: Porcelain or black stone. I don't know. I only saw it once for a few minutes. Floyd showed it to me when we first got hold of it.

SPADE (*smiling at her*): You are a liar!

BRIGID: I am. I've always been a liar.

SPADE: Well, don't . . . don't brag about it. Was there any truth at all in that yarn?

BRIGID: Some. Not very much.

SPADE: Well, we got all night. Coffee'll be ready soon. We'll have a cup and try again.

BRIGID (*clutching her head in exasperation*): Oh, I'm . . . I'm so tired, so tired of lying and making up lies, not knowing . . . (*She lies back on the sofa with her hand on her forehead.*)

226. CS: *Brigid.*

BRIGID: . . . what is a lie and what's the truth. I wish . . .

227. CS: *Spade, from a low angle, staring intently at her. He starts to bend down.*

228. CS: *Brigid and Spade. He bends down into the frame, preparing to kiss her. Suddenly he stops and looks through the fluttering curtains behind her. The camera moves past his head and we see what he is looking at. Wilmer*

*is standing in a doorway on the opposite side of the street and looking up
at Spade's window. Ominous music sounds on the soundtrack. Fade out.*

Exterior, day

229. C S : *sign: "Hotel Belvedere."*

Wipe.

Hotel Belvedere, interior, day

230. L S : *hotel lobby. Spade enters, walks over to the desk and picks up the
house phone. Camera moves in to a MS.*

    S P A D E : I want to talk to Mr. Cairo. Joel Cairo. (*He looks offscreen, notic-
ing someone.*)

231. L S : *rear angle of Wilmer, sitting in a lobby chair and reading a newspaper.*

232. M S : *Spade, as in the end of 230, still holding the telephone.*

    S P A D E : Oh, thanks. (*He places the receiver down and begins to walk out
of frame.*)

233. L S : *Spade and Wilmer. Wilmer is seated in the front of the frame with a
newspaper in front of his face. Spade walks toward him from the hotel desk
and sits in a chair placed at a right angle on Wilmer's left side.*

    S P A D E (*beginning to roll a cigarette*)): Where is he?

    W I L M E R (*dropping his paper so that his face faces the camera*): What?

    S P A D E : Where is he?

    W I L M E R : Who?

    S P A D E : Cairo.

    W I L M E R : What do you think you're doing, Jack? Kidding me?

    S P A D E : I'll tell you when I am. New York, aren't you?

    W I L M E R : Shove off! (*He begins reading the paper again.*)

    S P A D E : You're going to have to talk to me before you're through, sonny.
Some of you will, . . . (*He looks toward Wilmer.*) and you can tell the fat
man I said so.

    W I L M E R (*dropping his paper again*): Keep asking for it and you're going
to get it, plenty. I told you to shove off. Shove off!

    S P A D E (*standing up and looking directly at Wilmer*): People lose teeth
talking like that. If you want to hang around, you'll be polite. (*He begins
to walk back toward the desk.*)

234. M S : *Spade, signalling to someone offscreen.*

235. M S : *the hotel desk. A woman behind the counter tells Luke, the house detective, that Spade is signalling him. Luke looks offscreen and recognizes
Spade.*

236. L S : *hotel lobby. Luke, deep in the frame, walks to the right of the camera.
Spade comes into view and greets him. The camera dollies back as they
walk toward Wilmer.*

    L U K E : Hello, Sam.

    S P A D E : Hello, Luke.

    L U K E : Say, that was too bad about Miles.

SPADE: Yeah, it was a tough break. I want to show you something. (*The camera stops when Wilmer comes into view. Spade stands to his right, Luke to his left.*) What do you let these cheap gunmen hang around the lobby for, with their heaters bulging in their clothes?

LUKE (*looking at Wilmer*): What do you want here? (*Wilmer stands up.*) Well, if you don't want anything, beat it. . . .

237. CS: *Wilmer and Spade. Wilmer looks first offscreen at Luke, then glares at Spade.*

LUKE (*off*): . . . and don't come back.

WILMER: I won't forget you guys.

Spade slowly blows cigarette smoke into Wilmer's face.

238. MS: *Luke, Wilmer, and Spade. Wilmer sullenly walks off to screen left. Luke and Spade watch him as he disappears.*

LUKE: What is it?

SPADE: I don't know. I just spotted him.

LUKE: Say, what about Miles?

SPADE (*noticing something in the direction of the lobby desk and starting to walk in that direction*): I'll see you, Luke.

239. MS: *Cairo, looking disheveled and tired, walking up to desk clerk.*

CAIRO: 603.

DESK CLERK: Yes, sir.

Spade walks into frame. Cairo turns to greet him, but suspiciously.

SPADE: Good morning.

CAIRO: Good morning.

DESK CLERK: Here you are, sir.

The camera moves with Spade and Cairo as they walk away from the desk.

SPADE: Let's go some place where we can talk.

CAIRO: No, no, no. Our private conversations have not been such that I am anxious to continue them. Forgive my speaking so bluntly, but it is the truth.

SPADE: You mean last night? What else could I do? I had to throw in with her. I don't know where that bird is; neither do you. She does. How are we going to get it if I don't play along with her? (*They stop and face one another.*)

CAIRO: You always have a very smooth explanation . . .

240. MS: *Cairo, from rear, and Spade.*

CAIRO: . . . ready, hmm.

SPADE: What do you want me to do, learn to stutter? Dundy take you down to the station? How long did they work on you?

241. MS: *Cairo and Spade, reverse of 240.*

CAIRO (*rubbing his head*): Till a little while ago.

SPADE: What did they shake out of you?

CAIRO: Shake out? Not one thing. I adhered to the course you indicated earlier in your rooms, but I certainly wish you would have invented a more reasonable story. I felt distinctly like an idiot repeating it.

242. MS: *Cairo and Spade.*

SPADE: Well, don't worry about the story's goofiness. A sensible one would've had us all in the cooler. You sure you didn't tell 'em anything?

CAIRO: I did not.

SPADE: You'll want sleep if you've been standing up under a police grilling all night. I'll see you later. (*He walks off.*)

Wipe.

Spade's outer office, interior, day

243. LS: *Effie, standing up and on the phone. Spade enters.*

EFFIE: No, not yet. . . . Yes, I'll have him call you the minute he comes in. (*To Spade.*) That's the third time she's called this morning. Miss O'Shaughnessy's in there.

SPADE: Anything else?

EFFIE: The District Attorney's office called. Bryan would like to see you.

SPADE: Uh-huh.

EFFIE: And a Mr. Gutman called. And when I told him you weren't in, he said, "Would you please tell him that the young man gave me his message, and that I phoned and will phone again?"

The camera moves in for a CS *of Spade as he rubs his face, which has a look of pleased anticipation. He snaps his fingers as if something suddenly made sense.*

SPADE: Gutman, huh? Thanks, darling. (*The camera follows as he opens the door to his inner office.*)

Spade's inner office, interior, day

244. MS: *Brigid, standing in front of the window with "*SAMUEL SPADE*" on it. She turns to face the camera. Spade enters the frame and she comes up anxiously to him.*

BRIGID: Darling. Somebody's been in my apartment. It's all upside down, every which way. I changed as fast as I could and came right over here. You must have let that boy follow you there.

SPADE: Oh no, angel. I shook him off long before I ever went to your place. It might have been Cairo. (*She sits down, still looking up attentively at him.*) He wasn't at the hotel last night. He told me he'd been standing up under a police grilling. I wonder.

BRIGID: You saw Joel this morning?

SPADE: Yeah.

BRIGID: Why?

SPADE: Because, my own true love, I've got to keep in some sort of touch with all the loose ends of this dizzy affair *if* I'm ever going to make heads or tails of it. Now, we've got to find a new home for you.

BRIGID: I won't go back there!

Spade bends down and kisses her gently on the nose.

SPADE: I got an idea. Wait a minute. (*He walks out of the frame. She watches him.*)

Spade's outer office, interior, day

245. MS: *Spade walks back into his outer office and starts talking to Effie. The camera pans with him and she comes into the frame, seated at her desk. He sits on a wooden entrance gate.*

SPADE: What does your woman's intuition tell you about her?

EFFIE: She's all right. Oh, maybe it's her own fault for being in whatever the trouble is, but she's all right, if that's what you mean.

SPADE: That's what I mean. Are you strong enough for her to put her up for a few days?

EFFIE: You mean at home?

SPADE: Yeah.

EFFIE: Is she in any danger, Sam?

SPADE: I think she is.

EFFIE: Gee, that'd scare Mom into a green hemorrhage. I'd have to say she's a surprise witness or something you're keeping under cover until the last minute.

SPADE: You're a darling. (*He stands up and walks over to the door to his inner office. The camera follows him. He calls to Brigid and she appears at the door.*) Oh, Brigid, Effie here's offered to put you up for a few days.

BRIGID: Oh, that's very kind of you.

The camera pans left as the both of them walk over to Effie's desk and she reappears in the frame.

SPADE: You'd better start now. Go out the back entrance. There's usually a cab parked there by the alleyway. You ride part of the way with her over to the bridge, and make sure you're not followed.

Effie gets up and puts her hat on. Spade walks both of them to the outer door.

SPADE: You better change cabs a couple of times, just to be on the safe side.

EFFIE: I'll give Mom a ring.

SPADE: There's time enough for that when you get back. (*To Brigid.*) I'll call you later. (*They leave and the camera follows Spade as he walks back to his inner office.*)

Spade's inner office, interior, day

246. MS: *Spade. The camera follows as he walks from the door over to his desk, sits down, and dials his telephone.*

SPADE: Hello. This is Samuel Spade. Say, my secretary tells me Mr. Bryan wants to see me. Yeah, yeah. Ask him what time's most convenient for him. Spade. S-p-a-d-e. (*Spade looks up as Iva's arm and back appear in the frame.*) Hello, honey. (*He speaks again into the telephone.*) Yeah. Two-thirty. All right. Thanks. (*He looks up at her. As she starts talking, she moves around to the back of Spade's desk and the camera follows her, eventually bringing Spade back into the frame.*)

I V A : Oh, Sam, forgive me. Please forgive me. I sent those policemen to your place last night. I was mad, crazy with jealousy. I phoned them, if they went there, they'd learn something about Miles's murder.

S P A D E : What made you think of that?

I V A : I was mad, Sam, I wanted to hurt you.

He rises and walks over to the window near her.

S P A D E : Did you tell them who you were when you phoned?

I V A : Oh, no, Sam dearest, I . . .

S P A D E : Where'd you phone from?

247. C S : *Iva and the side of Spade's face.*

I V A : The drugstore across from your place.

248. C S : *Iva, from the rear, and Spade.*

S P A D E : You'd better hurry along home and think of something to tell the police. You'll be hearing from them and, . . .

249. C S : *Iva and Spade, as in 247.*

S P A D E : . . . by the way, where were you the night Miles was murdered?

I V A : Home. I was . . .

Spade shakes his head in disbelief.

S P A D E : No, . . .

250. C S : *Iva and Spade, as in 248.*

S P A D E : . . . but if that's your story, it's all right with me.

251. C S : *Iva and Spade, side angle.*

S P A D E : Now, you run along.

252. M S : *Spade, behind his desk with his back to the camera, watching Iva walk to the door and leave the office. The telephone rings and he answers it, turning to face the camera, which moves in for a C S as he speaks.*

S P A D E : Hello. Yeah, this is Spade. . . . Oh, yes, Mr. Gutman. I got it. Yeah. I been waiting to hear from you. . . . Now. The sooner, the better. Say, five minutes? Right. 12-C.

Wipe.

Gutman's hotel, interior, day

253. L S : *Spade, leaving elevator, nodding to the elevator operator and walking to his left down the corridor.*

E L E V A T O R O P E R A T O R : 12-C, to your left, sir.

The camera pans right to follow Spade as he walks to the end of the corridor.

254. M S : *Spade, rear angle, as he buzzes 12-C. The door is opened by Wilmer. Gutman is visible at the far end of the room. He comes toward the door to greet Spade.*

Gutman's hotel suite, interior, day

255. L S : *Gutman, Spade, and Wilmer. Gutman comes to greet Spade and shakes his hand.*

GUTMAN : Ah, Mr. Spade.

SPADE : How do you do, Mr. Gutman?

Gutman continues to hold Spade's hand and escorts him to the middle of the room while Wilmer, and the camera, follow. Gutman picks up a decanter of liquor and a glass, and nods to Wilmer. The camera follows as Wilmer goes into an interior room and closes the door, then the camera pans back to Spade and Gutman.

GUTMAN : You begin well, sir . . .

256. C S : *Spade, from the side rear, and Gutman.*

GUTMAN : . . . I distrust a man who says "when." He's got to be careful not to drink too much too much because he's not to be trusted when he does. (*He hands Spade a drink.*)

257. C S : *Spade and a rear view of Gutman.*

258. L S : *Spade and Gutman.*

GUTMAN : Well, sir, here's to plain speaking and clear understanding. *They drink, then Gutman motions to Spade to sit on a chair and sits himself on an adjacent chair. The camera moves in to a* M S *of them.*

GUTMAN : You're a close-mouthed man?

259. C S : *Spade.*

SPADE : No, I like to talk.

260. M S : *Spade and Gutman.*

GUTMAN : Better and better. I distrust a close-mouthed man. He generally picks the wrong time to talk and says the wrong things. Talking's something you can't do judiciously unless you keep in practice. (*Spade lights one of Gutman's cigars.*) Now, sir, we'll talk if you like.

261. M S : *Gutman, from a low angle which emphasizes his huge belly.*

GUTMAN : I'll tell you right out, I'm a man who likes talking to a man who likes to talk. (*He is also smoking a cigar.*)

SPADE (*off*): Swell, . . .

262. C S : *Spade.*

SPADE : . . . will we talk about the black bird?

263. M S : *Gutman, as in 261.*

GUTMAN (*laughing*): Hm, hm, hm. You're the man for me, sir. No beating about the bush. Right to the point. Let's talk about the black bird, by all means. First, sir, answer me a question: . . .

264. M S : *Spade and, from side rear, Gutman.*

GUTMAN : . . . Are you here as Miss O'Shaughnessy's representative?

SPADE : Well, there's nothing certain either way. It depends.

265. M S : *Gutman, as in 263.*

GUTMAN : It depends on? Maybe it depends on Joel Cairo.

266. MS: *Spade and Gutman, as in 264.*

    SPADE: Maybe.

    GUTMAN: The question is, then, which you represent. It'll be one or the other.

    SPADE: I didn't say so.

    GUTMAN: Who else is it?

    SPADE (*tapping his chest*): There's me.

267. MS: *Gutman, as in 266. He laughs and sits back in his chair.*

    GUTMAN: Aha, hmm, hmm. That's wonderful, sir, wonderful. I do like a man who tells you right out he's looking out for himself. Don't we all? I don't trust a man who says he's not.

268. CS: *Spade.*

    SPADE: Uh-huh. Now let's talk about the black bird.

269. MS: *Spade and Gutman, side angle, with glass decanter and drink mixers in the front bottom of the frame.*

    GUTMAN: Let's! Mr. Spade, have you any conception of how much money can be got for that black bird?

    SPADE: No.

    GUTMAN: Well, sir, if I told you, if I told you half, you'd call me a liar.

    SPADE: No, not even if I thought so. But you tell me what it is and I'll figure out the profit.

    GUTMAN: Hm, hm, hm. You mean, you don't know what that bird is?

270. CS: *Spade.*

    SPADE: Oh, I know what it's supposed to look like. (*He suddenly looks directly and sternly into Gutman's eyes.*) And I know the value in human life you people put on it.

271. MS: *Spade and Gutman, as in 269.*

    GUTMAN: She didn't tell you what it is? (*Spade shakes his head "No."*) Cairo didn't either?

    SPADE: He offered me ten thousand for it.

    GUTMAN (*contemptuously*): Ten thousand! Dollars, mind you, not even pounds!

272. CS: Gutman, as in 267. He sits forward in his chair.

    GUTMAN: ... Do they know what that bird is, sir? What is your impression?

273. CS: *Spade.*

    SPADE: Well, there's not much to go by. Cairo didn't say he did and he didn't say he didn't. She said she didn't, but I took it for granted she was lying.

274. CS: *Gutman, as in 272.*

    GUTMAN: Not an injudicious thing to do. (*He smiles grandly.*) If they don't know, I'm the only one in the whole wide, sweet world who does.

275. CS: *Spade.*

    SPADE: Swell, when you've told me, that'll make two of us.

276. C S : *Gutman, as in 274.*

GUTMAN: Mathematically correct, sir, but I don't know for certain that I'm going to tell you.

277. M S : *Spade and, from side rear, Gutman.*

SPADE: Oh, don't be foolish. You know what it is; I know where it is. That's why I'm here.

GUTMAN: Well, sir, where is it? (*Spade says nothing.*) You see? I must tell you what I know but you won't tell me what you know. . . .

278. C S : *Gutman, as in 276.*

GUTMAN: It's hardly equitable, sir. No, no, I don't think we can do business along those lines.

279. M S : *Spade, suddenly furious. The camera pulls back as he stands up and hurls his cigar onto the floor, near Gutman.*

SPADE: Well, think again and think fast! I told that gunsel of yours you'd have to talk to me before you're through. (*He points at Gutman.*) I'm telling you now, you'll have to talk to me today, or you *are* through. (*He flings his glass onto the coffee table, smashing the glass.*)

280. L S : *Gutman, sitting in the rear of the frame, and Spade, standing in the front right of the frame, his back to the camera.*

SPADE: What are you wasting my time for? I can get along without you. And another thing, . . . (*Wilmer enters the frame from the left and Spade glares at him briefly before returning his attention to Gutman.*) . . . keep that gunsel out of my way while you're making up your mind. I'll kill him if you don't, I'll kill him.

GUTMAN (*casually smoking his cigar, seemingly unaffected by this outburst*): Well, sir, I must say you have a most violent temper.

Spade stalks over to the right of the room to get his hat, and returns. The camera pans right and then back with him.

SPADE: Think it over. You've got till five o'clock. (*Spade then stalks over to the door and the camera follows him.*) Then you're either in or out, for keeps! (*He walks out of the room, slamming the door.*)

Hotel corridor, interior, day

281. L S : *Spade enters the hallway from Gutman's suite and walks toward the camera. He puts his hat on and takes his handkerchief out to wipe off his hands. His face breaks out into a self-satisfied smile as he nears the camera, which pans left with him and moves into a M S as he presses the elevator button. His hand is shaking. The camera moves back to L S as the door opens and Spade steps in. At exactly the same time, the elevator door to his left opens and Joel Cairo steps out and walks in the direction of Gutman's suite. Neither sees the other. Dissolve.*

District Attorney Bryan's office, interior, day

282. CS: *Bryan. The camera pulls back to a* LS *of Spade, the assistant district attorney, Bryan, and a stenographer.*

BRYAN: Who killed Thursby?

SPADE (*off*): I don't know.

BRYAN: Perhaps you don't, but you could make an excellent guess.

SPADE (*now visible*): My guess might be excellent, or it might be crummy, but Mrs. Spade didn't raise any children dippy enough to make guesses in front of a district attorney, an assistant district attorney, and a stenographer.

283. CS: *Bryan.*

BRYAN: Why shouldn't you, if you've nothing to conceal?

284. MS: *Spade and, from rear, Bryan.*

SPADE: Everybody has something to conceal.

285. CS: *Bryan, as in 283.*

BRYAN: I'm a sworn officer of the law, twenty-four hours a day, and neither formality nor informality justifies you withholding the evidence of crime from me, except, of course, on constitutional grounds.

286. LS: *Spade, the assistant district attorney, Bryan, and the stenographer, as at the end of 282. Spade stands up aggressively as he addresses Bryan over his desk, and the camera moves in for a tighter shot.*

SPADE: Now, both you and the police have as much as accused me of being mixed up in the other night's murders. Well, I've had trouble with both of you before and, as far as I can see, my best chance of clearing myself of the trouble you're trying to make for me is by bringing in the murderers all tied up, and the only chance I've got of catching them and tying them up and bringing them in is by staying as far away as possible from you and the police, because you'd only gum up the works. (*He suddenly turns and addresses the stenographer. His tone switches from one of outrage to one of polite solicitation.*) You getting this all right, son, or am I going too fast for you?

STENOGRAPHER: No, sir, I'm getting it all right.

SPADE: Good work. (*He turns back to Bryan and resumes his posture of outrage.*)

287. MS: *Spade and, from rear, Bryan.*

SPADE: Now, if you want to go to the board and tell them I'm obstructing justice and ask them to revoke my license, hop to it. You tried it once before and it didn't get you anything but a good laugh, all around.

288. CS: *Bryan.*

BRYAN: Now, look here.

289. MS: *Spade and Bryan, as in 287.*

SPADE: And I don't want any more of these informal talks. I've nothing to say to you or the police, and I'm tired of being called things by every

crackpot on the city payroll so, if you want to see me, pinch me or sub-
poena me or something, and I'll come down with my lawyer. (*The camera follows him as he takes his hat and walks out the door, closing it
behind him.*) I'll see you at the inquest, maybe!
Wipe.

Crowded city street, exterior, day

290. LS: *Spade walks briskly along a crowded sidewalk, the camera pans to
the right with him and stops when he sees Wilmer standing in a doorway.
He stands face to face with Wilmer.*

WILMER: Come on, he wants to see you.

SPADE: Well, I didn't expect you till five twenty-five. I hope I haven't
kept you waiting.

WILMER: Keep on riding me. They're going to be picking iron out of
your liver.

SPADE (*smirking*): The cheaper the crook, the gaudier the patter, huh?
Well, let's go.

*They walk back in the direction from which Spade came. The camera
follows.*
Wipe.

Gutman's hotel, interior, day

291. LS: *Spade and Wilmer. The camera tracks back as they leave the elevator
and walk toward both the camera and Gutman's hotel suite. Wilmer has his
hands deep in his overcoat pockets. Spade suddenly drops behind him and
yanks his overcoat shoulders down over his arms, immobilizing him. Spade
then pulls two automatic pistols from Wilmer's pockets and points toward
Gutman's rooms with a smirk.*

SPADE: Come on, this'll put you in solid with your boss. (*He follows Wilmer to Gutman's door and presses the buzzer.*)

292. LS: *Gutman, dressed now in a smoking robe, opens the door and Wilmer
and Spade enter.*

GUTMAN: Ah, come in, sir. Thank you for coming. Come in.

Spade hands Gutman Wilmer's guns. Gutman seems puzzled.

SPADE: Here. You shouldn't let him go around with these on him. He
might get himself hurt.

GUTMAN: Well, well, what's this?

SPADE: A crippled newsie took them away from him. I made him give
them back.

Gutman gives the guns to Wilmer, laughs robustly, and closes the door.

GUTMAN: By gad, sir, you're a chap worth knowing, an amazing character. Give me your hat. (*He takes Spade's hat and all go to the center of
the room. The camera follows and Wilmer exits to the left. Gutman
pours Spade a drink.*)

GUTMAN: Sit down. I owe you an apology, sir.

SPADE: Never mind that. Let's talk about the black bird.

GUTMAN: All right, sir, let's. Let's. (*He hands him the drink and a humidor of cigars.*) This is going to be the most astounding thing you've ever heard of, sir . . .

293. MS: *Gutman and Spade. Gutman replaces the humidor of cigars on the table and sits in a chair.*

GUTMAN: . . . and I say this knowing that a man of your caliber and your profession must have known some astounding things in his time. What do you know of the Order of the Hospital of Saint John of Jerusalem, later known as the Knights of Rhodes and other things?

SPADE: Crusaders or something, weren't they?

GUTMAN: Very good. Sit down. (*Spade sits on a couch and lights the cigar he accepted.*) In 1539, these crusading knights persuaded Emperor Charles the Fifth to give them the island of Malta. He made but one condition, that they pay him each year the tribute of a falcon in acknowledgment that Malta was still under Spain. Do you follow me?

SPADE: Uh-huh.

Gutman looks briefly off to his right, in the direction of the room where Wilmer is. He now speaks in a more confidential tone.

294. CS: *Gutman, looking back in Spade's direction.*

GUTMAN: Have you any conception of the extreme, the immeasurable wealth of the Order of that time?

295. CS: *Spade.*

SPADE: I imagine they were pretty well fixed.

296. MS: *Gutman and Spade.*

GUTMAN: "Pretty well" is putting it mildly. They were rolling in wealth, sir. For years they'd taken from the East nobody knows what spoils of gems, precious metals, silks, ivories, sir. We all know the Holy Wars to them were largely a matter of loot.

297. CS: *Gutman.*

GUTMAN: The Knights were profoundly grateful to the Emperor Charles for his generosity toward them. They hit upon the happy thought of sending him for his first year's tribute not an insignificant live bird . . . (*He looks furtively in the direction of Wilmer's room and leans forward in his chair, speaking now in a more confidential tone.*) . . . but a glorious golden falcon crusted from head to foot with the finest jewels in their coffers. Well, sir, what do you think of that?

298. CS: *Spade.*

SPADE: I don't know.

299. MS: *Gutman and Spade, as in 296.*

GUTMAN: These are facts, historical facts; not schoolbook history, not Mr. Wells's history, but history nevertheless.

300.   M S :   *Gutman, shot from a low angle to emphasize his girth. He is holding his glass.*

GUTMAN :   They sent this foot-high jeweled bird to Charles, who was then in Spain. They sent it in a galley commanded by a member of the Order. It never reached Spain. A famous admiral of buccaneers took the Knights' galley and the bird.

301.   M S :   *Spade, as in 298.*

GUTMAN (*off*):   In 1713 it turned up in Sicily.

302.   M S :   *Gutman and Spade.*

GUTMAN :   In 1840 it appeared in Paris. It had, by that time, acquired a coat of black enamel so that it looked nothing more than a fairly interesting black statuette. In that disguise, sir, it was, as you may say, kicked around Paris for over three score years by private owners too stupid to see what it was under the skin.

303.   C S :   *Gutman.*

GUTMAN :   Then, hrumph, in 1923 a Greek dealer named Charilaos Konstantinides found it in an obscure shop.

304.   M S :   *Gutman and Spade. While Gutman speaks, he stands up and pours a drink for Spade and hands it to him.*

GUTMAN :   No thickness of enamel could conceal value from his eyes. You begin to believe me a little?

SPADE :   I haven't said I didn't.

GUTMAN :   Well, sir, to hold it safe while pursuing his researches into its history, Charliaos re-enamelled the bird. (*The camera moves in on Gutman as he leans against the mantle.*) Despite this precaution, however, I got wind of his find. Ah, if I'd only known a few days sooner. . . .

305.   M S :   *Spade.*

GUTMAN (*off*):   . . . I was in London when I heard. I packed a bag, got on the boat train immediately. . . .

306.   C S :   *Gutman, from a low angle.*

GUTMAN :   . . . On the train I opened a paper, *The Times,* and read that Charilaos's establishment had been burglarized and him murdered. Sure enough, on arriving there I discovered the bird was gone. (*The camera follows as he starts to move back toward Spade.*) That was seventeen years ago. Well, sir, it took me seventeen years to locate that bird, but I did. I wanted it. I'm a man not easily discouraged . . .

307.   C S :   *Spade.*

GUTMAN'S VOICE :   . . . when I want something. I traced it to the home of a Russian general, . . .

308.   C S :   *Gutman, as in the end of 306.*

GUTMAN :   . . . one Kemidov, in an Istanbul suburb. He didn't know a thing about it. It was nothing but a black enamelled figure to him. His natural contrariness kept him from selling it to me, but I made an offer.

So I sent him some, er, agents to get it. Well, sir, they got it and I haven't got it, but I'm going to get it. (*He extends his hand.*)

309. M S : *Gutman and Spade.*

GUTMAN: Your glass? (*He pours another drink and hands it to Spade.*)

SPADE: Well, then, the bird doesn't really belong to any of you, but to a General Kemidov.

GUTMAN: Well, sir, you might as well say it belonged to the King of Spain. I don't see how you can honestly grant anyone else a clear title to it, except by right of possession. (*He sits next to Spade on the couch and confidentially places his hand on Spade's knee.*) And now, sir, before we start to talk prices, how soon can you, . . .

310. M S : *Gutman, from rear, and Spade.*

GUTMAN: . . . or how soon are you willing to produce the Falcon?

SPADE: A couple of days.

GUTMAN: That is satisfactory.

311. M S : *Gutman and Spade, reverse of 310.*

GUTMAN: Well, sir, here's to a fair bargain, profits large enough for both of us. (*Both drink.*)

SPADE: What's your idea of a fair bargain?

GUTMAN: I will give you twenty-five thousand dollars when you deliver the Falcon to me and another twenty-five thousand later on, or, I will give you one quarter of what I realize on the Falcon. . . .

312. M S : *Gutman and Spade, as in 310.*

GUTMAN: . . . That would amount to a vastly greater sum.

SPADE: How much greater?

GUTMAN: Who knows? Shall we say a hundred thousand? Will you believe me if I name a sum that seems the probable minimum?

SPADE: Why not?

GUTMAN (*placing his hand on Spade's knee again*): What would you say to a quarter of a million?

SPADE: Then you think the dingus is worth a million, huh?

GUTMAN: In your own words, "Why not?"

SPADE (*beginning to look groggy*): Hum, that's a lot of dough.

GUTMAN: A lot of dough.

SPADE (*trying to remain alert*): The minimum, huh? What's the maximum?

313. C S : *Gutman, out of focus, to simulate Spade's drugged point of view.*

GUTMAN: The maximum, I refuse to guess.

314. M S : *Gutman and Spade.*

GUTMAN: You'd think me crazy. I don't know. There's no telling how high it could go, sir. That is the one and only truth about it.

315. M S : *Gutman and Spade, from a slightly different angle. Spade gets up and starts to stagger around the room, knocking over a table with a vase of flowers upon it. The camera pulls back to* LS.

GUTMAN: Wilmer!

Wilmer enters from the left of the frame and trips Spade, who collapses on the floor. Gutman removes his smoking gown and walks toward a closet. Wilmer viciously kicks Spade in the head as Cairo enters the frame from the direction Wilmer had come. Cairo steps over Spade and then watches him on the floor.

316. MS: *Gutman, taking his suit jacket from a closet and then picking up his hat.*

317. LS: *Wilmer, Cairo, and Gutman walk toward and out the door as Spade remains unconscious on the floor. The camera follows Wilmer, Cairo, and Gutman.*
Fade out.
Fade in.

318. LS: *Spade, lying on the floor in Gutman's suite. It is now night and he staggers to his feet.*

319. MS: *The bathroom of Gutman's suite. Spade staggers in, turns on the light, and goes to the sink and splashes his face with water.*

320. MS: *Gutman's suite, outside the bathroom door. Spade comes in and begins to dial the telephone.*

321. CS: *Spade, occasionally grimacing with pain.*
     SPADE: Hello, Effie. It's me.
     EFFIE'S VOICE (*barely audible*): Yes, I know.
     SPADE: Let me talk to Miss O'Shaughnessy. . . . She isn't there? . . .
     What, she didn't show up? . . . Oh. Well, listen, you get on back to the
     office and wait there till I come or you hear from me. . . . Yeah, let's do
     something right for a change. *He hangs up and looks down. The camera
     tilts down and we see his hands open a container and go through a desk
     calendar.*
     Side wipe.

322. LS: *Gutman's bedroom. Spade is looking everywhere and overturning the
     mattress. The camera moves in for a* MS *as he sits down, looks at the night
     table drawer as well as objects on top of it, and finally picks up a dis-
     carded newspaper and looks through it.*

323. CS: *the camera moves in on the newspaper to the shipping news. Circled,
     under "Arriving Today," is "5:35 P.M.—La Paloma from Hong Kong."*
     Dissolve.

The harbor, exterior, night

324. LS: La Paloma *is on fire and firefighters are trying to put it out. One is
     climbing a ladder up the side of the ship. Sounds of sirens and commotion.*

325. LS: *the ship is listing in the water.*

326. LS: *fireman fighting the fire.*

327. LS: *a fireman climbing a ladder on the ship side.*

328. LS: *a fireman coming to assist another who is working a water cannon.*

329. LS: *the side of the burning ship, from the crowded dock. The backs of two
     policemen are in the front of the frame, with groups of men closer to the
     ship. After the initial background dialogue, Spade appears in front of the
     police and walks to the right. The camera follows him until he stops to
     question a harbor official.*
     MAN'S VOICE: It started in the hold aft, in the rear basement.
     SECOND MAN'S VOICE: What insurance was she carrying?
     MAN'S VOICE: Anybody burn?
     MAN'S VOICE: No.
     MAN'S VOICE: Only the harbor watch was aboard.
     SPADE: Someone I know came a . . .
     HARBOR OFFICIAL: What?
     SPADE: Someone I know came aboard this afternoon. I haven't seen her
     since. I'm worried.
     HARBOR OFFICIAL: No reason to be, mister. Everybody got off all right.
     SPADE: I wonder if you saw her. She's kind of small, about five foot uh. . . .
     HARBOR OFFICIAL: I couldn't, I couldn't tell you, mister, but if she
     came aboard, she got off all right. Only the harbor watch was aboard
     when the fire started.

Spade nods thanks and walks out of the frame.
Side wipe.

Spade's office, interior, night

330. M S :   *Spade and Effie. He is sitting back in his chair and she is tending to*
    his head wounds.

> S P A D E :   . . . Now you know as much about it as I do, precious. Maybe
> they went down to the ship, maybe they didn't.

> E F F I E :   The part about the bird is thrilling.

> S P A D E :   Heh-heh. Or ridiculous. (*Spade starts up at the sound of*
> *offscreen noises. The camera pans left to the door and Captain*
> *Jacoby comes in holding a newspaper-wrapped package. He knocks*
> *over a cabinet. Spade reappears in the frame, watching him. Jacoby*
> *drops the package.*)

> J A C O B Y :   You know . . .

331. C S :   *the package landing on the floor.*

332. M S :   *Jacoby and Spade, as at the end of 330.*

> J A C O B Y :   . . . Falcon. (*He stumbles over to a couch and collapses onto it.*
> *Spade follows and sits next to him.*)

> S P A D E :   Lock that door.

Effie races through the door to lock the door in the outer office.

333. M S :   *Jacoby and Spade, shot from a side angle. Spade goes through*
    Jacoby's pockets, finds a wallet, and looks through it.

334. M S :   *Jacoby and Spade in the foreground of the frame, as in the end of*
    332. Effie closes the inner door in the rear and then watches in horror.

> E F F I E :   Is, is he . . . ?

> S P A D E :   Yeah.

335. C S :   *Effie, horrified.*

336. M S :   *Jacoby and Spade, as in 333.*

> S P A D E :   Couldn't have come far with those holes in him. (*He stands up,*
> *walks across the room to a sink, and washes the blood from his hands.*
> *The camera pans right with him and we see Effie in the left of the*
> *frame.*) Why couldn't he have stayed alive long enough to tell us some-
> thing? (*He notices that Effie looks as if she is about to faint and rushes*
> *over to hold her arms. The camera follows and frames them in* M S .)
> Here, here, here, none of that now. Come on, can't pass out on me now.

> E F F I E :   All right, Sam.

Spade suddenly looks down at the package and starts to bend over.

337. C S :   *the package. Spade's hands pick it up and carry it over to place it on*
    his desk.

> E F F I E (*off*): Do you really think it's . . . *The camera pulls back to a* M S *of*
> *them as Spade takes out a knife and begins to open the package.*

338. M S :   *Effie and Spade, closer angle, featuring Spade. Spade excitedly cuts*
    at the wrappings, then smiles and grabs Effie's arm.

SPADE: We've got it, angel. We've got it.

339. MS: *Effie and Spade, featuring Effie, still horrified.*

EFFIE: You're hurting me.

The telephone rings.

SPADE: Answer the phone.

EFFIE (*into telephone*): Hello. Yes? . . . Who? . . . Oh, yes. . . . Where? . . . Yes, yes. (*A scream is heard over the telephone.*) Hello? Hello? Hello? (*Effie is utterly terrified. To Spade.*) It was Miss O'Shaughnessy! She wants you! She's in danger!

SPADE: Where is she?

EFFIE: Burlingame, 26 Ancho. Oh, Sam, . . . her voice, it was awful, and something happened to her before she could finish. Go help her, Sam. Why, you've got to go to her, don't you see? (*She looks in Jacoby's direction.*) He was helping her and they killed him and . . .

340. MS: *Effie and Spade, as at the end of 337.*

EFFIE: Oh, you've got to go, Sam!

SPADE: All right, I'll go. Now, after I've gone, you phone the police. (*She helps him on with his suit jacket and goes to get his overcoat.*) Tell them how it happened but don't drag any names in. You don't know. I got the phone call and I told you I had to go, but I didn't say where. Now, forget about this thing. Tell them how it happened, but without the bundle. Now, get that straight. (*She returns into the frame with his overcoat and helps him on with it.*) Everything happened exactly as it did happen, but without the bundle and I got the phone call, not you.

EFFIE: Yes, Sam.

SPADE: OK. (*He places the package under his arm and walks to the door. The camera and Effie follow him. He puts his hat on, opens the door, and turns to her.*) Shut this door and lock it behind me and don't open it till the police come.

EFFIE: Oh, do you know who he is? (*Both look in the direction of Jacoby's offscreen body.*)

SPADE: Yeah, yeah. He's Captain Jacoby, master of the *La Paloma*. (*Pats her arm and chucks her under the chin.*) You're a good man, sister. (*He leaves and she closes the door.*)

Side wipe.

Exterior, Union Bus Station, night

341. LS: *Spade, walking away from the camera across a busy street toward the Union Bus Station.*

Interior, lobby of the Union Bus Station, night

342. LS: *Spade walking into the lobby and toward the baggage counter. He places the package on the counter.*

343. MS: *Spade and the baggage clerk. Spade begins to fill out a baggage check.*

SPADE: Can I borrow your pencil?

CLERK: Sure.

Spade fills the form out and the clerk takes the package away.

344. CS: *Spade's hands writing "Box 589, P.O. Station C, City" on a stamped envelope. The camera pulls back as he places claim check 746 into the envelope.*

345. LS: *the camera pans left as Spade seals the envelope and walks over to a mailbox to deposit it.*

Side wipe.

Exterior, city street, night

346. LS: *Spade walking across the street toward the camera and a group of cab drivers standing on the sidewalk. As he comes near, two women walk past the cab drivers. As they pass, one makes a gesture as if he were shooting a rifle at them and another whistles. Spade smiles.*

347. MS: *Spade approaches one of the cab drivers and the camera dollies right with them as they walk toward his cab.*

SPADE: Say, Frank?

FRANK: Oh, hello, Mr. Spade.

SPADE: You got plenty of gas?

FRANK: Sure thing.

SPADE: Do you know where Ancho Street or Avenue is in Burlingame?

FRANK: Nope, but if she's there we can find her.

SPADE: Well, 26 is the number and the sooner the better.

FRANK: Correct! (*He opens the passenger door for Spade in a subservient gesture and Spade grabs him by the arm and guides him in first as if to say he is more of a friend than a customer.*)

Dissolve.

348. CS: *a spinning automobile wheel.*

Dissolve.

Exterior, deserted street in front of an old house, night

349. LS: *the cab pulls up and Spade climbs out and walks to the sidewalk.*

SPADE: Keep your motor running.

350. MS: *the camera dollies right as Spade walks down the deserted street and stops at a vacant lot. He waves to Frank to pull up.*

351. LS: *Frank's cab pulls up to Spade.*

FRANK: Bum steer, Mr. Spade?

SPADE: Yeah. (*He walks around the cab and climbs in.*) Let's get to a phone booth.

Dissolve.

Interior, telephone booth, night

352. CS: *Spade, talking into the telephone.*

SPADE: Hello, Mrs. Perine? Is Effie there? Yes, please. . . . Hello, precious. What's the good news? . . . No, no, it was a bum steer. Are you

sure that was her voice? . . . Well, it was hooey. Everything go all right?
. . . Nothing said about the bundle, huh? . . . That's swell. Did they take
you down to the hall? . . . Uh-huh. All right, precious. You'd better hit
the hay and get a good night's rest. You sound all in. . . . On, no. Save it
till tomorrow. I'm going on home. (*He hangs up the telephone.*)
Wipe.

Exterior, street outside Spade's apartment, night

353. L S :   *Frank's cab pulls up and Spade climbs out.*

S P A D E :   Thanks. Good night, Frank.

F R A N K :   Good night, Mr. Spade. *Spade walks up the stairs to the building
entrance and the camera pans left with Frank's cab as it pulls away, but
the camera stops on Brigid, who is hiding in a nearby doorway. It then
pans back right with her as she runs toward Spade and collapses in his
arms. He walks her into the building.*

B R I G I D :   I've been hiding in a doorway up the street. I thought you'd
never come.

Interior, Spade's building's lobby, night

354. M S :   *Spade and Brigid come into frame. The camera follows as they walk
to the elevator.*

S P A D E :   Can you make it all right or shall I carry you?

B R I G I D :   I'll be all right as soon as I can get some place where I can lie
down.

Dissolve.

Interior, Spade's apartment, night

355. L S :   *Brigid, Spade, and Wilmer. Spade opens the apartment door, enters
with Brigid, and turns on the light. Wilmer is hiding behind the door. The
camera pans right as Spade enters the living room of his apartment to find
Gutman and Cairo there (Gutman is seated). Wilmer comes up behind
Spade with a drawn pistol.*

G U T M A N :   Well, sir, we're all here. Now, let's come in and sit down and
be comfortable and talk.

S P A D E :   Sure.

*Wilmer pokes his automatic into Spade's back. Brigid is shocked and leaps
away. Spade turns and glares at Wilmer.*

B R I G I D :   Oh!

S P A D E :   Get away. You're not gonna frisk me.

W I L M E R :   Stand still. Shut up.

S P A D E :   Take your paws off me or I'll make you use that gun. Ask your
boss if he wants me shot up before we talk.

G U T M A N :   Never mind, Wilmer. You certainly are a most headstrong individual. Well, let's be seated.

*The camera pans right to follow Spade and Brigid as they walk into the
room and Brigid sits down.*

SPADE: Well, are you ready to make the first payment and take the Falcon off my hands?

GUTMAN: Well, sir, as to that . . . (*He takes an envelope from his vest-pocket and hands it to Spade.*) . . . as to that.

356. MS: *Spade, from a low angle, counting the money.*

SPADE: Ten thousand? We were talking about a lot more money than this.

357. CS: *Gutman.*

GUTMAN: Yes, sir, we were, but this is genuine coin of the realm. With a dollar of this you can buy ten dollars of talk. And there are more of us to be taken care of now.

358. MS: *Spade, as in 356.*

SPADE: Well, that may be, but I've got the Falcon.

359. CS: *Gutman and Cairo, who is standing behind Gutman and holding a small pistol.*

CAIRO: I shouldn't think it would be necessary to remind you, Mr. Spade, that you may have the Falcon, but we certainly have you.

360. LS: *Wilmer, Gutman, Cairo, Spade, and Brigid, as in the end of 355.*

SPADE: Naw, well, I'm trying not to let that worry me. We'll get back to the money later on. (*He hands the envelope to Brigid.*) There's something else to be discussed first. (*He removes his overcoat and throws it on a sofa, then sits down in a chair next to Brigid.*) We've got to have a fall guy.

361. CS: *Spade.*

SPADE: The police have got to have a victim, somebody they can pin those three murders on.

362. CS: *Gutman and Cairo.*

CAIRO: Three, but there's only two, because Thursby certainly killed your partner.

363. CS: *Spade, as in 361.*

SPADE: All right, only two then. What difference does it make? The point is, we've got to give the police . . .

364. CS: *Gutman.*

GUTMAN: Come, come, Mr. Spade, you can't expect us to believe at this late date that you're the least bit afraid of the police, or that you're not quite able to handle . . .

365. CS: *Spade. He abruptly leaps out of his seat and moves toward Gutman, bringing Gutman and Cairo into the frame. He cuts Gutman off and speaks in an angry tone.*

SPADE: I'm in this up to my neck, Gutman. I've got to find somebody, a victim, when the time comes. If I don't, I'll be it. (*He moves back and the camera moves with him. He looks offscreen in Wilmer's direction.*)

366. MS: *Wilmer.*

367. MS: *Spade, as in the end of 365.*

SPADE: Let's give them the gunsel. He actually did shoot Thursby and Jacoby, didn't he?

368. MS: *Wilmer, Gutman, and Cairo. Both Gutman and Cairo look at Wilmer, who glares at Spade.*

SPADE (*off*): Anyway, he's made to order for the part. Look at him . . .

369. MS: *Spade, as in 367.*

SPADE (*looking back toward Gutman*): Let's give him to them.

370. LS: *Wilmer, Gutman, Cairo, and Spade. Gutman bursts out laughing.*

GUTMAN: Ah, ha, ha, ha. By gad, sir, you are a character, that you are. There's never any telling what you'll say or do next, except that it's bound to be something astonishing.

SPADE: Why, it's our best bet. With him in their hands, the police will . . .

GUTMAN: But, my dear man, can't you see that if I, even for a moment, thought of doing such a thing. . . . That's ridiculous. I feel toward Wilmer here, just exactly as if he were my own son.

371. CS: *Gutman.*

GUTMAN: Really, I do. But if I, even for a moment, thought of doing what you propose, what in the world would keep Wilmer from telling the police every last detail about the Falcon and all. . . .

372. MS: *Spade.*

SPADE: Let him talk his head off. I'll guarantee you nobody'll do anything about it.

373. LS: *Wilmer, Gutman, Cairo, and Spade.*

GUTMAN: Ha, ha. Well, well, what do you think of this, Wilmer? Mighty funny?

WILMER: Mighty funny.

The camera moves in on Spade and then on Brigid as he sits next to her.

SPADE: How do you feel now? Any better, precious?

374. CS: *Spade and Brigid.*

BRIGID: Much better, but I'm frightened.

SPADE: Well, don't be. Nothing very bad's going to happen here. You want a drink, angel?

BRIGID (*shaking her head no*): Be careful, Sam.

375. MS: *Spade and Brigid, as at the end of 373. He stands up and walks toward Gutman, bringing Wilmer, Gutman, and Cairo into the frame. Spade sits down facing Gutman and we can no longer see Brigid.*

SPADE: Well?

GUTMAN: If you're really serious about this, the least we can do in common politeness is to hear you out. Now, how would you be able to fix it . . . (*He laughs jovially.*) . . . so that Wilmer couldn't do us any harm?

376. CS: *Spade.*

SPADE: I can show Bryan, our district attorney, that, if he goes around trying to collect everybody, he's going to have a tangled case, *but* if he sticks to Wilmer here, he can get a conviction . . .

377. MS: *Wilmer, looking furious. He advances toward Spade and the camera, into a* CS.

SPADE (*off*): . . . standing on his head.

378. CS: *Spade. Wilmer's hand and pistol appear in the front of the frame. Spade looks directly at him.*

379. CS: *Wilmer, shot from a low angle. He is fuming.*

WILMER: Get up on your feet. I've taken all the riding from you I'm gonna take. Get up and shoot it out.

380. LS: *Cairo, Gutman, Wilmer (from the back and hovering over Spade), and Spade. Spade looks at Wilmer in an amused way.*

SPADE: Young wild west! (*He looks at Gutman.*) Maybe you'd better tell him that shooting me before you get your hands on the Falcon's gonna be bad for business. (*He looks again directly at Wilmer.*)

GUTMAN: Now, now, Wilmer. We can't have any of that. . . .

381. CS: *Wilmer, as in 379.*

GUTMAN (*off*): . . . You shouldn't let yourself attach so much importance to these things.

WILMER: Then tell him to lay off me then.

382. LS: *Cairo, Gutman, Wilmer, and Spade.*

GUTMAN: Now, Wilmer. (*He tugs at Wilmer's arm and Wilmer slowly moves behind Gutman, still glaring at Spade and tensely holding his pistol. Gutman now addresses Spade.*) Your plan is, er, not at all satisfactory, sir. Let's not say anything more about it.

Spade stands up, throws his arms in the air in a slightly exasperated gesture, and walks over to the left of the frame. His back is now to the camera and he faces Cairo, Gutman, and Wilmer.

SPADE: All right, I've got another suggestion. It may not be as good as the first one, but it's better than nothing. Do you want to hear it?

383. CS: *Gutman and Cairo.*

GUTMAN: Most assuredly.

Spade leans into the frame, facing Gutman in a confidential manner. Cairo leans forward, his pistol pointing toward Spade. Spade points toward Cairo.

SPADE: Give them Cairo.

GUTMAN: Hm, hm (*Laughing.*) Well, by gad, sir.

CAIRO: And suppose we give them you or Miss O'Shaughnessy? How about that, huh?

SPADE: You want the Falcon. I've got it. The fall guy's . . .

384. LS: *Spade, Cairo, Gutman, and Wilmer, as at the end of 382.*

SPADE: ... part of the price I'm asking. (*He looks over toward Brigid, raises his arm, and walks toward her. The camera follows and brings her into the frame.*) As for Miss O'Shaughnessy, if you think she can be rigged for the part, I'm perfectly willing to discuss it with you. (*He places his arm on her shoulder and sits on the arm of her chair with his back to the camera.*)

CAIRO: You seem to forget that you are not in a position at all to insist upon anything.

GUTMAN: Now, come, gentlemen. Let's keep our discussion on a friendly basis. There certainly is something in what Mr. Cairo said.

385. CS: *Brigid and Spade. She looks at him; he looks offscreen directly at Gutman, leaning forward as he talks.*

SPADE: If you kill me, how are you gonna get the bird? And if I know you can't afford to kill me, how are you going to scare me into giving it to you?

386. MS: *Cairo, Gutman, and Wilmer.*

GUTMAN: Well, sir, there are other means of persuasion besides killing and threatening to kill.

387. LS: *Cairo, Gutman, Wilmer, Spade, and Brigid, as at the end of 384.*
Spade rises and walks over to sit next to Gutman, staring directly into his
face.
SPADE: Yes, that's . . . that's true, but . . .

388. CS: *Spade and Gutman, from side. Spade taps Gutman's arm for*
emphasis.
SPADE: . . . there're none of them any good unless the threat of death is
behind them. You see what I mean? If you start something, I'll make it a
matter of your having to kill me or call it off.

389. CS: *Spade, from rear, and Gutman, reverse angle of 388.*
GUTMAN: That's an attitude, sir, that calls for the most delicate judgment
on both sides because, as you know, sir, in the heat of action men are
likely to forget where their best interests lie and let their emotions carry
them away.

390. CS: *Spade and Gutman, as in 388.*
SPADE: Then the trick from my angle is to make my play strong enough
to tie you up, but not make you mad enough to bump me off . . .

391. CS: *Spade and Gutman, as in 390.*
SPADE: . . . against your better judgment.
GUTMAN (*admiringly*): By gad, sir, you are a character.
Cairo leans into the frame and whispers into Gutman's ear. Spade pulls
back, out of frame, and the camera moves right and up to show Wilmer,
watching.

392. MS: *Spade and Gutman, as in 389, but Spade is leaning back and smirk-*
ing at Wilmer.
SPADE: Six, two, and even, they're selling you out, sonny. (*He looks at*
Gutman.) I hope you're not letting yourself be influenced by the guns
these pocket edition desperados are waving around . . .

393. LS: *Spade, Cairo, Gutman, and Wilmer.*
SPADE: . . . because I've practiced taking guns away from these boys be-
fore . . . (*He stands up facing Wilmer.*) . . . so we'll have no trouble
there. Wilmer, here, is . . .
WILMER: All right . . . (*He is furious, and begins to advance on Spade.*
Gutman tries to restrain him.)
GUTMAN: Wilmer! Wilmer! . . .

394. CS: *Brigid, watching in amazement.*
GUTMAN (*off*): . . . Wilmer!

395. LS: *Spade, Gutman, Wilmer, and Cairo, as at the end of 393 except that*
Cairo has moved quietly behind Wilmer. Wilmer advances on Spade and
raises his pistol. Gutman grabs Wilmer's gun and Spade punches Wilmer,
knocking him over.

396. MS: *Brigid. The camera follows as she leans over and picks up the pistol*
that Wilmer dropped.

397. L S : *Gutman and Cairo, holding Wilmer down, and Spade. Spade looks in Brigid's direction, smiles, and walks over and takes the gun from her hands. The camera follows him and then pans back as he returns to the center of the room to help Cairo pick up Wilmer's body and drop it on the sofa. He then taps Cairo on the rear end with Wilmer's gun, searches him, and takes his pistol.*

398. C S : *Brigid, watching.*

399. L S : *Gutman, Spade, Cairo, and Wilmer, as at the end of 397. Spade takes Wilmer's other pistol from Wilmer's clothes, returns to Gutman and, smiling, speaks.*

> S P A D E : There's our fall guy. Now either you'll say yes right now or I'll turn the Falcon and the whole lot of you in.
>
> G U T M A N : Don't like that, sir.
>
> S P A D E : You won't like it. Well . . . (*Spade is laughing. Cairo moves behind and between both men.*)
>
> G U T M A N : You can have him.
>
> S P A D E : I won't be able to get the Falcon till daylight or maybe later.
>
> *Cairo sits quietly down and watches.*
>
> G U T M A N : It strikes me that it'd be best for all concerned if we did not get out of each other's sight until our business has been transacted. You have the envelope?
>
> S P A D E : Miss O'Shaughnessy has it. (*He looks in her direction.*) That's all right. Hang on to it. (*He walks over toward a lamp table and places the guns on it. The camera follows him to the left as he moves.*) We don't have to lose sight of each other; the dingus'll be brought to us here.

400. C S : *Gutman. The camera moves in for a tighter shot.*

> G U T M A N : Excellent, sir, excellent! Then in exchange for the ten thousand and Wilmer, you'll give us the Falcon and an hour or two of grace.

401. M S : *Spade and a side view of Gutman.*

> S P A D E : Now let's get the details fixed first. (*Spade points in Wilmer's direction.*) Why did he shoot Thursby and why and where and how did he shoot Captain Jacoby? You see, I've got to know all that happened so I can be sure the parts that don't fit are covered up.

402. C S : *Gutman, as in 400.*

> G U T M A N : I shall be candid with you, sir. Thursby was Miss O'Shaughnessy's ally. We believed that disposing of him in the manner we did would cause Miss O'Shaughnessy . . .

403. C S : *Brigid, eyes downcast.*

> G U T M A N (*off*): . . . to stop and think that perhaps it would be best to patch up her differences with . . .

404. C S : *Gutman, as in 402.*

> G U T M A N : . . . us, regarding the Falcon.

405. M S : *Spade and Gutman, as in 401. Spade lounges back on a table top.*

SPADE: Then you didn't try to make a deal with him before giving him
  the works?

406. MS: *Spade, from a side angle, and Gutman.*

  GUTMAN: We did. Yes, sir, we most certainly did. I talked to him myself that very night, but I could do nothing with him. He was quite
  determined to be loyal to Miss O'Shaughnessy . . . (*They look in
  Brigid's direction.*)

407. CS: *Brigid, looking down.*

408. MS: *Spade and Gutman, as in 406.*

  GUTMAN: . . . so Wilmer followed him back to the hotel and did what he
  did.

  SPADE: Ah, that sounds all right. Now, Jacoby.

  GUTMAN: Captain Jacoby's death . . . (*He rises and walks toward Brigid,
  towering over her. The camera moves with him.*) . . . was entirely Miss
  O'Shaughnessy's fault.

  SPADE (*off*):   Tell me what happened.

  GUTMAN: (*He walks over toward Spade and the camera follows, bringing Spade back into frame.*) Well, Cairo, as you must have surmised, got
  in touch with me after he left police headquarters yesterday night or
  morning. (*He now walks over to Cairo and the camera follows.*) He recognized the mutual advantage of pooling forces. Mr. Cairo is a man of
  nice judgment. The *Paloma* was his thought. He saw the notice of its arrival in the papers and remembered he had heard in Hong Kong that
  Jacoby and Miss O'Shaughnessy were seen together. (*He is walking
  back in Spade's direction and turns toward the sounds of moans that Wilmer is making.*)

409. MS: *Wilmer, lying unconscious.*

410. MS: *Spade and Gutman, as at the end of 408.*

  GUTMAN: Well, sir, he saw that notice and, putting two and two together,
  guessed the truth. She had given the bird to Jacoby to bring here for her.

  SPADE: And at that juncture you decided to slip me a mickey, huh? (*He
  is rolling a cigarette.*)

  GUTMAN: There was no place for you in our plans, sir . . . (*Spade
  laughs.*) . . . so we decided to spare ourselves any possible embarrass-
  ment. Mr. Cairo and Wilmer and I went to call on Captain Jacoby. (*He
  walks back, past Cairo and toward Brigid. The camera follows and
  again shows him towering over her.*) We were lucky enough to arrive
  while Miss O'Shaughnessy was there. In many ways, the conference
  was difficult, but we finally persuaded Miss O'Shaughnessy . . .

411. CS: *Brigid, looking embarrassed and terrified.*

  GUTMAN (*off*):   . . . to come to terms, or so we thought.

412. MS: *Gutman and Brigid, as at the end of 410.*

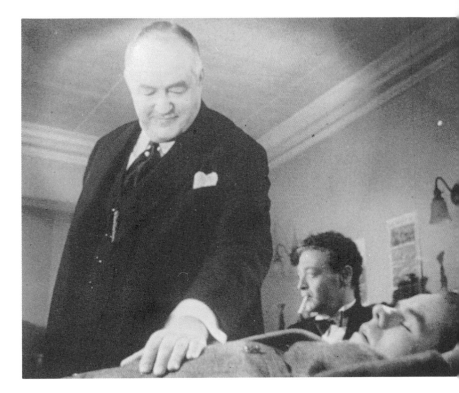

GUTMAN: We then left the boat and set out for my hotel, where I was to pay Miss O'Shaughnessy and receive the bird. Well, sir, . . . (*He laughs.*) . . . we mere men should have known better. En route, she, Captain Jacoby, and the Falcon slipped completely through our fingers. It was neatly done, sir, indeed it was. (*He glares at Brigid.*)

413. CS: *Spade, leaning against the wall and smoking.*
SPADE: You touched off the boat before you left?

414. MS: *Gutman and Brigid, as at the end of 412. As he speaks, Gutman moves toward Spade. The camera follows him, bringing Spade into frame and losing Brigid.*
GUTMAN: No, not intentionally. Though, I dare say we, or Wilmer at least, were responsible for the fire. While the rest of us were talking in the cabin, Wilmer went about the boat . . . (*He moves in Wilmer's direction.*)

415. MS: *Gutman, Cairo, and Wilmer, from an extreme low angle, showing the ceiling above Gutman's head.*
GUTMAN: . . . trying to find the Falcon. (*He pats Wilmer's stomach.*) No doubt he was careless with matches.

416. CS: *Spade, as in 413.*

   SPADE: Now about the shooting?

417. LS: *Cairo, Gutman, and Wilmer.*

   GUTMAN: We caught up with Miss O'Shaughnessy and Jacoby at her apartment. I sent Wilmer downstairs to cover the fire escape before ringing the bell and, sure enough, while she was asking us who we were through the door, and we were telling her, we heard a window go up. Wilmer shot Jacoby as he was coming down the fire escape, shot him more than once, but Jacoby was too tough to fall or drop the Falcon. He climbed down the rest of the way, knocked Wilmer over, and ran off. (*Laughing, he walks over to Brigid. The camera follows to show him and her. She squirms in her chair.*) We persuaded, that is the word, sir, we, er, persuaded Miss O'Shaughnessy to tell us where she had told Captain Jacoby to take the Falcon . . .

418. CS: *Brigid, squirming in her seat.*

   GUTMAN (*off*): . . . and we, uh, further persuaded her . . .

419. MS: *Gutman and Brigid, as at the end of 417.*

   GUTMAN: . . . to phone your office, in an attempt to draw you away before Jacoby got there but, unfortunately for us, it had taken us too long to persuade Miss O'Shaughnessy. (*He turns toward the sounds of Wilmer moaning.*) And you had the Falcon before we could reach you.

420. MS: *Wilmer, awakening and sitting up, stunned and puzzled.*

421. CS: *Gutman, from a low angle.*

422. CS: *Wilmer, as at the end of 420. He looks in Cairo's direction.*

423. CS: *Cairo, from a low angle.*

424. CS: *Wilmer, as at the end of 422. He looks in Spade's direction.*

425. CS: *Spade, watching.*

426. CS: *Wilmer, as at the end of 424. He looks in Brigid's direction.*

427. CS: *Brigid, watching.*

428. MS: *Gutman, Wilmer's back, and Cairo, from a very low angle.*

   GUTMAN: Well, Wilmer, I'm sorry indeed to lose you, but I want you to know I couldn't be fonder of you if you were my own son. But, well, if you lose a son, it's possible to get another. There's only one Maltese Falcon.

429. LS: *Cairo, Gutman, and Wilmer. Gutman walks toward Spade and returns to his chair. Cairo comforts Wilmer in the background. The camera follows Gutman and, when he sits, now shows just him and Spade.*

   GUTMAN: When you're young, you simply don't understand these things.

   SPADE (*laughing*): How about some coffee? . . .

430. CS: *Brigid.*

   SPADE (*off*): Put the pot on, will you, angel? I . . .

431. LS: *Spade and Gutman, as at the end of 429.*

   SPADE: . . . don't like to leave our guests.

BRIGID (*off*): Surely.

The camera moves to the right and in on Gutman, losing Spade and picking up Brigid as she walks past Gutman and, in the background, Cairo and Wilmer.

GUTMAN: Just a moment, my dear. Hadn't you better leave the envelope in here?

She stops, looks briefly in Spade's direction, and hands the envelope to Gutman.

BRIGID: Sit on it, if you're afraid of losing it.

GUTMAN: You misunderstand me; it's not that at all, . . . (*He opens the envelope and counts the bills.*) . . . but business should be transacted in a businesslike manner. (*He laughs and she enters the doorway in the back of the frame and turns on the interior light. Gutman hands the bills to Spade as the camera moves to the left to bring Spade into the frame. He now addresses Spade.*) For instance, there are only nine bills here now. There were ten when I handed them to you, as you very well know.

Spade looks at the bills, stands up and walks over toward Brigid and confronts her. The camera follows as Gutman returns the bills to the envelope and places it on the lamp table beside his chair.

SPADE: Well, . . .

432. MS: *Brigid, with the back of Spade's head and the top of Cairo's in the front of the frame.*

SPADE: . . . I want to know about this.

Brigid looks directly at him and shakes her head no.

433. LS: *Gutman, Spade, Cairo, Brigid, and Wilmer, as at the end of 431. Spade turns and walks over to Gutman and faces him in a confrontational manner.*

434. MS: *Gutman and Spade, from a low angle.*

SPADE: You palmed it.

GUTMAN: I palmed it?

SPADE: Yes. Do you want to say so or do you want to stand for a frisk?

GUTMAN: Stand for? . . .

SPADE: You're going to admit it or I'm gonna search you. There's no third way.

GUTMAN (*laughs*): By gad, sir, I believe you would. I really do. You are a character, if you don't mind my saying so.

SPADE: You palmed it.

435. LS: *Gutman, Brigid, Cairo, Spade, and Wilmer, as at the end of 433.*

GUTMAN: Yes, sir, that I did. (*He removes the bill from his vestpocket, laughs, and returns it to the envelope.*) I must have my little joke now and then and I was curious to know what you would do in a situation of this sort. I must say you passed the test with flying colors.

SPADE: Ah! That's the sort of thing I'd expect from somebody Wilmer's age.

GUTMAN: This will soon be yours. (*He offers Spade the envelope.*) You might as well take it.

SPADE: I ought to have more than ten thousand.

GUTMAN: Of course, sir. You understand this is the first payment. Later . . .

SPADE: Oh yes, later you'll give me millions, but, er, how's about fifteen thousand now?

GUTMAN: Frankly and candidly, upon my word of honor as a gentleman, ten thousand is all the money I can raise.

SPADE: But you didn't say positively.

GUTMAN: Positively. (*He looks around in Brigid's direction and then speaks to Spade in a confidential tone.*) I'd like to give you a word of advice.

SPADE: Go ahead. (*Gutman beckons him to come closer and Spade bends over.*)

GUTMAN: I dare say you're going to give her some money, but if you don't give her as much as she thinks she ought to have, my word of advice is, be careful.

SPADE: Dangerous?

GUTMAN: Very. (*Spade smiles, stands up, and calls to Brigid.*)

SPADE: How's the coffee coming, angel?

BRIGID (*off*): In a few minutes.

GUTMAN: It's almost daylight, Mr. Spade. Can you start getting it now?

SPADE: I guess so. (*He walks over to the telephone and dials. The camera follows.*)

436. CS: *Gutman, watching intently.*

437. LS: *Cairo, Brigid, Wilmer, and Spade, as at the end of 435. Spade speaks into the telephone.*

SPADE: Hello. . . . Hello, precious. I'm sorry to get you up so early. Now, listen carefully, here's the plot. In the Holland box at the post office there's an envelope with my scrawl. In that envelope there's a parcel room check for the bundle we got yesterday. . . . Uh huh. Now get that bundle and bring it here, P.D.Q. . . . Ah, that's a good girl. Now hustle. Bye.

Dissolve.

Spade's apartment, interior, day

438. LS: *overhead shot of Gutman reading a book, Cairo sleeping in a chair, Wilmer on a sofa, Brigid on another with her hand resting on the top, and Spade reading a newspaper. The room is much brighter, indicating daylight, and everyone looks like they have been up all night waiting. Spade rises, looks at a clock on a table, walks over and turns off the light switch,*

and returns to his seat. Gutman turns off the light on the table next to his chair and continues to read. The doorbuzzer sounds. Cairo gets up anxiously. Spade rises and goes to the door. The camera pans left with him and Gutman, following, comes into the frame. Spade opens the door to find Effie with the bundle. He takes it.

SPADE: Thanks, lady. Sorry to spoil your day of rest.

EFFIE: Not the first one you've spoiled. Anything else?

SPADE: No. No thanks.

EFFIE: Bye bye, then.

Spade closes the door, turns around, looks at Gutman, and reenters the room. The camera follows as he stops before a table. Cairo and Brigid rush up and all clear the table and Spade places the bundle on it.

439. MS: *Cairo, Brigid, and Gutman, from a low angle as they unwrap the bundle with intense concentration.*

SPADE (*off*): There you are.

440. CS: *hands removing layers of wrapping from the bundle.*

441. CS: *Gutman.*

GUTMAN: Now, after seventeen years. (*He looks up, the camera pans left to show Cairo and Brigid looking at him.*)

442. CS: *Spade, watching.*

443. CS: *Gutman's hands remove the wrapping to reveal the Falcon. He picks it up.*

444. MS: *Cairo, Brigid, and Gutman, staring at the statue and pushing the packing aside.*

445. CS: *Spade, watching.*

446. CS: *the statue, upright on the table. Cairo's hand touches it and Gutman's hands turn it around slowly. It is framed against Brigid's body. The camera pulls back as she sits down and we see Cairo, Brigid, Wilmer in the background, and Gutman in* MS.

GUTMAN: It is it. But we will make sure. (*He takes a pocketknife to it.*)

447. CS: *Spade, watching, as in 445.*

448. CS: *the Falcon, Gutman's hand chipping away at the surface with the pocketknife.*

449. MS: *Cairo, Brigid, and Gutman as Gutman chips away with a growing frenzy at the statue. Wilmer is seen moving to the right out of the frame. Gutman stands up, now wildly hacking at the statue. The camera pulls back and Spade is briefly seen at the left of the frame.*

450. CS: *Spade, watching.*

451. CS: *Gutman, looking down, stunned.*

452. CS: *the statue as Gutman's hand wildly hacks at it with the pocketknife.*

GUTMAN'S VOICE: Fake! It's a phony! It . . . it's lead! . . .

453. MS: *Spade, Cairo, Gutman, and Brigid. Gutman pushes the statue over.*

GUTMAN: . . . It's lead! It's a fake!

454. CS: *Spade, looking angrily in Brigid's direction.*
   SPADE: All right, you've had your little joke. Now tell us about it.
455. CS: *Brigid, frenzied.*
   BRIGID: No, Sam, no! That's the one I got from Kemidov. I swear it.
456. CS: *Cairo and, from the side, Gutman. Cairo glares at him furiously and speaks with a growing rage.*
   CAIRO: You! It's you who bungled it! You and your stupid attempt to buy it. Kemidov found out how valuable it was. Ha! No wonder we had such an easy time stealing it. You . . . you imbecile! You bloated idiot! . . .
457. MS: *Cairo and, from the side, Gutman. Cairo is now screaming at Gutman. Gutman seems dazed and about to totter over.*
   CAIRO: . . . You stupid fathead, you! (*He starts to weep, walks to frame right across the room and throws himself into a chair, still weeping. Gutman puts his left hand to the back of his neck and looks vaguely around, as if he is about to faint. He then looks back toward the statue, brings his hand down, gives a light chuckle, and bends over to set the statue upright. He looks at it and begins to laugh.*)

458. C S :   *the statue.*
459. C S :   *Gutman, from a side angle, as he looks down at the statue. He is now laughing uproariously.*
    G U T M A N :   Yes, it's the Russian's hand. There's no doubt about it. (*He turns to look offscreen toward Cairo and speaks with joyous optimism.*) Well, sir, what do you suggest? We stand here and shed tears and call each other names, or shall we go to Istanbul?
460. C S :   *Cairo, limp and exhausted in the chair, seems to awake with childlike interest.*
    C A I R O :   Are you going?
461. C S :   *Gutman.*
    G U T M A N :   Seventeen years I've wanted that little item, and I've been trying to get it.
462. M S :   *Gutman, from the rear, and Cairo, to the rear. As Gutman speaks, Cairo rises from the chair and approaches Gutman and the camera. Cairo is now smiling and glowing with enthusiasm.*
    G U T M A N :   If we must spend another year on the quest, well, sir, it will be an additional expenditure in time of only five and fifteen-seventeenths percent. (*He pivots around with an extravagant swagger as he speaks.*)
    C A I R O :   I'm going with you? (*As he speaks with awe-struck gratitude, Gutman suddenly looks offscreen with concern.*)
463. C S :   *the couch upon which Wilmer had been sleeping. His hat is still on it.*
464. M S :   *Gutman and Cairo, as at the end of 462. Gutman looks around and rushes into the open doorway at the back of the room.*
465. M S :   *Gutman entering the far doorway, looking around, and returning to the main room.*
466. M S :   *Gutman rushing into the bathroom, looking around, and rushing back into the main room.*
467. M S :   *Spade and Gutman. Gutman rushes toward Spade, with the statue on the table between them and the camera pulls back.*
    G U T M A N :   Wilmer?
468. C S :   *Spade, nodding to his right. The camera pans to show the open door to the hallway.*
469. M S :   *Spade and Gutman, as at the end of 467. Spade is laughing smugly.*
    S P A D E :   Ha, ha, ha. A swell lot of thieves!
    G U T M A N :   We've little enough to boast about, sir, but the world hasn't come to an end just because we've run into a little setback. (*He picks his hat up from the floor, places it on the table with the Falcon, and extends his hand to Spade.*) I must ask you for that envelope.
    S P A D E :   I held up my end. You got your dingus. It's your hard luck, not mine, it wasn't what you wanted.
    G U T M A N :   Now, come, sir, we've all failed and there's no reason for expecting any of us to bear the whole brunt. (*He places his derby on his*

head with his right hand and points a pistol at Spade with his left.) In
short, sir, I must ask you for my ten thousand.

470. CS: *Brigid, watching.*

471. MS: *Spade and Gutman, as at the end of 468. Spade takes a bill from the
envelope and holds it up with his right hand while extending the envelope
to Gutman with his left.*

SPADE: This will take care of my time and expenses.

Gutman nods his head, smiles, and accepts and pockets the envelope.

GUTMAN: Now, sir, we'll say goodbye to you, unless you care to under-
take the Istanbul expedition with us. (*Spade shakes his head "no."*) You
don't? (*The camera follows Gutman as he moves around the table, past
Cairo and Brigid, and comes face to face with Spade.*) Well, frankly, sir,
I'd like to have you along. You're a man of nice judgment and many
resources. Now that there's no alternative, I dare say you'll manage the
police without a fall guy.

SPADE: I'll make out all right.

GUTMAN: Well, sir, the shortest farewells are the best. Adieu. (*He bows
to Spade and then walks jovially toward the door, stopping in the entrance and turning back to face the room. The camera follows him.*) And
to you, Miss O'Shaughnessy, I leave the Rara Avis, on the table there, as
a little memento. (*He waves happily, turns, and leaves. Cairo follows
him out the door.*)

472. MS: *Spade. He walks past Brigid and picks up the phone. The camera follows, bringing her into the frame, and moves closer as he dials. Brigid
watches him intently. He smiles briefly at her and then speaks into the phone.*

SPADE: Hello. Sergeant Polhaus there? . . . Yeah, put him on. This is Sam
Spade. . . . Hello, Tom? Now listen, I've got something for you. Here it
is. Jacoby and Thursby were killed by a kid named Wilmer Cook. . . .
Yeah. He's about twenty years old, five foot six, wearing a gray overcoat. (*The camera moves in for a CS of Brigid, listening anxiously.*) He's
working for a man named Kasper Gutman. You can't miss Gutman, he
must weigh three hundred pounds. That fellow Cairo's in with them, too.

473. MS: *Spade.*

SPADE: They just left here for the Alexandria Hotel, but you'll have to
move fast. They're blowing town. Now watch yourself when you go up
against the kid. . . . Yes, that's right, *very.* . . . Well, good luck, Tom. (*He
hangs up, turns toward Brigid and begins to speak in an intensely anxious manner.*) Now, they'll talk, when they're nailed, about us. We're sitting on dynamite. (*He walks over and seizes her by the shoulders. The
camera follows, bringing her into the frame, and moves in for a CS.*)
We've got only minutes to get set for the police, Now give me all of
it fast. When you first came to my office, why did you want Thursby
shadowed?

474. CS: *Brigid and, from rear, Spade, reverse angle of 473.*
    BRIGID: I told you, Sam. I thought he was betraying me and I wanted to find out.
475. CS: *Brigid and Spade, as in 473.*
    SPADE: That's a lie! You had Thursby hooked and you knew it and you wanted to get rid of him before Jacoby came with the loot so you wouldn't have to split it with him, isn't that so?
476. CS: *Brigid and Spade, as in 474.*
    SPADE: What was your scheme?
    BRIGID: I thought that, if he knew someone was following him, he'd be frightened into going away. (*She is now avoiding eye contact with Spade.*)
477. CS: *Brigid and Spade, as in 475.*
    SPADE: Miles wasn't clumsy to be spotted the first night. You told Thursby he was being followed.
478. MS: *Brigid and Spade, side angle.*
    BRIGID: I told him. (*She stands up and walks across the room to put her cigarette out, then turns to look in Spade's direction. The camera follows her, removing Spade from the frame.*) I told him. Yes, but please believe me, Sam, I wouldn't have told him if I'd thought Floyd would kill him.
479. CS: *Spade.*
    SPADE: If you thought he wouldn't kill Miles, you were right, angel. Miles hadn't many brains but he'd had too many years experience as a detective to be caught like that by a man he was shadowing up a blind alley with his gun in his hip and his overcoat buttoned. . . .
480. MS: *Brigid and Spade, side angle. Spade advances on her and she backs up nervously.*
    SPADE: . . . But he'd have gone up there with you, angel. He was just dumb enough for that. He'd have looked you up and down and licked his lips and gone, grinning from ear to ear. . . .
481. CS: *Brigid, from rear, and Spade. She has her back against the wall and he is still advancing in a menacing manner, becoming more angry as he speaks.*
    SPADE: . . . Then you could have stood as close to him as you liked in the dark and put a hole through him with a gun you got from Thursby that evening.
    BRIGID: Don't, Sam! Don't say that! You know I didn't . . .
    SPADE: Stop it! The police'll be here any minute. Now talk!
    BRIGID: Oh, why do you accuse me of such a . . .
    SPADE: This isn't the time for that schoolgirl act! We're both of us sitting under the gallows! . . .
482. CS: *Brigid and Spade, reverse angle of 481.*
    SPADE: . . . Now, why did you shoot Miles?

BRIGID: I didn't mean to at first. Really, I didn't. But when I found out that Floyd couldn't be frightened, I . . . Oh, I can't look at you and tell you this, Sam! (*She turns away, weeping.*)

483. CS: *Brigid and Spade, as in 481, except that her face is to the wall and facing the camera.*

SPADE: You thought Thursby would tackle Miles and one or the other of them would go down. If Thursby was killed, you were rid of him. If it was Miles, you'd see that Thursby was caught and sent up for it, isn't that right?

BRIGID: Something like that.

SPADE: And when you found Thursby wasn't going to tackle him, you borrowed his gun and did it yourself, right? (*She nods.*) And when you heard Thursby was shot, you knew Gutman was in town! And you knew you needed another protector, someone to fill Thursby's boots, . . . so you came back to me. (*He now has a snarling look on his face.*)

484. CS: *Brigid and Spade, reverse angle of 483. She is writhing against the wall.*

BRIGID: Yes. Oh, sweetheart. It wasn't only that. I'd have come back to you sooner or later. From the very first instant I saw you, I knew. (*She desperately embraces him.*)

485. MS: *Brigid, from rear, and Spade.*

SPADE: Well, if you get a good break, you'll be out of Tahatchapi in twenty years, . . .

486. CS: *Brigid and Spade.*

SPADE: . . . and you can come back to me then. I hope they don't hang you, precious, by that sweet neck. (*Suddenly stunned, she stares into his eyes. He caresses her neck with his fingers.*)

BRIGID: You're not . . .

SPADE: Yes, angel, I'm going to send you over.

487. CS: *Brigid and Spade, as in 485.*

SPADE: The chances are you'll get off with life. That means, if you're a good girl, you'll be out in twenty years. I'll be waiting for you.

488. CS: *Brigid and Spade, as in 486.*

SPADE: If they hang you, I'll always remember you.

BRIGID: Don't, Sam! Don't say that, even in fun. (*She starts to laugh nervously.*) Ha, ha, ha. Oh, I was frightened for a minute. I really thought, . . . You do such wild and unpredictable things.

489. CS: *Brigid and Spade, as in 487.*

SPADE: Now, don't be silly. You're taking the fall.

She shoves him away and turns around. The camera follows and shows her in CS. *She is enraged.*

BRIGID: You've been playing with me, just pretending you cared, to trap me like this. You didn't care at all. You don't love me.

490. M S :   *Spade.*

    S PA D E :   I won't play the sap for you.

491. C S :   *Brigid, as at the end of 489.*

    B R I G I D :   Oh, you know it's not like that. You can't say that. (*She begins to plead with him. He moves into the frame, facing her, and we see him from the side rear. He is getting angrier as he speaks.*)

    S PA D E :   You never played square with me for half an hour at a stretch since I've known you.

    She clutches his arms.

    B R I G I D :   You know, down deep in your heart, that, in spite of anything I've done, I love you.

    S PA D E :   I don't care who loves who! I won't play the sap for you. I won't walk in Thursby's and I don't know how many others' footsteps!

492. C S :   *Spade and Brigid, reverse angle of 491.*

    S PA D E :   You killed Miles and you're going over for it. (*His rage has now subsided into a look of nauseated fatalism as he glares at her. She retreats out of the frame. He watches for a moment, takes a few steps and again glares. The camera follows him.*)

    B R I G I D (*off*): Oh, how can you do this to me, Sam? Surely Mr. Archer wasn't as much to you as . . . (*She weeps. Spade walks over to a chair near her, almost like a zombie, and sits down. Her heaving back is now visible in the frame as she weeps, holding her head on the arm of the couch.*)

493. M S :   *Spade, seated on a chair with the shadow of the fluttering window curtain on the wall behind him. He begins staring offscreen to his left at Brigid, but quickly turns his head and stares blankly ahead. His speech is slow and deliberate, almost as if he is drugged or somehow numbed. He looks as if he is repressing nausea.*

    S PA D E :   Listen. This won't do any good. You'll never understand me, but I'll try once and then give it up. . . .

494. M S :   *Spade, in side profile, is in the front left of the frame. Brigid is leaning, face down, on the couch to the rear and weeping. The open window with its fluttering curtain is behind her.*

    S PA D E :   . . . When a man's partner is killed, he's supposed to do something about it. It doesn't make any difference what you thought of him, he was your partner and you're supposed to do something about it. (*Brigid has now turned her head and is looking intently at Spade.*) And it happens we're in the detective business. Well, when one of your organization gets killed, it's . . . it's bad business to let the killer get away with it, bad all around, bad for every detective everywhere.

    B R I G I D :   You don't expect me to think that these things you're saying are sufficient reasons for sending me to the . . .

    S PA D E :   Wait till I'm through. Then you can talk.

495. MS: *Spade, as in 493.*
SPADE: I've no earthly reason to think I can trust you. And if I do this and get away with it, you'll have something on me that you can use whenever you want to. . . .

496. MS: *Spade and Brigid, as in 494.*
SPADE: . . . Since I've got something on you, I couldn't be sure that you wouldn't put a hole in me someday. . . .

497. MS: *Spade, as in 495.*
SPADE: All those are on one side. Maybe some of them are unimportant, I won't argue about that. But look at the number of them. And what have we got on the other side? . . .

498. CS: *Spade and Brigid, same angle as 494, but closer.*
SPADE: . . . All we've got is that maybe you love me and maybe I love you.
Brigid sits up with tears in her eyes and looks accusingly at Spade.
BRIGID: You know whether you love me or not.
He looks at her.
SPADE: Maybe I do.

499. MS: *Spade and Brigid, reverse angle of 498.*

    SPADE: Oh, I'll have some rotten nights after I've sent you over, but that'll pass. (*He has just looked away, but now turns and looks passionately at her again. He stands and brings her up with him. The camera moves to a low angle CS of them. Spade speaks more loudly, almost shouting in her face.*) If all I've said doesn't mean anything to you, then forget it and we'll make it just this. I won't because all of me wants to, regardless of consequences, and because you've counted on that with me, the same as you counted on that with all the others.

500. CS: *Spade and Brigid, reverse angle of the end of 499.*

    BRIGID: Would you have done this to me if the Falcon had been real and you'd got your money?

501. CS: *Spade and Brigid, reverse angle of 500.*

    SPADE: Don't be too sure I'm as crooked as I'm supposed to be. That sort of reputation might be good business, bringing high-priced jobs and making it easier to deal with the enemy, but a lot more money would have been one more item on your side of . . .

502. CS: *Spade and Brigid, as in 500.*

SPADE: ... the scales.

BRIGID: If you'd loved me, you wouldn't have needed any more on that side. (*She kisses him.*)

503. CS: *Spade and Brigid, as in 501. They are still kissing, but Spade begins to pull away.*

504. CS: *Spade and Brigid, as in 502. She is staring longingly at him. The doorbuzzer rings and she starts, looks away briefly, and then stares coldly and expectantly at him.*

SPADE: Come in.

505. LS: *the door to Spade's apartment opens and Dundy, Polhaus, and two other men enter. The camera pans right as they walk and brings Spade and Brigid into the frame.*

SPADE: Hello, Tom. Got 'em?

POLHAUS: Got 'em.

SPADE: Swell. (*He escorts Brigid over to them and then moves over to a table and hands items from it to Polhaus.*) Here's another one for you. She killed Miles. Oh, and I've got some exhibits: the boy's guns, one of Cairo's, ...

506. MS: *Polhaus, Spade, and Brigid. She stares blankly ahead.*

    SPADE: ... and a thousand-dollar bill I was supposed to be bribed with, and this black statuette here that all the fuss was about. (*He turns and looks smugly in Dundy's direction.*) What's the matter with your little playmate, ...

507. CS: *Dundy, looking embarrassed.*

    SPADE (*off*): ... he looks broken-hearted.

508. MS: *Polhaus, Spade, and Brigid, as in 506.*

    SPADE: I bet, when he heard Gutman's story, he thought he had me. (*He shifts his mocking gaze from Dundy to look thoughtfully at Brigid. Polhaus speaks sadly.*)

    POLHAUS: Cut it out, Sam.

    SPADE: Well, shall we be getting ...

509. LS: *Detective, Polhaus, Spade, Brigid, and Dundy. Spade briefly walks out of the frame to retrieve Brigid's coat and he returns into the frame to give it to Dundy, who helps Brigid on with it. Polhaus gathers up the evidence from the table.*

    SPADE: ... on down to the hall?

Dundy escorts Brigid toward the door and they leave the frame.

510. M S : *Polhaus, turning to side profile with the statuette in his hands.*
Spade, placing his hat on, walks into the frame.
P O L H A U S : Heavy. What is it?
Spade touches the statuette, looks first at Polhaus, then in Brigid's direction.
S P A D E : The, uh, stuff that dreams are made of.
P O L H A U S : Huh?
Spade takes the statuette and walks stolidly toward the camera. Soon we see only the statuette and his hands.

The hallway outside Spade's apartment, interior, day

511. M S : *Spade walks into the hallway holding the statuette and stops to watch Brigid being escorted into the elevator by a detective, who closes the elevator grate in front of her.*

512. C S : *Brigid, staring stolidly ahead as the elevator grate closes in front of her. The bars of the grate resemble prison bars.*

513. C S : *Spade, looking in her direction.*

514. C S : *Brigid, as in 512, looking as if she is about to cry.*

515. M S : *Spade looking at Brigid as the elevator door closes. Polhaus appears briefly between Spade and the camera as he descends the stairs and a detective is in the elevator with Brigid. When the door closes completely and the light indicates that the elevator is descending, Spade walks down the stairs. The camera pulls back for a long shot.*
Fade out.
Fade in.

516. C S : *"The End" and the Warner Brothers and First National logo over a darkly lit shot of the Maltese Falcon. These are followed by a cast list over the same shot.*
Fade out.

Contexts, Reviews, and Commentaries

Contexts

John Huston's choice of *The Maltese Falcon* for his first directorial project stemmed from his respect for Dashiell Hammett's novel combined with his conviction that the two earlier film adaptations of the novel had not capitalized upon its strengths. He claimed that he conceived of his script for the film as following the narrative line of the novel and, with this in mind, gave a copy of the novel to his secretary and asked her to transcribe it into screenplay format. Somehow Jack Warner saw this "script," liked it, and, as a result, approved Huston's project for production.

This section provides a brief segment from chapter seven of Hammett's novel: Samuel Spade's story of Mr. Flitcraft and the falling beam. Although this story was not used in the film, it is a justly famous piece that reads like a short story. It gives a fine sense of Hammett's prose style as well as what has been termed his existentialist perspective upon experience. It also reveals a good deal about Hammett's Sam Spade.

This is followed by Rudy Behlmer's "'The Stuff That Dreams Are Made Of': *The Maltese Falcon,*" which gives a detailed account of the origins and production of the movie. It draws heavily upon Warner Bros. archives to give fascinating information about Hammett's sources for characters in the novel, the 1931 and 1936 versions of the novel, censorship problems encountered during the making of Huston's film, difficulties in casting, the relatively easy time with shooting and retakes, and the film's effect upon Bogart's career.

The Story of Samuel Spade and Mr. Flitcraft
Dashiell Hammett

Spade sat down in the armchair beside the table and without any preliminary, without an introductory remark of any sort, began to tell the girl about a thing that had happened some years before in the Northwest. He talked in a steady matter-of-fact voice that was devoid of emphasis or pauses, though now and then he repeated a sentence slightly rearranged, as if it were important that each detail be related exactly as it had happened. At the beginning Brigid O'Shaughnessy listened with only partial attentiveness, obviously more surprised by his telling the story than interested in it, her curiosity more engaged with his purpose in telling the story than with the story he told; but presently, as the story went on, it caught her more and more fully and she became still and receptive.

A man named Flitcraft had left his real-estate-office, in Tacoma, to go to luncheon one day and had never returned. He did not keep an engagement to play golf after four that afternoon, though he had taken the initiative in making the engagement less than half an hour before he went out to luncheon. His wife and children never saw him again. His wife and he were supposed to be on the best of terms. He had two children, boys, one five and the other three. He owned his house in a Tacoma suburb, a new Packard, and the rest of the appurtenances of successful American living.

Flitcraft had inherited seventy thousand dollars from his father, and, with his success in real estate, was worth something in the neighborhood of two hundred thousand dollars at the time he vanished. His affairs were in order, though there were enough loose ends to indicate that he had not been setting them in order preparatory to vanishing. A deal that would have brought him an attractive profit, for instance, was to have been concluded the day after the one on which he disappeared. There was nothing to suggest that he had more than fifty or sixty dollars in his immediate possession at the time of his going. His habits for months past could be accounted for too thoroughly to justify any suspicion of secret vices, or even of another woman in his life, though either was barely possible. "He went like that," Spade said, "like a fist when you open your hand." . . .

Brigid O'Shaughnessy frowned and stirred in her chair, but did not say anything. Spade . . . told her: "Well, . . . I was with one of the big detective agencies in Seattle. Mrs. Flitcraft came in and told us somebody had seen a man in Spokane who looked a lot like her husband. I went over there. It was Flitcraft, all right. He had been living in Spokane for a couple of years as Charles—that was his first name—Pierce. He had an automobile-business that was netting him twenty or

From *The Maltese Falcon* (1930; reprint, New York: Vintage, 1972), 63–67.

twenty-five thousand a year, a wife, a baby son, owned his home in a Spokane suburb, and usually got away to play golf after four in the afternoon during the season."

Spade had not been told very definitely what to do when he found Flitcraft. They talked in Spade's room at the Davenport. Flitcraft had no feeling of guilt. He had left his first family well provided for, and what he had done seemed to him perfectly reasonable. The only thing that bothered him was a doubt that he could make that reasonableness clear to Spade. He had never told anybody his story before, and thus had not had to attempt to make its reasonableness explicit. He tried now. "I got it all right," Spade told Brigid O'Shaughnessy, "but Mrs. Flitcraft never did. She thought it was silly. Maybe it was. Anyway, it came out all right. She didn't want any scandal, and, after the trick he had played on her—the way she looked at it—she didn't want him. So they were divorced on the quiet and everything was swell.

"Here's what happened to him. Going to lunch he passed an office-building that was being put up—just the skeleton. A beam or something fell eight or ten stories down and smacked the sidewalk alongside him. It brushed pretty close to him, but didn't touch him, though a piece of the sidewalk was chipped off and flew up and hit his cheek. It only took a piece of skin off, but he still had the scar when I saw him. He rubbed it with his finger—well, affectionately—when he told me about it. He was scared stiff of course, he said, but he was more shocked than really frightened. He felt like somebody had taken the lid off life and let him look at the works."

Flitcraft had been a good citizen and a good husband and father, not by any outer compulsion, but simply because he was a man who was most comfortable in step with his surroundings. He had been raised that way. The people he knew were like that. The life he knew was a clean orderly sane responsible affair. Now a falling beam had shown him that life was fundamentally none of these things. He, the good citizen-husband-father, could be wiped out between office and restaurant by the accident of a falling beam. He knew then that men died at haphazard like that, and lived only while blind chance spared them. It was not, primarily, the injustice of it that disturbed him: he accepted that after the first shock. What disturbed him was the discovery that in sensibly ordering his affairs he had got out of step, and not into step, with life. He said he knew before he had gone twenty feet from the fallen beam that he would never know peace again until he had adjusted himself to this new glimpse of life. By the time he had eaten his luncheon he had found his means of adjustment. Life could be ended for him at random by a falling beam: he would change his life at random by simply going away. He loved his family, he said, as much as he supposed was usual, but he knew he was leaving them adequately provided for, and his love for them was not of the sort to make absence painful.

"He went to Seattle that afternoon," Spade said, "and from there by boat to San Francisco. For a couple of years he wandered around and then drifted back to the

Northwest, and settled in Spokane and got married. His second wife didn't look like the first, but they were more alike than they were different. You know, the kind of women that play fair games of golf and bridge and like new salad-recipes. He wasn't sorry for what he had done. It seemed reasonable enough to him. I don't think he even knew he had settled back naturally into the same groove he had jumped out of in Tacoma. But that's the part of it I always liked. He adjusted himself to beams falling, and then no more of them fell, and he adjusted himself to them not falling."

"How perfectly fascinating," Brigid O'Shaughnessy said.

"The Stuff That Dreams Are Made Of"
The Maltese Falcon
Rudy Behlmer

In an apartment on Nob Hill, a few blocks west of the Mark Hopkins Hotel in San Francisco, Dashiell Hammett wrote perhaps the best of all private-eye novels. *The Maltese Falcon* originally appeared as a five-part serial in the pulp detective magazine *Black Mask* beginning in September 1929. In 1930 the book was published and became a best seller. It has remained so over the years.

Warner Bros. bought the rights to *The Maltese Falcon* the year it was published in book form for $8,500 and produced two film versions within the next six years. By 1941, John Huston, the son of actor Walter Huston, was doing particularly well at Warners collaborating on the scripts for such films as *Jezebel, The Amazing Dr. Clitterhouse, Juarez, Dr. Ehrlich's Magic Bullet, High Sierra,* and *Sergeant York.* But he wanted to direct. When he occasionally visited sets and watched directors working with his material, he realized he would never be happy unless he could interpret the ideas himself.

"They indulged me rather," Huston told author Gerald Pratley. "They liked my work as a writer and they wanted to keep me on. If I wanted to direct, why they'd give me a shot at it, and if it didn't come off all that well, they wouldn't be too disappointed as it was to be a very small picture. They acted out of friendship for me, out of good will. This was Jack Warner, but largely [executive producer] Hall Wallis and [producer] Henry Blanke." When Huston was asked what subject he would like to do he told them *The Maltese Falcon,* which the studio still owned and which could be done in a relatively inexpensive manner. "There was something in the *Falcon* that attracted me," Huston has said, "that hadn't been done in the other versions."

Henry Blanke by his own account was at first apprehensive about a third time around with the material, having produced the less-than-successful 1936 version. But Huston wanted to stick closely to the novel. "We took two copies of the book, tore each page and just pasted it together on script pages and edited it a little," Blanke has said. The producer understood what Huston wanted to do with the material and became a strong supporter. Huston had worked with Blanke on *Jezebel* (1938) and *Juarez* (1939) and they had become good friends.

An account given by Huston and verified by writer Allen Rivkin, who at the time shared a secretary with Huston, goes as follows: Huston gave the novel to the

From Rudy Behlmer, *Behind the Scenes: The Making of . . .* (Hollywood: Samuel French Trade), and Rudy Behlmer, *America's Favorite Movies: Behind the Scenes* (New York: Frederick Ungar Publishing Company, 1982), 135–153.

secretary and told her to recopy the text, but to break it down routinely into script format with the usual scene numbers and shot descriptions. According to this version, a copy somehow appeared on Jack Warner's desk. Warner looked over the "adaptation," was pleased, and gave Huston a go-ahead.

Eventually Huston tightened the narrative and eliminated a few scenes, a rather lengthy parable, and two minor characters—the daughter of the Fat Man, Kasper Gutman (one scene), and Sam Spade's attorney (two scenes)—but he retained an unusually large amount of the dialogue, style, and ambience used by Hammett, the founder of the hard-boiled school of detective fiction. Fortunately, the novel lends itself to dramatization, being primarily a series of brilliant dialogues.

As was the custom, the temporary script was sent automatically for approval to the Production Code Administration, the film industry's self-regulatory body. Joseph I. Breen wrote back to Jack L. Warner that while the basic story was acceptable under the code, there were certain objectionable details. Too much drinking, a few damns and hells, and instances of "gruesomeness"—meaning brutality. The point was made that "it is essential that Spade should not be characterized as having had a sex affair with Iva [his partner's widow]. Accordingly, we request that you cut down the physical contact indicated . . . and that the following lines must be deleted or changed to get away from such inference: 'You shouldn't have come here today, darling. It wasn't wise,' and Iva's line, 'You'll come tonight?' with Spade's reply, 'Not tonight.'"

Regarding the character subsequently played by Peter Lorre, the letter stated that "we cannot approve the characterization of Cairo as a pansy as indicated by the lavender perfume, high pitched voice, and other accoutrements. In line with this, we refer you to page 148, where Cairo tries to put his arm around the boy's [Wilmer] shoulder and is struck by the boy for so doing. This action, in the light of Cairo's characterization, is definitely unacceptable. . . .

"There must be no indication that Brigid [Mary Astor] and Spade are spending the night together in Spade's apartment," and, referring to a later scene in the script, "Brigid's line, 'Not after what we've been to each other . . .' should be changed to get away from the reference to an illicit sex affair."

The final script and film reflected these requests for changes. One scene from the novel that was used in the 1931 film version, when the old Production Code was quite loosely enforced, had been dropped early in the 1941 adaptation due to the strong censorship situation at that time: In Spade's apartment, the detective forces Brigid (or "Miss Wonderly")* to remove her clothes in front of him (off camera) in order to find out if she stole a thousand-dollar bill from an envelope containing several thousand dollars brought by Gutman.

Huston has said that Warner, Wallis, and Blanke "helped me marvelously with the casting." As was the custom, the casting department drew up a list of possibil-

---

*In the novel and in the Huston version, "Miss Wonderly's" real name is revealed to be Brigid O'Shaughnessy. In the 1931 version she was referred to only as "Miss Wonderly" or "Ruth Wonderly."

ities for each of the roles and circulated the sheet to Huston and the key executives. The list is an interesting one for various reasons, not the least of which is speculation on how certain roles would have been played by other performers. At the top of the roster of possible actors to play Sam Spade was George Raft, then under contract to Warners; in second position was Bogart, followed by Edward G. Robinson, Richard Whorf, Franchot Tone, Fred MacMurray, Fredric March, Henry Fonda, Brian Donlevy, Warner Baxter, Paul Muni, and some others.

On May 19, 1941, Hal Wallis sent a memo to Henry Blanke instructing him to send George Raft his two weeks' notice to report for work. "It will not be necessary for you to tell Raft at this time what his picture is to be, but for your own information, he will do *The Maltese Falcon*." Raft turned down the role on the advice of his agent. Also, Raft was uneasy about working with an inexperienced director, and his contract called for no remakes.

So, once again Bogart was second choice after a Raft refusal. The interesting and convoluted sequence of events leading up to Bogart being case in *The Maltese Falcon* is worth noting in some detail: A few years earlier, producer Samuel Goldwyn and director William Wyler had wanted Raft for the role of the gangster in *Dead End* (1937) but Raft turned it down because he thought the character unsympathetic, and he had an aversion to being killed at the picture's conclusion. Arrangements were made to borrow Bogart from Warners. Then Raft was wanted for *It All Came True* (1940) at Warners. On October 17, 1939, Raft wrote to Jack L. Warner:

When I saw you at your house, you told me . . . that I would not have to play any dirty heavies and if anyone at your studio ever submitted a script to me in which I was to play a dirty heavy I was to bring the script to you and you would take me out of it. I remarked at the time to you that I was afraid the studio would put me into parts that Humphrey Bogart should play and you told me that I would never have to play a Humphrey Bogart part.

Bogart did *It All Came True* and then *High Sierra* (1941) which Paul Muni and other Warners players had refused, followed by the lead in *The Wagons Roll at Night* (1941). Raft had turned down that one also. On January 16, 1941 Bogart wired Jack Warner:

DEAR JACK: IT SEEMS TO ME I AM THE LOGICAL PERSON ON THE LOT TO PLAY "GENTLE PEOPLE." I WOULD BE VERY DISAPPOINTED IF I DIDN'T GET IT.

Bogart was referring to the important role of the gangster in the studio's upcoming adaptation of Irwin Shaw's 1939 play, which later was retitled *Out of the Fog* (1941). However, there was some disagreement at the studio regarding the casting. Ida Lupino was slated to play the leading woman's role, and she did not want to work with Bogart again (they recently had made *High Sierra* together). Hal Wallis, Henry Blanke, and Lupino favored John Garfield for the part. Jack Warner wanted Bogart to do it, and Bogart agreed. Blanke said in an interoffice memo to

Jack Warner on January 31, 1941, that "casting Garfield for the part of Goff would, as you know, relieve us of the problem of convincing Lupino to play with Bogart." And on February 3, Blanke wrote to casting director Steve Trilling that "you witnessed my last conversation with Mr. Warner in which he insisted it was Bogart, and you had better straighten out the Lupino-Bogart situation."

Ida Lupino was in a strong position at the time, having just completed outstanding performances in three particularly good Warner films in a row: *They Drive by Night* (1940), *High Sierra* (1941), and *The Sea Wolf* (1941). (George Raft turned down the part eventually played by John Garfield in *The Sea Wolf.*) She won her point regarding Bogart, and Garfield was cast opposite her in *Out of the Fog.* Then Bogart was assigned to *Manpower* (1941) with George Raft and Marlene Dietrich. Bogart sent a telegram to Hal Wallis on March 6, 1941:

DEAR HAL: . . . I HAVE NEVER HAD ANYTHING BUT THE VERY FINEST FEELINGS OF FRIENDSHIP FOR GEORGE. I UNDERSTAND HE HAS REFUSED TO MAKE THE PICTURE IF I AM IN IT. . . . GEORGE HAS ALSO TOLD MY AGENT SEVERAL WEEKS AGO THAT HE DIDN'T THINK I SHOULD DO THIS PART AS IT WAS COMPLETELY WRONG FOR ME. . . . I FEEL VERY MUCH HURT BY THIS BECAUSE IT'S THE SECOND TIME I HAVE BEEN KEPT OUT OF A GOOD PICTURE AND A GOOD PART BY AN ACTOR'S REFUSING TO WORK WITH ME.

Bogart was replaced in *Manpower* by Edward G. Robinson. On March 13, a script of *Bad Men of Missouri* (1941) was delivered to Bogart and he was notified that he had been given the role of Cole Younger in that production. On March 17, a messenger returned the script with a memo attached to Steve Trilling: "Are you kidding? This is certainly rubbing it in. Since Lupino and Raft are casting pictures maybe I can."

For refusing *Bad Men of Missouri,* which was given to Dennis Morgan, Bogart was placed on suspension. Meanwhile, after finishing *Manpower,* George Raft was assigned to *The Maltese Falcon.* He wrote Jack Warner on June 6: "As you know, I strongly feel that *The Maltese Falcon,* which you want me to do, is not an important picture and, in this connection, I must remind you again before I signed the new contract with you, you promised me that you would not require me to perform in anything but important pictures." Bogart was put in *The Maltese Falcon* shortly before filming was to begin on June 9th. He had been on suspension for two months.*

Possibilities for the role of Brigid were Olivia de Havilland, Loretta Young, Rita Hayworth, Geraldine Fitzgerald, Mary Astor, Paulette Goddard, Brenda Marshall,

---

*Later, in July, Raft was assigned to *All Through the Night* (1942), which he refused. Bogart's agent, Sam Jaffe (not the actor) wrote Steve Trilling: "I had a long discussion about *All Through the Night* with him [Bogart] and I felt this would make a pretty fair picture though he didn't exactly think so. . . . A story should be prepared for which they have Bogart in mind and no other actor because it seems that for the past year he's practically pinch-hit for Raft and been kicked around from pillar to post." Bogart did *All Through the Night,* but soon afterward when it came time for *Casablanca,* the tables were turned.

Janet Gaynor, Joan Bennett, Betty Field, Ingrid Bergman, and a few others. Geraldine Fitzgerald (*Dark Victory, Wuthering Heights*) seemed to be favored for a time. But on May 19, Blanke sent a memo to Wallis, saying:

> I had Mary Astor in on Friday and gave her the script on *Maltese Falcon*. . . . She called me this morning saying that she thinks *Maltese Falcon* is a "humdinger" and would love to do it. . . . We are waiting to hear from [Geraldine] Fitzgerald today . . . so that we can then make up our minds.

Later that day, in a memo to Blanke, Wallis said, "If we do not get an okay from Geraldine Fitzgerald on *The Maltese Falcon*, we will use Mary Astor." The inference is that Fitzgerald had certain contractual approvals, since almost immediately thereafter the decision was made to go with Mary Astor. She had recently signed a two-picture contract with Warners. Mary Astor had been in films since 1921. While still a teenager, she had played opposite John Barrymore in *Beau Brummel* (1924) and *Don Juan* (1926) and Douglas Fairbanks in *Don Q, Son of Zorro* (1925). Other memorable films include *Red Dust* (1932), with Gable; *Dodsworth* (1936), with Walter Huston; *The Prisoner of Zenda* (1937); and *Midnight* (1939). At the time Mary Astor was set for *The Maltese Falcon*, she had just scored a considerable success with a major role in a Bette Davis vehicle, *The Great Lie* (1941).

Peter Lorre was first choice for Joel Cairo in *The Maltese Falcon*, with Martin Kosleck, Sam Jaffe, Curt Bois, and Elia Kazan as follow-ups. (Kazan was also considered for Wilmer.)

Sydney Greenstreet, who at the age of sixty-one had never made a film, was the prime choice for the Fat Man, Kasper Gutman. Other possibilities included Laird Cregar, Edward Arnold, George Barbier, Lee J. Cobb, Gene Lockhart, Eugene Pallette, Akim Tamiroff, S. Z. Sakall, Guy Kibbee, Alan Hale, Broderick Crawford, and Billy Gilbert, the character comedian whose trademark was his crescendo sneeze. Greenstreet had been acting on the stage, both in his native England and in America, since 1902. He had spent over six years with Alfred Lunt and Lynn Fontanne and was touring with them in *There Shall Be No Night* when John Huston saw him at the Biltmore Theater in Los Angeles and persuaded him to break his rule about doing films. He was primarily a character comedian on the stage, but his screen career was to consist mainly of villains. Warners signed Greenstreet for $1,000 a week with a four-week guarantee. The principal players were now set for *The Maltese Falcon*.

In the first film version of the novel, *Dangerous Female,** made in early 1931, Ricardo Cortez played a tough but rather suave and elegant Sam Spade, given to wearing a silk lounging robe in his apartment. Bebe Daniels was a more vulnerable Ruth Wonderly, Dudley Digges a less ominous Gutman, Otto Matiesen a relatively colorless Joel Cairo, and Dwight Frye a rather perfunctory Wilmer (Elisha Cook, Jr., in 1941), compared with the portrayals in the Huston version.

---

*Retitled for TV to avoid confusion with the 1941 version.

Although it was reasonably faithful to Hammett's novel in plot, the first film did not have the advantage of the style, marvelous casting, and beautiful mesh of elements that prevail in the classic 1941 version. A 1936 Warners variation on the theme, called *Satan Met a Lady,* took considerable liberties and transposed an item or character here and there. Warren William was a slick, flamboyant Spade (changed to Ted Shane), Bette Davis a revamped Miss Wonderly, or Brigid, called Valerie Purvis, and the Fat Man had the most dramatic metamorphosis—he became a woman, Madame Barabbas, in the person of Alison Skipworth. The Falcon was now an ancient hunting horn crammed with jewels, and the whole enterprise emerged as a misguided attempt at comedy-melodrama.

Dashiell Hammett had based some facets of his *Maltese Falcon* characters on real people he had encountered while working as a Pinkerton detective for several years: "I followed Gutman's original in Washington," Hammett said, "and I never remember shadowing a man who bored me so much. He was not after a jeweled falcon, of course; but he *was* suspected of being a German spy. Brigid was based, in part, on a woman who came in to Pinkerton's to hire an operative to discharge her housekeeper." And she was also patterned on Peggy O'Toole, Hammett's assistant in the advertising department of Albert Samuel's jewelry company in San Francisco, where Hammett worked after leaving Pinkerton's. "The Cairo character I picked up on a forgery charge in 1920. Effie, the good girl [Spade's secretary, played by Lee Patrick], once asked me to go into the narcotic smuggling business with her in San Diego. Wilmer, the gunman, was picked up in Stockton, California; a neat small smooth-faced quiet boy of perhaps twenty-one. He was serenely proud of the name the papers gave him—'The Midget Bandit.'" Hammett stated that Sam Spade had no original. He was "idealized . . . in the sense that he is what most of the private detectives I've worked with would *like* to have been."

Hammett told author James Thurber that he was influenced by Henry James's 1902 novel *The Wings of the Dove* when writing *The Maltese Falcon.* James, with his polished prose styling, influenced the history of the novel by emphasizing psychological character analysis. "In both novels," related Thurber, "a fabulous fortune—jewels in *Falcon,* inherited millions in *Dove*—shapes the destinies of the disenchanted central characters, and James's designing woman, Kate Croy, like Hammett's pistol-packing Brigid O'Shaughnessy, loses her lover in a Renunciation Scene."

Concentrating on abiding moral themes, James admitted into his stories and novels only what could be represented as the perception or experience of his characters. Huston followed this technique. He said that "the book was told entirely from the standpoint of Sam Spade, and so too is the picture, with Spade in every scene except the murder of his partner. The audience knows no more and no less than he does. All the other characters are introduced only as they meet Spade, and upon their appearance I attempted to photograph them through his eyes."

Recalling his initial opportunity to direct a film, John Huston told Gerald Pratley: "I still remember going on the floor for the first day. . . . As I hadn't been on the set very often when I was a writer, directing was something that came instinctively. I knew almost exactly what I was going to do. I made drawings of every set-up, through the whole picture from beginning to end. I made the drawings myself. I showed the pictures and the drawings to [director] Willy Wyler and he criticized them, and whatever ideas he had I incorporated them if they seemed to be good." Wyler was an old friend and professional associate. He had directed the first film Huston worked on as a writer, *A House Divided* (1931) and was directly responsible for bringing Huston to Warners to work as a writer on *Jezebel* (1938).

"Before going on the set," said Huston, "Henry Blanke gave me the best advice I ever had, that any young director could have, in my opinion. That was: each scene, as you go to make it, is the best scene in the picture . . . the most important." Blanke worked closely with Huston and helped him with the fundamental techniques of film making before he stepped on the stage.

But, as shooting began, there was some concern on the part of the executives. Hal Wallis, in a memo sent to Blanke on June 12, 1941 (with a copy to Huston), said, in part, that:

> Huston's second day's dailies* are better than the first, but I still feel that they are too leisurely in tempo. I think my criticism is principally with Bogart, who has adopted a leisurely, suave form of delivery. . . . Bogart must have his usual brisk, staccato manner. . . . All of the action seems a little too slow and deliberate. . . . The actual scene, the setups, etc. are fine. It is primarily a matter of tempo and delivery.

Huston replied to Wallis in a memo:

> I am shrinking all the pauses and speeding up all the action. You understand, of course, that so far I have done only the slow scenes of the picture. . . . After the sequence I am doing at present—Brigid's apartment—the story really begins to move. By the time we reach the Cairo-Brigid-copper sequence in Spade's apartment, it will be turning like a pinwheel. . . . As I am making each scene, I am keeping the whole picture in mind. This picture should gain in velocity as it goes along. . . . Nevertheless, I am. . . . making Bogart quick and staccato and taking the deliberateness out of his action.

Blanke recalls screening for Huston the daily scenes of a picture director Anatole Litvak was shooting on the lot at the same time, *Blues in the Night,* and pointing out the difference in pacing, with Litvak's fast tempo being presented as an example.

Of course, the dominant aspect of the Warners style during the 1930s and 1940s was the furious pacing. The credo was to move everything as fast as possible without anything remaining on screen a fraction of a second longer than necessary.

---

*The material shot the previous day that had been developed and printed.

Scripts were usually pared down to the minimum prior to shooting, performers talked rapidly and picked up their cues, and editors ruthlessly cut frames; next Hal Wallis (and, before he left Warners in 1933, Darryl Zanuck) trimmed even more footage. Then Jack L. Warner had his crack at it. There were exceptions to this, particularly after the initial release of *Gone With the Wind* (1939) and during the World War II years, when long-drawn-out features were in vogue.

Mary Astor thought that "it helped a great deal that we shot the picture [to a large extent] in sequence. . . . Because John's script was well prepared, and because he took time in rehearsal, the shooting went very quickly. Often there is much time lost in lack of preparation. There was and is too much of 'Let's rehearse with film,' in the hopes that something might happen that would be spontaneous and fresh, and wouldn't happen again."

One of Mary Astor's approaches to the role of Brigid, the slightly psychopathic, congenital liar, was to breathe rather rapidly to emphasize the unstable quality. "So, I hyperventilated before going into most of the scenes. It gave me a heady feeling, of thinking at cross purposes."

In a memo to Henry Blanke on June 24, Wallis said:

> The scene in the apartment with Bogart, Astor, and Peter Lorre is very good. I don't think it is too slow. . . . One thing that bothers me, however, is the way in which Mary Astor is speaking her lines. She seems to be playing it just a little too coy and ladylike. I think she is going overboard a little on this, in the soft quality of her voice, and obviously playing a part for all the characters with whom she comes in contact in the picture, and I think she overdoes it to the point of where the people she is playing with would know that she was putting on an act.

On June 30, Wallis said in another memo to Blanke that "Sydney Greenstreet is wonderful in the part, but just a little difficult to understand. Will you ask Huston to watch him a little on this, and have just a little clearer enunciation."

As a good-luck gesture, Walter Huston worked one day in the unbilled bit role of Captain Jacobi, who staggers into Spade's office and hands the Falcon over before dying. Most people in the audience did not recognize him.

After thirty-four days of filming, on July 18, 1941, *The Maltese Falcon* completed shooting—two days ahead of schedule. Jack Warner requested a few changes after the film was edited. First, there was a very brief additional scene—not in the book, script, or any previous movie version—showing Spade's partner, Archer (Jerome Cowan), being murdered. This was to be photographed using the subjective camera technique, with the camera being the killer. Second, there was a new ending. The ending originally planned was the same as that of the book: After Brigid is turned over to the police in Spade's apartment, the scene shifts to the next morning in Spade's office. There is a short dialogue between Sam and his secretary, Effie. She says to him, "Iva is here" (Gladys George). Spade, looking at nothing, nods almost imperceptibly and says, "Yes. . . ." He shivers, and then says, "Well. . . . send her in." Fade out.

In the revised ending, the latter part of the scene in Spade's apartment was reshot in early August, including a new non-Hammett line in reference to the Falcon—"the stuff that dreams are made of." Lieutenant Dundy (Barton Mac-Lane) and Brigid exit the room first, but this time they continue in the corridor to the elevator. Spade follows. As Brigid descends in the open elevator, Spade takes one last look at her from the corridor and starts down the stairway. The end.*

This revision contributes to the general softening of Sam Spade's character, some of which was already accomplished by the necessary editing of the overall text, some of which was implicit in Bogart's somewhat vulnerable manner. The new ending allows the audience to believe that, although he may have seemed as corrupt as Gutman, Spade was always playing a role in order to solve the crime.

James Naremore in his 1973 essay, "John Huston and *The Maltese Falcon*," points out that "Bogart is the visual opposite of Hammett's Sam Spade. Spade, Hammett tells us, is a tall man with an 'almost conical' body. When he takes off his shirt, 'the sag of his big rounded shoulders' makes him resemble 'a bear.' . . .

"Sydney Greenstreet . . . is not so flabby or bombastic as the Gutman of the novel, and he lacks 'dark ringlets' of hair. Peter Lorre is properly Levantine, but less effeminate and less bejeweled than Hammett's Joel Cairo. . . . Hammett's Brigid O'Shaughnessy is little more than a sexy dame. . . . Mary Astor, on the other hand, has a lovely but almost matronly face and build, and she brings a sophistication to the role that is entirely lacking in the novel."

Jack Warner also requested a short written prologue giving the background and history of the Falcon on a title following the opening credits. The background was partially based on fact. Hammett stated that "somewhere I had read of the peculiar rental agreement between Charles V [of Spain] and the Order of the Hospital of St. John of Jerusalem [the Knights of Malta]." This agreement of 1530 specified that rent for the island of Malta would be an annual tribute on All Saint's Day of a single falcon. The rest of the history seems to be Hammett's romantic embellishment.

Warners staff composer Adolph Deutsch was assigned the film and created a subtle and properly mysterious score that was devoid of bombast. The Warners music style of that time usually was thick textured, with heavy brass and strings surging to the foreground. Deutsch was relatively unobtrusive in his approach and gave the edge more to the mood and colorings his use of woodwinds evoked. He told me recently that he consciously avoided "the Wagnerian approach" and that he did not want obvious leitmotifs overpowering the picture. He said that he did not screen the film with Huston, Blanke, or Wallis and Warner, but discussed the music and where it would be used in the film only with Leo F. Forbstein, the head of the studio's music department.

---

*In the 1931 version, the audience learns by means of a newspaper insert shot that at the trial Spade produced a Chinese merchant, the only eyewitness to Archer's murder, who positively identified Ruth Wonderly as the murderess. Then Spade visits her in jail, announcing that he has been made a special investigator for the district attorney's office. "You helped me get it," he says. "If they don't hang you, I'll be waiting for you." The picture ends with Spade leaving the jail.

The Maltese Falcon was previewed on September 5, 1941, and the next morning Jack Warner sent a memo to Hal Wallis in which he said:

Last night after the preview, I thought for about an hour, and believe we should positively make over the opening closeups of Mary Astor [in Spade's office] and tell the audience what the hell it is all about instead of picking up with a lot of broken sentences with confusing words. . . .

Many of the [preview] cards stated they were very confused in the beginning, and I am sure we throw them off. Therefore, why be so clever, as we have a hell of a good picture under the name *The Maltese Falcon,* which I have already wired New York we are going to use.* We should do these retakes the first thing Monday.

On September 10, Bogart was excused from the shooting of his next picture, *All through the Night,* and along with Mary Astor and Jerome Cowan, reported to Stage 6 to retake the opening scene in the office of Spade and Archer. Brigid's speech regarding her sister and Floyd Thursby was rewritten and simplified by Huston. For example, in the original shooting the dialogue began:

SPADE

Now what can I do for you, Miss Wonderly?

MISS WONDERLY

(hurriedly)

Could you—? I thought—I—that is—

SPADE

Suppose you tell me about it from the very beginning.

MISS WONDERLY

That was in New York.

SPADE

Yes?

MISS WONDERLY

I don't know where she met him in New York. She's five years younger than I—only seventeen—we didn't have the same friends. I don't suppose we've ever been as close as sisters should be. Mama and Papa are in Europe. It would kill them. I've *got* to get her back before they come home.

In the revised scene, the exposition was much clearer:

SPADE

Won't you sit down, Miss Wonderly?

MISS WONDERLY

Thank you. I inquired at the hotel for the name of a reliable, private detective. They mentioned yours.

---

*There had been some thought given to calling the film, "The Gent from Frisco."

> SPADE

Suppose you tell me about it from the very beginning.

> MISS WONDERLY

I'm from New York.

> SPADE

Uh-huh.

> MISS WONDERLY

I'm trying to find my sister. I have reason to believe that she's here in San Francisco with a man by the name of Thursby, Floyd Thursby. I don't know where she met him. We've never been as close as sisters ought to be. If we had, perhaps Corinne would have told me that she was planning on running away with him. Mother and Father are in Honolulu. It will kill them. I've got to find her before they get back home. They're coming home the first of the month.

The entire scene up to Archer's entrance was modified in this way. Seven camera set-ups—photographed by Ernest Haller, substituting for the original cameraman, Arthur Edison, who was on another assignment—were completed by 4:00 P.M.

Less than a month later, this modest little film, which cost $381,000, according to the studio records, opened in New York. Within two days Wallis wrote Jack Warner, who was on vacation in Hot Springs, Arkansas:

> According to some of the reviews and other press notices from New York on *The Maltese Falcon,* the picture came in "under wraps," "on rubber heels," "was a delightful surprise because it came in unheralded," etc. etc.
>
> You probably have seen the reviews, which are wonderful, and have seen the figures, which are also wonderful, and it is too bad that they [Warners' New York headquarters] were apparently not sufficiently sold on the picture in New York to get behind it importantly.
>
> Now that it has opened and has proven to be a hit, I thought perhaps you might want to give them a slight goose and let them get behind this picture in other situations and give it the importance which it deserves.

The Maltese Falcon was the forerunner of a number of films over the next several years that were a direct, if somewhat belated, result of its influence. Hammett, Raymond Chandler, James M. Cain, and similar authors of the hard-boiled school became fashionable in Hollywood. *The Glass Key* (1942), *Murder My Sweet* (1944), *Double Indemnity* (1944), and others were big box office. Bogart even returned to the private detective genre a few years later as Philip Marlowe in Chandler's *The Big Sleep* (1946).

In early 1943, Henry Blanke wrote Roy Obringer, head of the studio legal department that several years ago we purchased an original, called *Three Strangers,* from John Huston. . . .

To the characters John Huston had, we have added a private detective on the order of the one played by Humphrey Bogart in *The Maltese Falcon.* It would enrich my story manifold if we could make him identically the same character as in *The Maltese Falcon* and even give him the same name. . . .

The question . . . is whether or not I have the legal right to use this character's name.

Obringer replied (in part):

I find that "Detective Spade" is a character which has been used on more than one occasion by Dashiell Hammett. . . . In other words, the author did not divest himself of the privilege of using the character "Spade" when he sold us *The Maltese Falcon,* as this character is one which appears to have established a secondary meaning in the public mind, and which character cannot be used by the buyer of a book containing such character for the purpose of sequels. We have no sequel rights on *The Maltese Falcon.*

When Warner Bros. first announced their intention of filming *Three Strangers* in October 1942, the plan was to reunite Bogart with Sydney Greenstreet and possibly Mary Astor, if she could be borrowed from MGM by the time filming was to begin. John Collier had been signed to write the screenplay and Blanke was to produce. By the time the picture was released in early 1946, it had a new producer and writer, there was no character named Sam Spade, and Mary Astor and Bogart were not in the cast.

Before becoming a star of the first magnitude, Humphrey Bogart spent several years under contract to Warner Bros. playing mostly tough, ruthless gangsters. He supported Warners' main gangster fixtures—James Cagney, Edward G. Robinson, George Raft—in addition to carrying the load by himself in a few minor films. These were all stock roles with little opportunity for dimension and shading, but Bogart played them better than anyone else and built a reputation as a reliable actor with a distinctive style. *The Maltese Falcon* solidified further aspects of the emerging Bogey character that had been tentatively projected in *Dead End* (1937) and *High Sierra* (1941). In *The Maltese Falcon* Bogart presented the classic loner: weathered, tough, disillusioned (or perhaps nonillusioned), somewhat sadistic, cutting right through to the bare bones of his women, and yet true to his own sense of ethics and professional integrity.

According to Mary Astor, Bogart "was a hard-working guy, a good craftsman. . . . His technical skill was quite brilliant. His precision timing was no accident. He kept other actors on their toes because he *listened* to them, he watched, he *looked* at them.

He never had that vague stare of a person who waits for you to finish talking, who hasn't heard a word you have said."

Following *The Maltese Falcon,* all that was now needed to complete the Bogart mystique was a strong romantic element. Bogart's love interest in *Falcon,* brilliantly played by Mary Astor, was a tough and striking figure of feminine deceit and betrayal, but the relationship, while intriguing and offbeat, did not project the necessary romantic aura to capture the public's imagination. Then came *Casablanca.*

Reviews

The early reviews of *The Maltese Falcon* in the United States and, five years later, in France, established the basic parameters of the ways in which the movie has been perceived ever since. Bosley Crowther's *New York Times* review is fairly typical of the initial American response in its unanticipated but wholesale enthusiasm for the film and for Huston's debut as well as in its perception of the movie as unusually tough, unsentimental, and violent.

Otis Ferguson's *New Republic* review shares Crowther's praise for the film as well as for Huston's work, while also making special note of Bogart's contribution. Ferguson's somewhat bewildered description of Mary Astor's "black widow" character points to the newness of this character type at the time, a newness that is particularly interesting since similar characters so quickly became so central to *film noir.*

Film noir is arguably the most influential American film style. It was first identified by the French after World War II and their term has defined it

ever since. However, little of the actual French commentary has ever appeared in English and, consequently, the two important responses to *The Maltese Falcon* by Nino Frank reprinted here fill a major gap.

The first is Frank's review of the movie for *L'Écran Français.* It is a positive review but, unlike many American reviews which tended to focus upon Huston's debut or the brutality of the film, Frank treats the film as springing almost entirely from Dashiell Hammett's novel and, by extension, the distinctively American hard-boiled detective story.

Three weeks after his review appeared, Frank published another essay that placed *The Maltese Falcon* within a much larger context, that of "a new kind of detective story" or, as he termed it, *"film noir."* Citing half a dozen films that had just appeared in France (including *Double Indemnity, Laura,* and *Murder, My Sweet*), he describes the detective film as moving in entirely new directions, away from the elaborate but arid puzzles in films based upon the novels of S. S. Van

Dine and Sir Arthur Conan Doyle and toward the enigmatic psychological complexity, violence, misogyny, and narrational density of *film noir.* The term than carried with it associations of "black" French films of the 1930s (such as Marcel Carne's *Hôtel du Nord* or *Le Jour se lève*) as well as Marcel Duhamel's *Serie Noire* books.

As in the earlier essay, Frank gives dominating importance to the literary sources of the films, particularly the novels of Hammett and Raymond Chandler. In many ways, Frank's two essays mark the beginning of the cottage industry of film discourse that has sprung up around *film noir.*

The *New York Times*
Bosley Crowther

T he Warners have been strangely bashful about their new mystery film, "The Maltese Falcon," and about the young man, John Huston, whose first directorial job it is. Maybe they thought it best to bring both along under wraps, seeing as how the picture is a remake of an old Dashiell Hammett yarn done ten years ago, and Mr. Huston is a fledgling whose previous efforts have been devoted to writing scripts. And maybe—which is somehow more likely—they wanted to give everyone a nice surprise. For "The Maltese Falcon," which swooped down onto the screen of the Strand yesterday, only turns out to be the best mystery thriller of the year, and young Mr. Huston gives promise of becoming one of the smartest directors in the field.

For some reason, Hollywood has neglected the sophisticated crime film of late, and England, for reasons which are obvious, hasn't been sending her quota in recent months. In fact, we had almost forgotten how devilishly delightful such films can be when done with taste and understanding and a feeling for the fine line of suspense. But now, with "The Maltese Falcon," the Warners and Mr. Huston give us again something of the old thrill we got from Alfred Hitchcock's brilliant melodramas or from "The Thin Man" before he died of hunger.

This is not to imply, however, that Mr. Huston has imitated anyone. He has worked out his own style, which is brisk and supremely hardboiled. We didn't see the first "Falcon," which had Ricardo Cortez and Bebe Daniels in its cast. But we'll wager it wasn't half as tough nor half as flavored with idioms as is this present version, in which Humphrey Bogart hits his peak. For the trick which Mr. Huston has pulled is a combination of American ruggedness with the suavity of the English crime school—a blend of mind and muscle—plus a slight touch of pathos.

Perhaps you know the story (it was one of Mr. Hammett's best): of a private detective in San Francisco who becomes involved through a beautiful but evasive dame in a complicated plot to gain possession of a fabulous jeweled statuette. As Mr. Huston has adapted it, the mystery is as thick as a wall and the facts are completely obscure as the picture gets under way. But slowly the bits fall together, the complications draw out and a monstrous but logical intrigue of international proportions is revealed.

Much of the quality of the picture lies in its excellent revelation of character. Mr. Bogart is a shrewd, tough detective with a mind that cuts like a blade, a temperament that sometimes betrays him, and a code of morals which is coolly

From the *New York Times,* October 4, 1941.

cynical. Mary Astor is well-nigh perfect as the beautiful woman whose cupidity is forever to be suspect. Sidney Greenstreet, from the Theatre Guild's roster, is magnificent as a cultivated English crook, and Peter Lorre, Elisha Cook Jr., Lee Patrick, and Barton MacLane all contribute stunning characters. (Also, if you look closely, you'll see Walter Huston, John's father, in a bit part.)

Don't miss "The Maltese Falcon" if your taste is for mystery fare. It's the slickest exercise in cerebration that has hit the screen in many months, and it is also one of the most compelling nervous-laughter provokers yet.

The New Republic
Otis Ferguson

T he *Maltese Falcon* is the first crime melodrama with finish, speed, and bang to come along in what seems ages, and since its pattern is one of the best things Hollywood does, we have been missing it. It is the old Dashiell Hammett book, written back in the days when you could turn out a story and leave it at that, without any characters joining the army, fleeing as refugees, or reforming bad boys, men, or women. It is hokum, all right—about a historic image so costly with gold and jewels that people follow it all over the world, plotting to get it away from other people similarly employed, the various forces finally converging in the territory of Sam Spade, a detective. But John Huston has written the screenplay and directed the picture so that a fast pace and direct, vigorous approach give a surface meaning to each situation as it follows another.

The story is one of the few cases where they have their cake and eat it too, for the detective *is* in love with the mystery woman, and she *might* turn out in the end to be another case of (a) innocence wronged, (b) the most trusted agent of the United States Government. But she doesn't and he sends her up for twenty years. There is bound to be a little confusion in this, for an audience likes to know where it stands, and neither Mary Astor's lines nor her abilities above them quite get over the difficulty of seeming black and then seeming white, and being both all along.

Scene by scene, the picture has many good services—first of all those of the director, who has a genuine sense of suggestion and picture motion, Peter Lorre is never dull though much too often typed. There are Ward Bond, Barton MacLane, Gladys George, and Jerome Cowan, but the key man in the supporting cast is Sydney Greenstreet, who does a marvelous and veteran creation, solid in the center of each scene, as the genial and menacing fat man. There is character in the picture and this, as well as the swift succession of its contrived excitements and very shrewd dialogue, is what gives the temporary but sufficient meaning required by its violent fantasy.

And outside of the writer-director, the chief character influence in the story is Humphrey Bogart, a man of explosive action in an iron mask. He is not a villain here, though a pretty hard type; but it doesn't make any difference: he has some of that magnetism you can feel through the screen; he is a villain with appeal. He has a good part here, a steady outlet for that authority and decision and hard, level talk of his. But he fills it without trying and you're with him.

From *The New Republic,* October 20, 1941.

An Exciting . . . Put-You-to-Sleep Story, *L'Écran Français*

Nino Frank

I will not insult my reader by telling him who Dashiell Hammett is: a private detective turned writer. The few books (novels or stories) that he had published before Hollywood made use of his services were enough to establish his mastery. If he did not have the literary quality of Faulkner or Dos Passos or Caldwell, the social value of Hemingway or of Steinbeck, his name was not at all unworthy of being cited among them, for his influence has been and remains profound. In place of the detective story, which was a pleasant substitute for crossword puzzles, with a crime at the beginning, a long and complicated journey among the suspects, and a discovery of the killer in the last chapter, he put the crime novel with its astounding documentary character, and the reader must, above all else, attempt to understand what has happened, for the author shows his characters in action, but does not at all concern himself with explaining what they know and what their intentions are. His prodigiously exciting works, such as *The Thin Man, The Glass Key,* or *The Maltese Falcon,* were a great success in France as well as in America.

This last novel has already been made into a film several years ago. It is the story of a precious object that enigmatic persons covet with the reluctant help of a no less enigmatic private detective. This new version directed by John Huston reflects the economy of the production methods characteristic of the studio [Warner Bros.] from which it comes: The camera and the characters move as little as possible; action is reduced to bare essentials; everything takes place in a limited number of sets. The single bold technique was to find a way to shoot Sydney Greenstreet, with his monumental stomach and his strange watch chain, from an unusual angle.

In this way dialogue is foregrounded. Actually, dialogue is not that which is most convincing in Hammett. But the prominence of the film's dialogue makes it possible, by a certain transfiguration, to give an idea of the author's style.

When you think about it, the whole effect adds up to a story that puts you to sleep, a perfectly unrealistic story arranged in a harum-scarum way. I would not be able to summarize it. But, once again, this inconstancy only appears after you think about it. During the screening (or the reading), I defy anyone to resist the grip of the story or to fail to recognize its improbable truth.

This film illustrates the three essential themes of Dashiell Hammett: the work of the American private detective who lives on the fringe of the law and on the fringe of crime; an essential brutality compounded of whiskey, tobacco, vomiting, and

From *L'Écrán Français*, no. 58 (August 7, 1946), 10. Translated by Connor Hartnett.

hasty eroticism (which the screen has toned down, of course), none of which excludes a certain cordiality in the personal relationships; and finally a determined misogyny conveyed by the unsparing depiction of the female characters, and by the pitiless and unrelieved Cornelian character of the epilogue.

The acting is correct: the dangerous fragility of Mary Astor, the photogenic paunch of Sydney Greenstreet, the curls and the faces of Peter Lorre. All that appears old hat, but what is natural is never out of place with Dashiell Hammett. As to the leading man, it is Humphrey Bogart: He is good, but not how we imagine this author's heroes (no more, it may be added, would the William Powell type). That's Hollywood.

A New Kind of Detective Story, *L'Écrán Français*

Nino Frank

For a year now, following a series of American films of poor quality, it has been assumed that Hollywood was exhausted. Today we are led to another conclusion. The opening of a half dozen good works from California forces one to write and attest that American cinema is more prodigious than ever. Our cinema people are decidedly cyclomythic.

Seven new American films are said to be wonders: *Citizen Kane, The Little Foxes, How Green Was My Valley,* then *Double Indemnity, Laura,* and, to a certain degree, *The Maltese Falcon* and *Murder, My Sweet.* The first three are films that belong to an exceptional category. One cannot take them into consideration if one wishes to understand Hollywood's normal production. Let's take a further look at the four others.

They belong to what one used to call the detective genre, but it would be better to use the term criminal adventure or, better yet, criminal psychology. It is one of the great cinematographic genres that have replaced the Western; and there would be an amusing conclusion to draw from this displacement of the dynamism of the chase and the stirring idyll by the dynamism of violent death and the enigma to be clarified. And don't forget the replacement of the decor of vast and romantic nature by the decor of the "contemporary fantastic."

This kind of film has developed vigorously these days in America in the wake of the novel in which the reign of Dashiell Hammett succeeded the reign of S. S. Van Dine. Poe, since Corbiau, and Conan Doyle, acquainted us with the formula of the detective story: a mysterious crime, suspects, and, at the end, the discovery of the guilty party thanks to a shrewd mind. The formula has been brought to the point of perfection; the detective story (and the film), having been the Sunday replacement of the crossword puzzle, has sunk into boredom. However, I don't know any enlightened "amateur" who has claimed that the reading of the first fifty pages or the viewing of the first two reels was enough for him.

In the film, the handicap was bigger. First drawback: the long explanations come at the end, at the moment in which a film, its action over, is no longer of interest to the spectator. Another drawback: if the characters are able to live and dream, the hero, that is, the detective, is only a thinking machine and, in the best case (Maigret), a thinking machine sniffing and filling his pipe. They fall back on sets, humor, supplementary crimes—and that can't last.

We are witnesses to the death of this formula. Of the four works cited above, only *Laura* belongs to this old-fashioned type, but Otto Preminger and his collab-

From *L'Écrán Français*, no. 61 (August 28, 1946), 8–9, 14. Translated by Connor Hartnett.

orators attempted to renew the formula by slipping into it a pleasant study of sets and faces, narrative devices, the ordinary but charming character of a perverse writer, and, above all, endowing their detective with a love life. That makes, in effect, a film devoid of originality but perfectly entertaining and, in a word, successful.

It's different for the three others. They are to the usual detective film what the novels of Dashiell Hammett are to those of Van Dine and Ellery Queen. They convey what people call "life." The detective is not a machine but the protagonist; that is to say, the character who matters the most to us. Thus the heros of *The Maltese Falcon* and of *Murder, My Sweet* practice that strange trade of private detective which (in America) has nothing to do with the bureaucratic and is, as a matter of fact, completely outside the law, the law of the police as well as that of the "gang." The essential question is no longer to discover who committed the crime, but to see how the protagonist behaves (you don't even have to understand, in detail, the stories in which he is involved). Only the enigmatic psychology of one or the other counts, at the same time friends and enemies. Even more important, the sock on the jaw or the pistol shot plays no role until the end. And it is certainly no accident that the two films end the same way, the cruelest of all—the heroines take it on the chin. These stories are tough and misogynous, like much of present day American literature.

I will not swear that they have succeeded: If *The Maltese Falcon* is exciting as can be (it was based on a novel by Dashiell Hammett), *Murder, My Sweet* is very uneven and, at times, empty (although it makes a good case for the novel of Raymond Chandler that is its source).

We find this toughness, this misogyny again in *Double Indemnity*. Here there's no mystery; we know everything from the beginning; we follow the preparation of a crime, its execution, its effects (as in *Suspicion* of Alfred Hitchcock, which is taken from a novel of Francis Iles, and an absolute failure). The interest then centers on the characters and the story is astonishingly clear and constantly sustained. It is Billy Wilder, the director who has done more than slavishly transpose the narrative scheme of the novel of James Cain on which the film is based. He began by writing with Raymond Chandler a magisterially precise scenario, which details adroitly the movements and the reactions of the characters. The film follows the scenario faithfully.

Thus these "black" films have nothing in common with the unusual detective films. Clearly psychological stories, action, whether violent or lively, counts here less than the faces, the behavior, the words—therefore the truth of the characters, this "third" dimension of which I have just spoken. And that's great progress: after films like these the characters in the usual detective films seem like puppets. Today's audience is particularly sensitive to this impression of life, of life as it is lived, and to certain atrocities that actually exist and that no good purpose is served in hiding. The struggle for life is not a present-day invention.

Parallel to this internal evolution, one ought to notice another, purely formal one, in the treatment of the story: A narrator or a commentator is introduced and that permits the fragmentation of the story, the rapid gliding over the various transitional elements. This permits the emphasis on life as it is lived. It is evident that this procedure helps to get the story moving, and it also allows for the introduction of energy in a psychological portrait that is a bit static.

Sacha Guitry first employed this procedure in the *Story of a Trickster* (*Le Roman d'un tricheur*). The creators of the films which I have just cited (save for *The Maltese Falcon*) have used this technique and have thereby demonstrated both its flexibility as well as the way it lends depth to the style of the story. I notice, however, that Preminger in *Laura* has the story narrated at the beginning by a person who cannot know, later on, how things develop or, more logically, their conclusions.

Has Hollywood definitively outclassed Paris?

It seems to me that we have reached this conclusion a bit too quickly.

Without doubt, after these films, it will not be easy to produce detective stories of the usual kind. Without doubt it will be necessary for us to work at and fill out a bit more seriously our scenarios and to give up the beautiful image, the fancy camerawork and other technical minuets that diminish the importance of the third dimension on the screen for the benefit of trompe-l'oeil and the "Cinema" (in the bad sense of this word). Without doubt we see emerging in Hollywood a new series of producers, the Billy Wilders, the Premingers, the Chandlers, the John Hustons, who promise to send the old men out to pasture: the John Fords, the Wylers, and even the Capras.

But from all that to conclude that French cinema has to fold its tent. . . .

There is, though, a matter to which we ought to draw the special attention of our cinema people: the primacy of the script and the fact that a film must be first of all a somber story, well constructed and presented in an original manner. I have read just the opposite of what I have just said from the pen of my old friend George Charensol regarding *How Green Was My Valley*. Charensol and other critics seem to long for the silent film, and to judge a film on the number of stagecoach attacks it has. I really fear that it would be useless to contradict them: the fatal evolution of the movies will be burdened with a future in which the making of a film might tend more and more to become a function of the scenario and one in which today there is more dynamism in the static shot than in a majestic pan.

The proof? Admirable films like *How Green Was My Valley* or *The Little Foxes*, admirable and profoundly tedious, of a clearly outmoded kind. In the first, mise-en-scène in capital letters, photographic beauty, paternalism in the moving camera, a boredom distilled preciously by the camera. In the second, filmed theater in all its splendor made possible by a special lens, a ballet in a private chamber magnificently filmed, prodigiously animated, that you view with a yawn. Both are void of life, of truth, of depth, of charm, of atmosphere, of authentic vitality, of the third dimension that I care about. Trompe l'oeil and filmed theater, those two revolutionary and antithetic formulas joined together, lead us to state, alas, that very great fine fellows such as John Ford and William Wyler are already museum artifacts. The use of the face in *Laura* or in *Double Indemnity*—it is perhaps sad to say, but let's say it—touches us more than the photographic eloquence of the former and the learned staging of the latter.

Above all, don't make me say that the future belongs only to detective films told in the first person.

Commentaries

The essays in this section present a variety of cultural and historical perspectives on *The Maltese Falcon*. The first is by James Agee, an important early champion of Huston's work. Agee called *The Maltese Falcon* "the best private-eye melodrama ever made"; this essay, entitled "Undirectable Director," appeared nearly ten years after that film and indicates the cult of personality that was beginning to form around Huston. Agee calls him "the most inventive director of his generation" and describes him as doing more than anyone since D. W. Griffith to invigorate American films. The essay is historically interesting because it places *The Maltese Falcon* not as much within the context of the detective film or *film noir* as within the context of Huston's career.

In the 1970s, academic film studies first became a widespread discipline in American universities. James Naremore's article, "John Huston and *The Maltese Falcon*," was one of the first and remains one of the most impressive appraisals of the film from

within the field. Writing more than twenty years after Agee, Naremore charts the critical decline of Huston's reputation and presents his analysis of *The Maltese Falcon* as a corrective. He describes the film as "typical of Huston's themes" and "the finest achievement of his visual style." He is careful to distinguish Huston's achievement from that of Hammett's novel as well as from that of the 1931 film based upon it, and he makes a strong case for Huston as a visual stylist.

The Maltese Falcon was very much a product of the Hollywood studio system at its peak. My essay, "Tracking *The Maltese Falcon:* Classical Hollywood Narration and Sam Spade," discusses the film as an example of classical Hollywood narration, taking a close look at its narrative strategies and formal motifs. It also examines a number of its thematic strategies, such as its xenophobia, its presentation of sexual deviation, its construction of masculinity and femininity, the ways in which major characters deceptively assume different roles and contrive different narratives for themselves and the relationship of this to the film's sense of diverse ways to see history.

Jean-Loup Bourget, writing in France in 1975, reveals a disposition similar to that of Nino Frank thirty years earlier to link the film's value with that of its literary source in the very title of his "On the Trail of Dashiell Hammett (The Three Versions of *The Maltese Falcon*)." Bourget's article compares the three adaptations of Hammett's novel on the grounds that "it would be wrong to give the impression (false, in my opinion) that the Huston version is practically the only one and in any case the best." Defying traditional evaluations, Bourget makes a case for the 1936 *Satan Met a Lady* as the best of the three films. He discusses a number of narrative, stylistic, character, and thematic transmutations among the novel and three films, and considers the films representative of cinematic trends of the decades in which they were made—the first two reflecting the buoyancy and spirit of the 1930s and Huston's film the more somber tone of the 1940s.

Ilsa J. Bick's essay, "The Beam That Fell and Other Crises in *The Maltese Falcon*," also discusses the novel and the three film adaptations but from the perspective of contemporary film theory. She uses as her jumping-off point the most oft-cited passage in Hammett's novel, Spade's story of Mr. Flitcraft and the falling beam, a story that has never been used in any of the film adaptations of the novel. She develops the story's fatalistic notion of the repetitive circularity of characters' destinies as central to Hammett's novel but largely absent from Huston's film. To discuss the significance of this deviation from Hammett's fatalism, she contextualizes Huston's film within a discussion of the two earlier films, centering upon the emphasis in all four works upon seduction. She then differentiates the unrestrained and ebullient sexuality of the Spade characters in the 1930s films from the constrained and dangerous sexuality of Spade in Huston's film. She places these shifts within developments in American film and culture, such as the influence of psychoanalysis, of war trauma, and of genre shifts like that from the gangster films of the early 1930s to the screwball comedies of the late 1930s. A central focus throughout is the ways in which the films reveal shifting constructions of femininity and masculinity.

Undirectable Director, *Life*

James Agee

The Ant, as every sluggard knows, is a model citizen. His eye is fixed unwaveringly upon Security and Success, and he gets where he is going. The grasshopper, as every maiden ant delights in pointing out, is his reprehensible opposite number: a hedonistic jazz-baby, tangoing along primrose paths to a disreputable end. The late Walter Huston's son John, one of the ranking grasshoppers of the Western Hemisphere, is living proof of what a lot of nonsense that can be. He has beaten the ants at their own game and then some, and he has managed that blindfolded, by accident, and largely just for the hell of it. John was well into his twenties before anyone could imagine he would ever amount to more than an awfully nice guy to get drunk with. He wandered into his vocation as a writer of movie scripts to prove to a girl he wanted to marry that he amounted to more than a likeable bum. He stumbled into his still deeper vocation as a writer-director only when he got sick of seeing what the professional directors did to his scripts. But during the ten subsequent years he has won both Security aplenty (currently $3,000 a week with MGM and a partnership in Horizon Pictures with his friend Sam Spiegel) and Success aplenty (two Oscars, a One World Award, and such lesser prizes as the Screen Directors' Guild quarterly award, which he received last week for his *Asphalt Jungle*).

Yet these are merely incidental attainments. The first movie he directed, *The Maltese Falcon,* is the best private-eye melodrama ever made. *San Pietro,* his microcosm of the meaning of war in terms of the fight for one hill town, is generally conceded to be the finest of war documentaries. *Treasure of the Sierra Madre,* which he developed from B. Traven's sardonic adventure-fable about the corrosive effect of gold on character, is the clearest proof in perhaps twenty years that first-rate work can come out of the big commercial studios.

Most of the really good popular art produced anywhere comes from Hollywood, and much of it bears Huston's name. To put it conservatively, there is nobody under fifty at work in movies, here or abroad, who can excel Huston in talent, inventiveness, intransigence, achievement, or promise. Yet it is a fair bet that neither money, nor acclaim, nor a sense of dedication to the greatest art medium of his century have much to do with Huston's staying at his job: he stays at it because there is nothing else he enjoys so much. It is this tireless enjoyment that gives his work a unique vitality and makes every foot of film he works on unmistakably his.

Huston seems to have acquired this priceless quality many years ago at the time of what, in his opinion, was probably the most crucial incident in his life. When he

From *Life*, September 18, 1950.

was about twelve years old he was so delicate he was hardly expected to live. It was interminably dinned into him that he could never possibly be quite careful enough, and for even closer protection he was put into a sanitarium where every bite he ate and breath he drew could be professionally policed. As a result he became virtually paralyzed by timidity; "I haven't the slightest doubt," he still says, "that if things had gone on like that I'd have died inside a few more months." His only weapon was a blind desperation of instinct, and by day not even that was any use. Nights, however, when everyone was asleep, he used to sneak out, strip, dive into a stream which sped across the grounds, and ride it down quite a steep and stony waterfall, over and over and over. "The first few times," he recalls, "it scared the living hell out of me, but I realized—instinctively anyhow—it was exactly fear I had to get over." He kept at it until it was the one joy in his life. When they first caught him at this primordial autotherapy the goons were of course aghast; but on maturer thought they decided he might live after all.

The traits revealed in this incident are central and permanent in Huston's character. Risk, not to say recklessness, are virtual reflexes in him. Action, and the most vivid possible use of the immediate present, were his personal salvation; they have remained lifelong habits. Because action also is the natural language of the screen and the instant present is its tense, Huston is a born popular artist. In his life, his dealings and his work as an artist he operates largely by instinct, unencumbered by much reflectiveness or abstract thinking, or any serious self-doubt. Incapable of yessing, apple-polishing, or boot-licking, he instantly catches fire in resistance to authority.

Nobody in movies can beat Huston's record for trying to get away with more than the traffic will bear. *San Pietro* was regarded with horror by some gentlemen of the upper brass as "an antiwar picture" and was cut from five reels to three. *Treasure,* which broke practically every box-office law in the game and won three Oscars, was made over the virtually dead bodies of the top men at Warners' and was advertised as a Western. *The Asphalt Jungle* suggests that in some respects big-town crime operates remarkably like free enterprise. Huston seldom tries to "lick" the problem imposed by censorship, commercial queasiness, or tradition; he has learned that nothing is so likely to settle an argument as to turn up with the accomplished fact, accomplished well, plus a bland lack of alternative film shots. And yet after innumerable large and small fights and a fair share of defeats he can still say of his movie career, "I've never had any trouble." Probably the whitest magic that protects him is that he really means it.

Nonetheless his life began with trouble—decorated with the best that his Irish imagination, and his father's, could add to it. He was born John Marcellus Huston on August 5, 1906, in Nevada, Missouri, a hamlet which his grandfather, a professional gambler, had by the most ambitious version of the family legend acquired in a poker game. John's father, a retired actor, was in charge of power and light and was learning his job, while he earned, via a correspondence course. Before the postman had taught him how to handle such a delicate situation, a fire broke out in town. Walter overstrained the valves in his effort to satisfy the fire department, and the Hustons decided it would be prudent to leave what was left of Nevada before morning. They did not let their shirttails touch their rumps until they hit Weatherford, Texas, another of Grandfather's jackpots. After a breather they moved on to St. Louis (without, however, repeating the scorched-earth policy), and Walter settled down to engineering in dead earnest until a solid man clapped him on the shoulder and told him that with enough stick-to-itiveness he might well become a top-notch engineer, a regular crackerjack. Horrified, Walter instantly returned to the stage. A few years later he and his wife were divorced. From there on out the child's life lacked the stability of those early years.

John divided his time between his father and mother. With his father, who was still some years short of eminence or even solvency, he shared that bleakly glamorous continuum of three-a-days, scabrous fleabags, and the cindery, ambling day coaches between, which used to be so much of the essence of the American theater. John's mother was a newspaperwoman with a mania for travel and horses (she was later to marry a vice-president of the Northern Pacific), and she and her son once pooled their last ten dollars on a 100-to-1 shot—which came in. Now and then she stuck the boy in one school or another, but mostly they traveled—well off the beaten paths.

After his defeat of death by sliding down the waterfall, there was no holding John. In his teens he became amateur lightweight boxing champion of California. A high-school marriage lasted only briefly. He won twenty-three out of twenty-five fights, many in the professional ring, but he abandoned this promise of a career to join another of his mother's eccentric grand tours. He spent two years in the Mexican cavalry, emerging at twenty-one as a lieutenant. In Mexico he wrote a book, a puppet play about Frankie and Johnny. Receiving, to his astonishment, a $500 advance from a publisher, he promptly entrained for the crap tables of Saratoga where, in one evening, he ran it up to $11,000, which he soon spent or gambled away.

After that Huston took quite a friendly interest in writing. He wrote a short story which his father showed to his friend Ring Lardner, who showed it to his friend H. L. Mencken, who ran it in the *Mercury.* He wrote several other stories about horses and boxers before the vein ran out. It was through these stories, with his father's help, that he got his first job as a movie writer. He scripted *A House Divided,* starring his father, for William Wyler. But movies, at this extravagant stage of Huston's career, were just an incident. At other stages he worked for the New York *Graphic* ("I was the world's lousiest reporter"), broke ribs riding steeplechase, studied painting in Paris, knocked around with international Bohemians in London, and went on the bum in that city when his money ran out and he was too proud to wire his father. At length he beat his way back to New York where, for a time, he tried editing the *Midweek Pictorial.* He was playing Abraham Lincoln in a Chicago WPA production when he met an Irish girl named Leslie Black and within fifteen minutes after their meeting asked her to marry him. When she hesitated he hotfooted it to Hollywood and settled down to earn a solid living as fast as possible. Marrying Leslie was probably the best thing that ever happened to him, in the opinion of Huston's wise friend and studio protector during the years at Warner Brothers, the producer Henry Blanke. Blanke remembers him vividly during the bachelor interlude: "Just a drunken boy; hopelessly immature. You'd see him at every party, wearing bangs, with a monkey on his shoulder. Charming. Very talented but without an ounce of discipline in his make-up." Leslie Huston, Blanke is convinced, set her husband the standards and incentives which brought his abilities into focus. They were divorced in 1945, but in relation to his work he has never lost the stability she helped him gain.

At forty-four Huston still has a monkey and a chimpanzee as well, but he doesn't escort them to parties. His gray-sleeted hair still treats his scalp like Liberty Hall and occasionally slithers into bangs, but they can no longer be mistaken for a Bohemian compensation. He roughly suggests a jerked-venison version of his father, or a highly intelligent cowboy. A little over six feet tall, quite lean, he carries himself in a perpetual gangling-graceful slouch. The forehead is monkishly puckered, the ears look as clipped as a show dog's; the eyes, too, are curiously animal, an opaque red-brown. The nose was broken in the prize ring. The mouth is large mobile, and gap-toothed. The voice which comes out of this leatheriness is surprisingly rich, gentle, and cultivated. The vocabulary ranges with the careless ease of a mountain goat between words of eight syllables and of four letters.

Some friends believe he is essentially a deep introvert using every outside means available as a form of flight from self-recognition—in other words, he is forever sliding down the waterfall and instinctively fears to stop. The same friends suspect his work is all that keeps him from flying apart. He is wonderful company, almost anytime, for those who can stand the pace. Loving completely unrestrained and fantastic play, he is particularly happy with animals, roughhousers, and children; a friend who owns three of the latter describes him as "a blend of Santa Claus and the Pied Piper." His friendships range from high in the Social Register to low in the animal kingdom, but pretty certainly the friend he liked best in the world was his father, and that was thoroughly reciprocated. It was a rare and heart-warming thing, in this Freud-ridden era, to see a father and son so irrepressibly pleased with each other's company and skill.

He has an indestructible kind of youthfulness, enjoys his enthusiasms with all his might and has the prompt appetite for new knowledge of a man whose intelligence has not been cloyed by much formal education. He regrets that nowadays he can read only two or three books a week. His favorite writers are Joyce, his friend Hemingway (perhaps his closest literary equivalent), and above all, O'Neill; it was one of the deepest disappointments of his career when movie commitments prevented his staging the new O'Neill, *The Iceman Cometh*. His other enjoyments take many forms. He still paints occasionally. He is a very good shot and a superlative horseman; he has some very promising runners of his own.

He likes money for the fun it can bring him, is extremely generous with it and particularly loves to gamble. He generally does well at the races and siphons it off at the crap tables. He is a hard drinker (Scotch) but no lush, and a heavy smoker. Often as not he forgets to eat. He has a reputation for being attractive to women, and rough on them. His fourth wife is the dancer, Ricky Soma; their son Walter was born last spring. He makes most of his important decisions on impulse; it was thus he adopted his son Pablo in Mexico. The way he and his third wife, Evelyn Keyes, got married is a good example of Huston in action. He suggested they marry one evening in Romanoff's a week after they met, borrowed a pocketful of money from the prince, tore out to his house to pick up a wedding ring a guest had mislaid in the swimming pool, and chartered Paul Mantz to fly them to Las Vegas where they were married that night.

Huston's courage verges on the absolute, or on simple obliviousness to danger. In Italy during the shooting of *San Pietro*, his simian curiosity about literally everything made him the beau ideal of the contrivers of booby traps; time and again he was spared an arm, leg, or skull only by the grace of God and the horrified vigilance of his friend Lieutenant Jules Buck. He sauntered through mine fields where plain men feared to tread. He is quick to get mad and as quick to get over it. Once in Italy he sprinted up five flights of headquarters stairs in order to sock a frustrating superior officer; arriving at the top he was so winded he could hardly stand. Time enough to catch his breath was time enough to cool off; he just wobbled downstairs again.

Huston is swiftly stirred by anything which appeals to his sense of justice, magnanimity, or courage; he was among the first men to stand up for Lew Ayres as a conscientious objector, he flew to the Washington hearings on Hollywood (which he refers to as "an obscenity"), and sponsored Henry Wallace (though he voted for Truman) in the 1948 campaign. Some people think of him, accordingly, as a fellow traveler. Actually he is a political man chiefly in an emotional sense: "I'm against *anybody*," he says, "who tries to tell anybody else what to do." The mere sight or thought of a cop can get him sore. He is, in short, rather less of a Communist than the most ultramontane Republican, for like perhaps five out of seven good artists who ever lived he is—to lapse into technical jargon—a natural-born antiauthoritarian individualistic libertarian anarchist, without portfolio.

A very good screen writer, Huston is an even better director. He has a feeling about telling a story on a screen which sets him apart from most other movie artists and from all nonmovie writers and artists. "On paper," he says, "all you can do is say something happened, and if you say it well enough the reader believes you. In pictures, if you do it right, *the thing happens, right there on the screen.*"

This means more than it may seem to. Most movies are like predigested food because they are mere reenactment of something that happened (if ever) back in the scripting stage. At the time of shooting the sense of the present is not strong, and such creative energy as may be on hand is used to give the event finish, in every sense of the word, rather than beginning and life. Huston's work has a unique tension and vitality because the maximum of all contributing creative energies converge at the one moment that counts most in a movie—the continuing moment of committing the story to film. At his best he makes the story tell itself, makes it seem to happen for the first and last time at the moment of recording. It is almost magically hard to get this to happen. In the *Treasure* scene in which the bandits kill Bogart, Huston wanted it to be quiet and mock-casual up to its final burst of violence. He told two of his three killers—one a professional actor, the other two professional criminals—only to stay quiet and close to the ground, and always to move when Bogart moved, to keep him surrounded. Then he had everyone play it through, over and over, until they should get the feel of it. At length, one of them did a quick scuttling slide down a bank, on his bottom and his busy little hands and feet. A motion as innocent as a child's and as frightening as a centipede's, it makes clear for the first time in the scene that death is absolutely inescapable, and very near. "When he did that slide," Huston says, "I knew they had the feel of it." He shot it accordingly.

Paradoxically in this hyperactive artist of action, the living, breathing texture of his best work is the result of a working method which relies on the utmost possible passiveness. Most serious-minded directors direct too much: "Now on this word," Huston has heard one tell an actor, "I want your voice to break." Actors accustomed to that kind of "help" are often uneasy when they start work with Huston. "Shall I sit down here?" one asked, interrupting a rehearsal. "*I* dunno," Huston replied, "You tired?" When Claire Trevor, starting work in *Key Largo,* asked for a few pointers, he told her, "You're the kind of drunken dame whose elbows are always a little too big, your voice is a little too loud, you're a little too polite. You're very sad, very resigned. Like this," he said, for short, and leaned against the bar with a peculiarly heavy, gentle disconsolateness. It was the leaning she caught onto (though she also used everything he said); without further instruction of any kind, she took an Oscar for her performance. His only advice to his father was a whispered, "Dad, that was a little too much like Walter Huston." Often he works with actors as if he were gentling animals; and although Bogart says without total injustice that "as an actor he stinks," he has more than enough mimetic ability to get his ideas across. Sometimes he discards instruction altogether; to get a desired expression from Lauren Bacall, he simply twisted her arm.

Even on disastrously thin ice Huston has the peculiar kind of well-earned luck which Heaven reserves exclusively for the intuitive and the intrepid. One of the most important roles in *Treasure* is that of the bandit leader, a primordial criminal psychopath about whom the most fascinating and terrifying thing is his unpredictability. It is impossible to know what he will do next because it is impossible to be sure what strange piece of glare-ice in his nature will cause a sudden skid. Too late for a change, it turned out that the man who played this role, though visually ideal for it, couldn't act for shucks. Worried as he was, Huston had a hunch it would turn out all right. It worked because this inadequate actor was trying so hard, was so unsure of what was he doing and was so painfully confused and angered by

Huston's cryptic passivity. These several kinds of strain and uncertainty, sprung against the context of the story, made a living image of the almost unactable, real thing, and that had been Huston's hunch.

In placing and moving his characters within a shot Huston is nearly always concerned above all else to be simple and spontaneous rather than merely "dramatic" or visually effective. Just as he feels that the story belongs to the characters, he feels that the actors should as fully as possible belong to themselves. It is only because the actors are so free that their several individualities, converging in a scene, can so often knock the kinds of sparks off each other which cannot be asked for or invented or foreseen. All that can be foreseen is that this can happen only under favorable circumstances; Huston is a master at creating such circumstances.

Each of Huston's pictures has a visual tone and style of its own, dictated to his camera by the story's essential content and spirit. In *Treasure* the camera is generally static and at a middle distance from the action (as Huston says, "It's impersonal, it just looks on and lets them stew in their own juice"); the composition is—superficially—informal, the light cruel and clean, like noon sun on quartz and bone. Most of the action in *Key Largo* takes place inside a small Florida hotel. The problems are to convey heat, suspense, enclosedness, the illusion of some eighteen hours of continuous action in two hours' playing time, with only one time lapse. The lighting is stickily fungoid. The camera is sneakily "personal"; working close and in almost continuous motion, it enlarges the ambiguous suspensefulness of almost every human move. In [*We Were*] *Strangers* the main pressures are inside a home and beneath it, where conspirators dig a tunnel. Here Huston's chief keys are lighting contrasts. Underground the players move in and out of shadow like trout; upstairs the light is mainly the luminous pallor of marble without sunlight; a cemetery, bank interior, a great outdoor staircase.

Much that is best in Huston's work comes of his sense of what is natural to the eye and his delicate, simple feeling for space relationships; his camera huddles close to those who huddle to talk, leans back, a proportionate distance, relaxing, if they talk casually. He loathes camera rhetoric and the shot-for-shot's-sake; but because he takes each moment catch-as-catch-can and is so deeply absorbed in doing the best possible thing with it he has made any number of unforgettable shots. He can make an unexpected closeup reverberate like a gong. The first shot of Edward G. Robinson in *Key Largo,* mouthing a cigar and sweltering naked in a tub of cold water ("I wanted to get a look at the animal with its shell off") is one of the most powerful and efficient "first entrances" of a character on record. Other great shots come through the kind of candor which causes some people to stare when others look away: the stripped, raw-sound scenes of psychiatric interviews in *Let There Be Light.* Others come through simple discretion in relating word and image. In *San Pietro,* as the camera starts moving along a line of children and babies, the commentator (Huston) remarks that in a few years they'll have forgotten there ever was a war; then he shuts up. As the camera continues in silence along the terrible frieze of shock and starvation, one realizes the remark was not the inane optimism it seemed; they, forgetting, are fodder for the next war.

Sometimes the shot is just a spark—a brief glint of extra imagination and perception. During the robbery sequence in *Asphalt Jungle* there is a quick glimpse of the downtown midnight street at the moment when people have just begun to hear the burglar alarms. Unsure, still, where the trouble is, the people merely hesitate a trifle in their ways of walking, and it is like the first stirrings of metal filings before the magnet beneath the paper pulls them into pattern. Very often the fine shot comes because Huston, working to please himself without fear of his audience, sharply condenses his storytelling. Early in *Strangers* a student is machine-gunned on the steps of Havana's university. A scene follows which is breath-taking in its surprise and beauty, but storytelling, not beauty, brings it; what seems to be hundreds of young men and women, all in summery whites, throw themselves flat on the marble stairs in a wavelike motion as graceful as the sudden close swooping of so many doves. The shot is already off the screen before one can realize its full meaning. By their trained, quiet unison in falling, these students are used to this. They expect it any average morning. And that suffices, with great efficiency, to suggest the Cuban tyranny.

Within the prevailing style of a picture, Huston works many and extreme changes and conflicts between the "active" camera, which takes its moment of the story by the scruff of the neck and "tells" it, and the "passive" camera, whose business is transparency, to receive a moment of action purely and record it. But whether active or passive, each shot contains no more than is absolutely necessary to make its point and is cut off sharp at that instant. The shots are cantilevered, sprung together in electric arcs, rather then butted together. A given scene is apt to be composed of highly unconventional alternations of rhythm and patterns of exchange between long and medium and close shots and the standing, swinging, and dollying camera. The rhythm and contour are very powerful but very irregular, like the rhythm of good prose rather than of good verse; and it is this rangy, leaping, thrusting kind of nervous vitality which binds the whole picture together. Within this vitality he can bring about moments as thoroughly revealing as those in great writing. As an average sample of that, *Treasure*'s intruder is killed by bandits; the three prospectors come to identify the man they themselves were on the verge of shooting. Bogart, the would-be tough guy, cocks one foot up on a rock and tries to look at the corpse as casually as if it were fresh-killed game. Tim Holt, the essentially decent young man, comes past behind him and, innocent and unaware of it, clasps his hands as he looks down, in the respectful manner of a boy who used to go to church. Walter Huston, the experienced old man, steps quietly behind both, leans to the dead man as professionally as a doctor to a patient and gently rifles him for papers. By such simplicity Huston can draw the eye so deep into the screen that time and again he can make important points in medium shots, by motions as small as the twitching of an eyelid, for which most directors would require a close-up or even a line of dialogue.

Most movies are made in the evident assumption that the audience is passive and wants to remain passive; every effort is made to do all the work—the seeing, the explaining, the understanding, even the feeling. Huston is one of the few movies artists who, without thinking twice about it, honors his audience. His pictures are not acts of seduction or of benign enslavement but of liberation, and they require, of anyone who enjoys them, the responsibilities of liberty. They continually open the eye and require it to work vigorously; and through the eye they awaken curiosity and intelligence. That, by any virile standard, is essential to good entertainment. It is unquestionably essential to good art.

The most inventive director of his generation, Huston has done more to extend, invigorate, and purify the essential idiom of American movies, the truly visual telling of stories, than anyone since the prime of D. W. Griffith. To date, however, his work as a whole is not on the level with the finest and most deeply imaginative work that has been done in movies—the work of Chaplin, Dovzhenko, Eisenstein, Griffith, the late Jean Vigo. For an artist of such conscience and caliber, his range is surprisingly narrow, both in subject matter and technique. In general he is leery of emotion—of the "feminine" aspects of art—and if he explored it with more assurance, with his taste and equipment, he might show himself to be a much more sensitive artist. With only one early exception, his movies have centered on men under pressure, have usually involved violence, and have occasionally verged on a kind of romanticism about danger. Though he uses sound and dialogue more intelligently than most directors, he has not shown much interest in exploring the tremendous possibilities of the former or in solving the crippling problems of the latter. While his cutting is astute, terse, thoroughly appropriate to his kind of work, yet compared with that of Eisenstein, who regarded cutting as the essence of the art of movies, it seems distinctly unadventurous. In his studio pictures, Huston is apt to be tired and bored by the time the stages of ultrarefinement in cutting are reached, so that some of his scenes have been given perfection, others somewhat impaired, by film editors other than Huston. This is consistent with much that is free and improvisatory in his work and in his nature, but it is startling irresponsibility in so good an artist.

During his past few pictures Huston does appear to have become more of a "camera" man, and not all of this has been to the good. The camera sometimes imposes on the story; the lighting sometimes becomes elaborately studioish or even verges on the arty; the screen at times becomes rigid, overstylized. This has been happening, moreover, at a time when another of Huston's liabilities has been growing: thanks to what Henry Blanke calls his "amazing capacity for belief," he can fall for, and lose himself in, relatively mediocre material. Sometimes—as in *Asphalt Jungle*—he makes a silk purse out of sow's ear, but sometimes—as in parts of *Strangers* and *Key Largo*—the result is neither silk nor sow.

Conceivably Huston lacks that deepest kind of creative impulse and that intense self-critical skepticism without which the stature of a great artist is rarely achieved. A brilliant adapter, he has yet to do a Huston "original," barring the war documentaries. He is probably too much at the mercy of his immediate surroundings. When the surroundings are right for him there is no need to talk about mercy: during the war and just after he was as hard as a rock and made his three finest pictures in a row. Since then the pictures, for all their excellence, are like the surroundings, relatively softened and blurred. Unfortunately no man in Hollywood can be sufficiently his own master or move in a direct line to personally selected goals. After *Treasure,* Huston was unable to proceed to *Moby Dick* as he wanted to; he still is awaiting the opportunity to make Dreiser's *Jennie Gerhardt* and Dostoevski's *The Idiot* although he is at last shooting Stephen Crane's *The Red Badge of Courage,* which he has wanted to make for years. "This has got to be a masterpiece," he recently told friends, "or it's nothing."

There is no reason to expect less of it than his finest picture yet, for the better his starting material, the better he functions as an artist: he is one of the very few men in the world of movies who has shown himself to be worthy of the best. He has, in abundance, many of the human qualities which most men of talent lack. He is magnanimous, disinterested, and fearless. Whatever his job, he always makes a noble and rewarding fight of it. If it should occur to him to fight for his life—his life as the consistently great artist he evidently might become—he would stand a much better chance of winning than most people. For besides having talent and fighting ability, he has nothing to lose but his hide, and he has never set a very high value on that.

John Huston and *The Maltese Falcon*

James Naremore

John Huston's reputation was in decline during the heyday of auteurism, chiefly because of *The List of Adrian Messenger, Casino Royale,* and *The Bible,* but also because of critics who attacked him in order to praise Vincente Minnelli or Howard Hawks. He was often described as an "adapter" rather than an auteur (his public statements about his craft tended to justify this description), and even his earliest success was subtly damned. Thus Andrew Sarris described *The Maltese Falcon* as an actor's picture, owing more to "casting coups than to directorial acumen." The film, he said, was an "uncanny matchup of Dashiell Hammett's literary characters with their visual doubles: Mary Astor, Humphrey Bogart, Sydney Greenstreet, Peter Lorre, and Elisha Cook, Jr. Only Stendhal's Julien Sorel in search of Gerard Philipe can match *Falcon's* Pirandellian equation."[1]

First let me say I have deep respect for Sarris. He is a remarkably fine critic, greatly responsible for our serious interest in American popular cinema; but in this case he was in error. Even if his remarks were true, he should have given Huston more credit for assembling such presences. In fact, however, the actors can hardly be regarded as "visual doubles" for people in the novel. Consider Hammett's opening paragraph:

> Samuel Spade's jaw was long and bony, his chin a jutting v under the more flexible v of his mouth. His yellow-gray eyes were horizontal. The v motif was picked up again by thickish brows rising outward from twin creases above a hooked nose, and his pale brown hair grew down—from high flat temples—in a point on his forehead. He looked rather pleasantly like a blond satan.

Clearly Humphrey Bogart is the visual opposite of Hammett's Sam Spade. Spade, Hammett tells us, is a tall man with an "almost conical" body. When he takes off

This essay, which originally appeared in *Literature/Film Quarterly,* is nearly two decades old, and was my first attempt to write anything about the movies. I fear it has become something of an antique, even though it conveys the admiration I still feel for *The Maltese Falcon.* I have changed the tenses of a few sentences to indicate that Huston is no longer living, but otherwise I decided not to revise the text. Some of my later ideas about Hammett and Huston are contained in two other articles: "Dashiell Hammett and the Poetics of Hard-Boiled Fiction," in *Essays on Detective Fiction,* ed. Bernard Benstock (London: Macmillian, 1983); and "Return of the Living Dead," in *James Joyce Literary Supplement* (May 1991).
1. Andrew Sarris, *The American Cinema: Directors and Directions, 1929–1968* (New York: E. P. Dutton, 1968), 156.

From *Literature/Film Quarterly* 1, no. 3 (1973), 239–249.

his shirt, "the sag of his big rounded shoulders" makes him resemble "a bear." Bogart's slight, swarthy appearance, his menacing smile, to say nothing of his famed low-life New York accent (he calls the falcon a "black boid") evoke an altogether different personality.

In a less absolute sense, the same point can be made about the casting of every actor in the film. Sydney Greenstreet, in a beautifully restrained performance, is not so flabby or bombastic as the Gutman of the novel, and he lacks "dark ringlets" of hair. Peter Lorre is properly Levantine, but less effeminate and less bejeweled than Hammett's Joel Cairo. Elisha Cook, Jr., has the right stature for the "boy" Wilmer, but he seems always to have had the pinched face of an old man. Most unusual of all is Huston's choice of Mary Astor, who, far from being a double, is actually cast against the grain of her character. Hammett's Brigid O'Shaughnessy is little more than a sexy dame; indeed, one problem with the book is that it gives us no good reason why Spade should be in love with Brigid. She is wonderful to sleep with, but she is obviously not to be trusted, her only quality besides good looks being her transparent deceitfulness. Mary Astor, on the other hand, has a lovely but almost matronly face and build, and she brings a sophistication to the role that is entirely lacking in the novel. She fits nicely Raymond Durgnat's description of Maggie Smith; a blend of "brimming feminine sensitivity, of superior intelligence, and of something mockingly autonomous."[2]

2. Raymond Durgnat, *Films and Feelings* (Cambridge: MIT Press, 1970), 149.

Like the character in the novel she is a tease, but she is a tease of a distinctly upper-class sort. Perhaps that is why she never became a great star. In any case, the scenes between her and Bogart have a humor and intelligence that seem to run beneath the surface of the words, so that lines Hammett wrote flatly and seriously gain a new dimension. When Astor tosses her head back on a soft couch, gazes up at the ceiling, and gives a description of Floyd Thursby ("He never went to sleep without covering the floor around his bed with crumpled newspaper so nobody could come silently into his room"), her manner—and Huston's framing of her face—is so outrageous and chic that we smile with delight. As Spade would say, now she's *really* dangerous.

One could go on in this vein, celebrating the changes that the film makes in even the minor roles (Jerome Cowan is a different Miles Archer than the one described by Hammett—slicker, more ironically treated), but there is no need to mention all the ways that Huston's characters are different. If these discrepancies between text and film prove anything, it is that Huston has gained ascendancy over Hammett. It is easy to forget that Sam Spade was not actually the visual double for Bogart, because we feel he should have been.

Moreover, while many people deserve credit for the success of *The Maltese Falcon,* its special quality owes chiefly to John Huston's style, a style so recognizable and individual that it is anything but the sign of a "competent craftsman." This statement may seem paradoxical, since Huston is widely regarded as an oblique, nearly styleless director, and especially since the movie is a fairly literal rendition of the novel. Huston claimed that before beginning work on a screenplay he gave Hammett's book to a secretary, asking her to break it down into shots, scenes, and dialogue. A copy of the secretary's work was shown to Jack Warner, who, thinking he had a complete script, gave Huston his blessing for capturing the flavor of the original.[3] The finished screenplay is less an adaptation than a skillful editing of the novel, which is mostly dialogue anyway. Huston economizes beautifully, telescoping scenes, cutting away some of the minor characters (including Kasper Gutman's daughter), and making slight changes in a few places to get past the censors or heighten the irony. The picture is leaner, quicker than the novel, but with few exceptions the words are Hammett's own.

And yet the result is a phenomenon much like the one observed by André Bazin, speaking of Jean Renoir's *Madame Bovary* and *Une partie de campagne:* "What strikes us about the fidelity of Renoir is that paradoxically it is compatible with complete independence from the original. The justification for this is of course that the genius of Renoir is certainly as great as that of Flaubert or Maupassant. The phenomenon we face here is comparable then to the translation of Edgar Allan Poe by Baudelaire."[4] Huston was no Flaubert, but with the aid of cameraman Arthur Edeson, art director Robert Haas, and a brilliant group of players, he made

3. See William F. Nolan, *John Huston: King Rebel* (Los Angeles: Sherbourne Press, 1965), 40.
4. André Bazin, *What is Cinema?* vol. 1 (Berkeley: University of California Press, 1967), 67.

from *Falcon* one of the classics of dark cinema, a film that is not only "faithful" but also constitutive of his own signature.

The very choice of *Falcon* was consistent with the personality Huston would convey in nearly all his subsequent work—perhaps *Falcon* even determined that personality to some degree. Notice how neatly it fits into the Huston oeuvre: Most of his good films—*The Treasure of the Sierra Madre, Key Largo, We Were Strangers, The Asphalt Jungle, The Roots of Heaven, Beat the Devil, The Misfits, Fat City*—depend on simple visual symbolism and sharp contrasts of character. They are all quasi-allegorical adventures about groups of exotic, eccentric people, and, as several commentators have observed, they usually end on a note of great, ironic failure. Even *The African Queen,* which isolates two completely different character types, is barely an exception to these rules; it merely has a smaller cast and a more optimistic comedy, an act of God intervening to save the protagonists. It would be a more typical film if it ended about fifteen minutes earlier, at the point where Bogart and Hepburn collapse with exhaustion as the camera rises above high grass to show the open sea only a few feet away. Ultimately, however, Huston was less interested in success or failure than in the moments of truth that an adventurous quest leads up to. As a result, the point in his version of *Falcon* is not the bird itself, nor the fact that it ends up being a phony. Huston wants to show the greed, the treachery, and sometimes the loyalty of his characters. The focus at the end of the picture is on Sam Spade's curious integrity, and on Sydney Greenstreet as he taps a bowler hat on his head and gaily wanders off in search of the real bird.

Huston's films also show his admiration for a male world, though he was sometimes more ambivalent toward that world than a director like Hawks. Raymond Durgnat has rightly pointed out that "*Treasure of Sierra Madre* and *The Misfits* are 'tragic critiques' of the Hawksian ideal, respecting it, fairly, but going beyond their tough conformism to a profounder humanism."[5] *Falcon* is hardly an example of profound humanism, but Huston does seem more conscious than Hammett of the male myth which underlies the novel. The film is more emphatic, more stylized than the book, and it shows us very clearly that the underworld characters are foils for Spade's masculinity. A single room tells us that Spade scorns luxury; he is not effeminate like Cairo, and he has no soft belly like Gutman. This contrast is elaborated by other details: Spade does not need to carry a gun, but the "boy" Wilmer—whose very name sounds prissy—ludicrously brandishes two big forty-fives in a desperate and unsuccessful attempt to assert manhood. More important, Spade's professional ethics, his willingness to turn in a woman he loves out of loyalty to a dead partner he never liked much anyway, is at bottom a victory for the "male" ethic. It is true that in the past he cuckolded Archer (mostly, we suspect, at the insistence of Archer's wife), but his behavior as we actually see it is fundamentally different from Brigid O'Shaughnessy's or Mrs. Archer's. As in

---

5. Durgnat, *Films and Feelings,* 84.

most private-eye stories, the women in Huston's film are fickle and dangerous killers, and they have to be rejected or sent off to prison at the end if the hero wishes to survive. *The Maltese Falcon* is one of the purest examples of this classic form; significantly, the one trustworthy female in the movie is Effie Perine, whom Spade treats like a little sister. She sits on his desk and rolls his cigarettes, and at one point he calls her a "good man."

But if *Falcon* is typical of Huston's themes, it is also the finest achievement of his visual style. In this respect we can see most clearly the difference between his work and Hammett's. Hammett's art is minimalist and deadpan, but Huston, contrary to his reputation, is a highly energetic and expressive storyteller who likes to make comments through his images. In his treatment of settings, for example, he usually employs the same principle of vivid contrast that governs his approach to character. In *We Were Strangers* he takes us from the sunny, white-washed streets of Havana to the inside of a house filled with revolutionaries, where the light has what James Agee called "the luminous pallor of marble." Beneath the house the conspirators are desperately burrowing a tunnel, and all we see in the darkness is a occasional sweaty face. In *Freud* we move from the dark, heavily draped, and tapestried background of Freud's household to the sunny, spacious, flowered boudoir of a young blond patient. *Falcon* has a similar structure, though it is more subtly realized. Most of the action takes place inside four rooms—Spade's office, his apartment, and the hotel rooms of Brigid O'Shaughnessy and Kasper Gutman. These rooms are roughly the same size, and the last three contain ornate mantlepieces of the same proportions but with different designs, as if Huston and his decorator were stressing a parallel to establish a basic contrast. Spade's apartment embodies a tough, masculine ethos: it is predictably Spartan, except for a big chair upholstered in glittering leather and a series of horse-racing photographs in the far distance over his mantlepiece (a touch surely provided by Huston himself). There are a couple of lighted lamps and several unlit fixtures. Books and papers are scattered around, and to one side is a rumpled bed with a plain iron bedstead. A window is always open, though it is cold enough outside for everyone to wear overcoats. The rooms of Brigid and Gutman, on the other hand, are feminine and luxurious, the walls nearly as bare as Spade's, but the furniture all satiny and decorated with stripes. A fire burns in Brigid's hearth; the windows are closed, and flowers stand around in cut-glass vases. Gutman's room is similar but more expensive, with oriental lamps and a few French provincial furnishings. It is also the whitest room in the film, its lightness accentuating Greenstreet's bulky, black-clothed body.

These settings have been criticized as being less accurate than the ones in Roy Del Ruth's 1931 version of *Falcon*.[6] It is true that the sets in the Huston movie are extremely simple, and the exteriors in particular have a false, studioish aura that is typical of Warners in the early 1940s. Still, Huston uses the *mise-en-scène* with

---

6. John Baxter, *Hollywood in the Thirties* (New York: Paperback Library, 1970), 200–201.

great intelligence, first to emphasize the contrast between Spade's "maleness" and the "femininity" of the other characters, and second to give the film much of its remarkable feeling of spatial unity. Ninety percent of the action is played out against the same architecture, even though the decorative arrangement of each setting is different, and we seldom see all of a room in a given shot. *Falcon* is not so potentially claustrophobic a movie as *Twelve Angry Men* or *Lifeboat,* but it does have the same circumscribed, nearly allegorical world and the same technical problem of maintaining interest. Huston seems aware of the problem—thus the pace of the acting, the speed of the editing, the variety of the camera setups—but he also knows that the *Black Mask* detective genre is among the most fetishistic of fictions, and therefore close interiors can be as important to it as open vistas are to the Western. The classic private-eye story benefits from intimacy, and it fascinates us with all kinds of objects: in Huston's film, for example, we have the leather swivel chair in Bogart's office, his roll-your-own cigarettes, the gadget on his desk from which he can withdraw lighted matches, the little neon signs outside his window that glow KLVW or DRINK. We also have Brigid's fur wrap, Gutman's watch fob, Cairo's enameled cane, and of course Wilmer's pistols. The atmosphere is heightened, so that a splash of whiskey in a glass is more important than the sound of gunfire.

Even Dashiell Hammett, whose prose style is extremely bare, occasionally lends atmosphere to his tale by listing objects. For example, in the first awkward moment of Brigid O'Shaughnessy's interview with Spade, we find this description:

> On Spade's desk a limp cigarette smouldered in a brass tray. . . . Ragged grey flakes of cigarette-ash dotted the yellow top of the desk and the grey blotter and the papers that were there. A buff-curtained window, eight or ten inches open, let in from the court a current of air. . . . The ashes on the desk twitched and crawled.

A bit later in the novel, when Spade receives a phone call about the death of Archer, Hammett pays fond attention to the things in the room: "a packet of brown papers and a sack of Bull Durham tobacco," a "pigskin-and-nickel lighter," a "tinny alarm clock insecurely mounted on a corner of Duke's *Celebrated Criminal Cases of America,*" and "cold steamy air" blowing in from two open windows. The deep-focus lenses of the early 1940s were well suited for adapting this technique; they brought clarity and perspective into the movie image and allowed objects to take on the ambience of character. Thus, one of the most effective and memorable shots in Huston's film is our first view of Spade's room, a view which is suggested by the descriptions in the novel. We have just seen Archer's murder, and immediately we cut to an in-depth composition featuring a bedside table in the foreground, in the distance an open window, its transparent curtains waving slowly in the cold night breeze. At first we are in darkness, the objects on the table a shadowy pyramid sculpted by pale light from the window. We see an old-fashioned tall black telephone, Hammett's "tinny alarm clock," a legal book, a newspaper, a sack of Bull Durham, and the shade of an unlighted lamp. The telephone is ringing, and a hand comes into the picture to remove it. The camera keeps the table precisely framed while we hear Bogart's voice and watch the somewhat ghostly curtains waving in the background. At last Bogart sits up from his bed, the camera moving back slightly to get the edge of his face. He is learning about the murder. He puts down the base of the phone and switches on the lamp. Now the whole depth of the composition has been lighted; the clock face reads 2:05, as in the novel, and an old patterned drapery is visible in the distance behind Bogart's head. We see the shiny surfaces of the alarm and the telephone, Bogart's full profile up close, and swaying curtains in the background at the left of the frame. It is an extraordinary shot, one tiny section of the room evoking the entire hardboiled style of life. Furthermore, as in Hammett's novel, none of the atmosphere is achieved at the expense of the story. The time of night is established, Spade's character is suggested, and the sinister consequences of Archer's death are conveyed immediately and powerfully.

Here, as nearly everywhere else, the film is even more economical than the novel, and the force of its imagery is simpler, more nearly symbolic. It is perhaps fitting that the black bird itself, fetishist object around which all the other objects are organized, should be presented to us at the very opening, beneath the credits, so that its dark exotic shape can preside over the later scenes like a symbol. Probably Huston is not responsible for the credits, but in some ways they are in keeping with the stylized quality of the rest of the film. Huston's approach in *Falcon* is neither utilitarian (as in Hawks's *The Big Sleep*) nor arty (as in Edward Dmytryk's *Murder, My Sweet*); and yet, for a director who was widely reputed to conceal his technique, he shows a decided flair for iconography. This was the only time in his career when he made preliminary sketches for the camera setups, and these resulted in a number of bold flourishes. Perhaps the most famous example of visual symbolism comes at the very end, where the iron bars of an elevator grille close across Mary Astor's beautiful tear-stained face, foreshadowing the years she is going to spend at Tehachapi. A long shot follows, and as the lighted elevator cage descends, Bogart, purely for the sake of the metaphor, walks slowly down a stairway at the left of the frame, descending to his own kind of sorrow.

There are several such moments, including the little tableau on the night table. Indeed, even the first sequence of the picture is stylishly rounded off by a pair of camera movements which underline the irony of Archer's subsequent death. It begins with a pan shot, moving downward from the reversed SPADE AND ARCHER sign of the window above Bogart's desk. At the end of the sequence, the camera is set very low, looking up at Archer as he stands examining the money left by Brigid O'Shaughnessy. His greed and lechery are stressed by the squint of his eye, his little smile, and the cigarette hanging from his mouth; above him, the odd line of a beam on the ceiling creates a disquieting note. As Bogart walks into the frame the camera pulls back and up to a more normal view; then, as the two men walk across the room we pull back even more, until they stop at their desks. Their figures are composed at either side of the screen, and Spade's cramped little office now looks as big as an empty ballroom. They sit down, the SPADE AND ARCHER sign between them and about three-quarters of the floor visible, with nothing between the camera and the far-off desks. It is an extremely unrealistic shot; the real space of the office has been violated, as if we were looking through a proscenium onto a stage. As Spade jokes with Archer ("You're got brains. Yes you have.") the screen darkens a bit and the camera moves down again, panning to the floor, aimed at the lighted rectangle cast by a window, the SPADE AND ARCHER sign visible again in bold dark shadow, its letters returned by the light to their normal left-right order. In the next sequence, of course, we will see Archer's murder.

The close-ups, too, are deliberately stylized. In its own way, *Falcon* is nearly as preoccupied with the landscape of faces as Carl Theodor Dreyer's *Passion of Joan of Arc,* though Huston's images are sometimes more like good cartoons, they give the movie much of its grotesque comedy and its feeling of a moral tale. Nearly every close-up is designed to make a statement about character—Peter Lorre brushing the tip of his fancy walking stick across his lips; Elisha Cook's psychotic eyes brimming with tears; Greenstreet's countenance appearing just above his stomach. Our first view of Mary Astor's face is meant to contrast her with the drab walls of Spade's office: Daylight from a window at the upper right of the frame sets off the little black hat perched atop her head, her fur wrap, and the line of her shoulder. Most of the composition is in gray or black, except for Astor's white collar and her face, a soft triangle of flesh at the very center of the picture. At the end of the film, when Spade informs Brigid he is turning her over to the law, a harsh dawn light breaks through the windows of his room, the curtains waving still, but now seeming to underline the agitation of the characters. Bogart literally pushes Astor up against a white wall, flat light washing the shadows out of her face as, for the first time, she loses control.

Huston's expressive, almost comic-strip style can be seen best in a sequence that comes midway in the first reel, when Lieutenant Dundy and Detective Tom Polhaus (Barton MacLane and Ward Bond) pay a call at Spade's apartment to discuss the murders of Archer and Floyd Thursby. Dundy is a smart, rather mean cop who disliked Spade. Polhaus is relatively slower and very uncomfortable, caught between his superior officer and his old acquaintance. The interview begins on a fairly uneasy note and then leads to an aggressive exchange between Dundy and Spade. Ultimately, when Spade sees that the police are not sure he is the killer, he relaxes somewhat, and the scene ends with the three men having a drink together. It is not one of the more important sequences of the film, but it is relatively brief and extremely well realized, showing how a powerful narrative is generated from Edeson's photography and Huston's rather mannered placement of actors and camera. Those who are interested may compare the film treatment with the equivalent passage in Hammett's novel. Huston has cut some speeches, trimmed others to their essence, and added a new line at the end. Hammett writes very well (the monosyllabic talk and the tough accents of his characters are indispensable), but in comparison the book seems a bit pale, without the edge of visual wit and the almost electric tension of the film. The sequence begins with two leisurely panning movements, taken from different angles and accompanied by foreboding music, emphasizing the decor of Spade's room and the unfettered bodies of the actors. Thereafter we have a fairly rapid series of tight, three-figured compositions and occasional close-ups. The coats and hats of the policemen are made to contrast with Bogart's open white shirt and bare head, and the players are cunningly positioned within the frame. We see Bogart reclining on his bed in front of two seated figures or sitting up in the bed with a figure beyond each shoulder. We watch him rise and cross between his visitors, trying to escape their menace, or we look down on his hair as the hats of the two detectives gather around. The montage of relatively static images gives the scene a frustrated energy that is perfectly in keeping with the dramatic situation.

Throughout the sequence, Edeson's lighting effects are low-key and melodramatic, making full use of the lamps, overcoats, and pulled-down hats that are the stock-in-trade of detective films, but investing all this paraphernalia with an uncommon intensity. It is only through a willed alienation that we can be aware of his skill. He keeps the entire room illuminated, using an extremely short focal-length lens (21 mm) to increase perspective, creating atmosphere with the *tone* of light and by ingeniously setting hats and coats off from their backgrounds. Except for occasional shots of night streets of completely darkened rooms, no shadows in *Falcon* are very deep—as they are, say, in Stanley Kubrick's heavy-handed, pseudo-Wellesian *The Killing,* where whole sections of a room will be blacked out while others are sharply lit, or where two characters will huddle ridiculously over the top of a lighted lamp in order to have a conversation. Throughout *Falcon,* the relatively cramped spaces of the interiors are completely visible; the strongest blacks and whites belong to the characters themselves, while the play of light and shadow on the walls makes subtler, grayer contrasts.

The film never sledgehammers us with effects, and yet Huston's camera is at once more energetic and more stylized than the lighting (which he left mainly to Edeson) or the acting. There is, for example, a relatively large amount of cutting in the sequence I have been describing—most of it toward the end, where the tempo of the editing matches the heat of the conversation—and also a marked propensity for shooting at the ceiling, for framing tight compositions, and for looking at faces from slightly odd angles. The camera jumps about the room, moving along with the characters and always making comments on the action by pointing up at a face or by peering through a doorway. It is this camera style, together with Huston's positioning of the actors, which creates overtly sinister effects and the feeling that we are viewing the scene through the eyes of some witty observer. Notice, for instance, how Huston makes the sequence a near comedy by exaggerating the contrasts between the characters. Bond and MacLane are set off from one another by their clothing, by the way they walk into the room, by the chairs they select, by their every move. As MacLane enters, he keeps his eyes trained hard on the back of Bogart's neck, his overcoat neatly belted and buttoned, his hands not too deeply in the coat pockets. Bond moves slowly, a few steps to the rear, coat spread open, hands in his pants pockets, his eyes sliding over and around the room. MacLane switches on a lamp and chooses Spade's comfortable leather chair, while Bond takes a hard seat off to the right. At first, the camera stands back and watches them, but then it begins to stress their respective traits by shooting up at one and down at the other. The close, three-figured compositions are just as expressive. The camera moves in to show the dark shapes of the police leaning inward toward Bogart's white shirt, or it sits back just far enough to show MacLane's hand resting idly on the leather chair while Bond nervously rubs his palms.

Some people, who strain to follow all the plot turns and the rapid flow of the dialogue in *Falcon*, regard the film as a bit talky; in fact, the important events are always clear, and the viewer does better to let many of the long speeches slide by while he reads Huston's sharp, simple images. Huston has been called a realist, but here and in much of the rest of the film his methods are closer to caricature. Though in casting the major roles he has been less flamboyant than Hammett, and though his camera is never radically expressive in the manner of an Orson Welles or a Max Ophuls, there is a streak of the showman in his character. He will not dolly a camera right past a wall, or photograph a character from behind a piece of furniture, as Kubrick does, but all the same his images tend to be rigidly stylized. Especially in his treatment of minor figures like Miles Archer and his wife, Huston likes to underline meaning: Jerome Cowan as Archer sits on the top of Bogart's desk, crosses his legs, and leers at Mary Astor. Later, Bogart walks into his office and meets the sudden embrace of Archer's widow, dressed all in black. Or compare the Barton MacLane role in the film with Hammett's version of the character. In the novel Lieutenant Dundy is a compact, round-headed fellow with a grizzled mustache, a five-dollar gold piece in his necktie, and a Masonic emblem pinned to his lapel. Huston, on the other hand, makes him a big, dark man with his hat brim jerked down—a wonderfully sinister image which is nevertheless dangerously near cliché.

The mannered style, which can be seen nearly everywhere in the film, is at odds with the common notion that Huston was an antirhetorical director. The late James Agee, one of Huston's best critics, was perhaps chiefly responsible for establishing such an idea. "He loathes camera rhetoric," Agee wrote. "In placing and moving his camera within a shot Huston is nearly always concerned above all else to be simple and spontaneous rather than merely 'dramatic' or visually effective." As an example of what Agee meant, here is his description of a moment he loved from *The Treasure of the Sierra Madre*. An intruder has been killed by bandits:

> The three prospectors come to identify the man. . . . Bogart, the would-be tough guy, cocks one foot up on a rock and tries to look at the corpse as casually as if it were fresh-killed game. Tim Holt, the essentially decent young

man, comes past behind him and, innocent and unaware of it, clasps his hands as he looks down, in the respectful manner of a boy who used to go to church. Walter Huston, the experienced old man, steps quietly behind both, leans to the dead man . . . and gently rifles him for papers.[7]

It is a fine touch, true enough, and it may have been achieved by Huston's casual, nondirective approach to the actors, but even in Agee's description it sounds as calculated and symbolic as a ballet.

There are nearly equivalent moments in *Falcon*. For example, there is the scene where Elisha Cook, Jr., awakes from being knocked out by Bogart. As he looks around the room at the faces of the other characters (all shown in vivid close-ups), he realizes he has been made a scapegoat and will be delivered to the police. He buries his head in his hands, and subsequently in a medium shot Huston shows Greenstreet and Bogart discussing the price of the falcon while Mary Astor goes to the kitchen to make coffee. Only Peter Lorre, as the homosexual, pays attention to Cook's sorrow. The camera barely seems to notice Lorre as he stands withdrawing an unlit cigarette from his mouth, his great frog eyes staring with pity, a hand reaching down to pat Cook on the shoulder. Of such effects Agee remarks, "Huston can draw the eye so deep into the screen that time and again he can make important points in medium shots . . . for which most directors would require a close-up or even a line of dialogue."[8] The point is well taken. It is true that Huston's compositions are oblique compared to those of a director like Alfred Hitchcock, who focuses unremittingly on the center of visual interest. Huston will sometimes have an actor stand off to the side of the screen in a long shot and do an intimate bit of business. But this does not constitute the absence of rhetoric, and in any case the absence of rhetoric is not always a virtue (vide Hitchcock). Agee's emphasis on casualness and spontaneity creates a somewhat false impression; certainly next to a Hawks or a Roberto Rossellini, Huston seems an almost Mandarin stylist.

In the good Huston films, nearly everything—the actor's movements, the camera setups, the editing—works to create a somewhat emphatic quality. Huston's camera never retards or works against the power of a script by utterly meaningless bravura, and usually he generates such interest that we don't care to analyze his technique. But clearly he does not eschew rhetoric, and the effect he produces on the screen seldom looks truly spontaneous. Thus Manny Farber, the eulogist of tough guys and termite art, gives an account of Huston's style that is both radically different and in some ways superior to Agee's: Farber overdoes it when he calls Huston the "Eisenstein of the Bogart thriller" (though notice the montage of greedy faces and hands as the coveted falcon is being unwrapped by Greenstreet, Astor, and Lorre). Still, he is right in saying that Huston's work is characterized by a "statically designed image" and a "mobile handling of close three-figured

7. James Agee, *Agee on Film*, vol. 1 (New York: Grosset & Dunlap, 1967), 327–329.
8. Ibid., 329.

shots." Farber does not much care for this style, but he is often good at describing it. He observes that Huston "rigidly delimits the subject matter that goes into a frame, by chiaroscuro or by grouping his figures within the square of the screen so that there is hardly room for an actor to move an arm."[9] Actually, Huston is somewhat less rigid in his late films, such as *Freud,* where he lets the camera slide a little here and there to catch an actor who has strayed out of the frame. In a movie like *Falcon,* however, the actors are used like models—an unusual attribute, coming as it does from a director who was always happy to let the characters find their own way.

I bring out these qualities of Huston's work not because they are defects but because they help define a temperament. L. B. Mayer believed that Huston was a realist because *The Asphalt Jungle* was filled with seamy detail and a morbid sense of humor. Actually, Huston's world was no more ultimately real than that of Hawks or Minnelli. His best films had tough, even grimy settings, and he always rigorously excluded Hollywood romance; but he could not avoid what Agee called a "romanticism about danger," and he loved to point a moral. Chiefly with his camera style, he loaded male adventure stories with allegorical significance, and many of his pictures, despite their superficial realism, are like existentialist morality plays. Even his filming of *Moby Dick* forsakes Melville's visionary manner and turns the novel into a typical Huston movie—a cautionary tale about a group of odd characters engaged in a quest. It is no surprise that the last line of *The Maltese Falcon,* Bogart's remark about the black bird ("the stuff that dreams are made of"), is Huston's invention. But the same quality of mind that put that sentimental comment in the film is responsible for much of what is good about it, namely the sheer liveliness of the images, the way they give Hammett's fairly straight crime novel the air of dark comedy. There is subtlety and understatement in some of Hammett's language, in the acting of players like Greenstreet and Bogart, and in Edeson's photography. Yet against all this, and somehow enhancing it, is the overt drama of Huston's camera. The film is just stylized enough to present the private-eye story as it has to be presented—as a male myth rather than as a slice of life; and Huston's wit is just sly enough to humanize the film without destroying the power of its melodrama.

9. Manny Farber, *Negative Space* (New York: Praeger, 1971), 33–34.

Tracking *The Maltese Falcon:*
Classical Hollywood Narration and Sam Spade
William Luhr

T**he *Maltese Falcon* is often cited as a milestone film. Its unexpected success not only solidly launched John Huston's career as a director and provided a major stepping stone in Humphrey Bogart's climb from contract player to major star but it also, with *Citizen Kane* in the same year (1941), became a progenitor of *film noir.* It is frequently shown in revival houses and on television but despite its popularity has seldom attracted detailed scholarly attention. As a partial corrective, this essay explores aspects of the film's narrative organization and indicates useful areas for further investigation.

The Maltese Falcon was made by Warner Bros. during the peak period of the production mode known as the studio system. That system used the narrative paradigm within which this film operates, and since that paradigm is the dominant one in fiction film production, it is useful here to outline some of its presumptions and techniques.

Classical Hollywood narration became regularized around the time of World War I, is still operative, and functions in distinctly different ways from other narrative modes, such as the international art cinema and many avant-garde cinemas.[1] It focuses upon an individual or small group of individuals who early on encounter discrete and specific goals that are either clearly attained or clearly unattained by the film's end. The goals tend to exist in two spheres, and their pursuit is developed along parallel and often interdependent plot lines. One sphere is private, generally a heterosexual romance; the second is public—a career advance, the obliteration of an enemy, a mission, a discovery, and the like. In *The Maltese Falcon,* for example, Samuel Spade explores a romance with Brigid O'Shaughnessy as well as the case of the Maltese Falcon, and the two are interrelated. He resolves both in separate scenes at the film's end.

Causality provides the prime unifying principle in classical narration. Plot construction tends to be linear, one scene clearly leading to the next. The major hermeneutics raised near the beginning of the film (Will Shane, in *Shane,* bring

---

1. Much of the best work on classical Hollywood narration appears in David Bordwell, *Narration in the Fiction Film* (Madison: University of Wisconsin Press, 1985) and David Bordwell, Janet Staiger, and Kristin Thompson, *The Classical Hollywood Cinema: Film Style and Mode of Production to 1960* (New York: Columbia University Press, 1985). My summary here draws significantly upon the first book, particularly chapters 4, 5, and 9.

From *Close Viewings: Understanding Films,* ed. Peter Lehman (Gainesville: University Press of Florida, 1990), 7–22.

peace to the valley? Will Marty, in *Marty,* find true love?) are developed, complicated, and then neatly resolved by the film's ending. This does not mean that classical narration requires a happy ending; a definitive failure to attain a goal is as clear a resolution as a success, but the spectator should know the outcome one way or the other.

A distinction between the notions of story and plot is useful here. Plot is the sequence of events as presented in the film whereas story is the causal/chronological sequence of events as they theoretically would have occurred in actuality. The plot may begin near the end of the story sequence as a main character nears death and then backtrack to reveal the events that led up to this point, as in *Double Indemnity* or *Citizen Kane.* A story sequence for a film that runs 1–2–3–4–5 may be presented to the viewer as plot sequence 4–1–3–2–5, with the reshuffled event structure indicating part of the film's strategy for evoking spectator response. Classical narration often uses its plot to generate confusion, but it invariably clears up all such confusion by the end. It seldom allows for ambiguous presentation of story elements, something that commonly occurs in the international art cinema in films such as *Persona.*

The spatial, temporal, and sonic techniques of classical narration reinforce this story clarity. The spaces that are shown and the sounds that are heard are subordinated to the logic of the narrative. We seldom see space, for example, that we can not situate in relation to the film's characters. A character may be seen in the space or may be looking at it, and the linkage is generally quite clear. Objects are similarly subordinated to narrative causality. In differentiating the narrative strategies of Ozu from those of the classical paradigm, Kristin Thompson and David Bordwell use *The Maltese Falcon* to underline precisely this point: "John Huston wouldn't think of cutting away from Sam Spade and Brigid O'Shaughnessy to a shot of the coat-rack in the corner of the office unless the hats on it had some significance (e.g., in the unravelling of the enigma). Yet in *There Was a Father,* Ozu does cut to a coat-rack to begin a sequence in a *go*-parlor, without ever drawing the hats or the space of the rack into the narrative action" (1976, 46).

In classical narration the camera pretends to be an invisible and ideal observer of preexistent events. We get the best views, cued by codes of lighting, framing, and movement, of the most significant actions necessary to further the plot. We see punches thrown and, from a different perspective, received; dialogue spoken and responded to; rockets fired and, miles away but seconds later, hitting their target. The events are presented as having their own integrity and not, as in some Godard films, as being developed with an intimate and formative relationship to the filmmaking apparatus. We do not see camera equipment in the rear of the shot or reflected in mirrors, and actors do not acknowledge the camera's presence. The process of production is concealed; the camera is omnipresent. The individual shots are stitched together according to the highly coded principles of classic continuity editing that emphasize clarity of action and story continuity according to realist norms.

Classical narration has not only changed over time but it also incorporates a wide range of options. It includes a number of genres whose norms of realism vary. A character in a comedy or musical may much more directly acknowledge the camera's presence or defy gravity than one in an historical epic; character options and motivations may be much different in a Western than in a detective film.

As a mystery, *The Maltese Falcon* works to confuse the viewer in ways that films in other genres, such as war films or romances, do not. Virtually all classical narrative tries to keep the viewer guessing as to what will happen next, but the mystery foregrounds this and also makes the viewer wonder what has happened in the past and even question the significance of what is happening right now. The project of the film's plot, as well as of the detective, is to uncover its story, and the plot reveals story information in often confusing and apparently contradictory ways. Little can be taken at face value when it appears, although all major story and plot elements become retrospectively consistent at the film's end.

The plot of *The Maltese Falcon* is linear and follows the involvement of the private detective Samuel Spade (Humphrey Bogart) with Brigid O'Shaughnessy (Mary Astor) and the case of the Maltese Falcon. It limits itself primarily to his point of view; with minor exceptions, new information appears as he learns it and events progress according to his participation in them. The film begins when O'Shaughnessy enters his office, moves chronologically forward as he becomes more deeply involved with her and with the complexities of the case, and ends when he turns her over to the police.

Spade must constantly process, question, and reformulate the often deceptive information he receives, and the sinister characters he encounters are developed with reference to deviations from cultural norms only hinted at in the dialogue. His triumph over mystery and danger lies at the center of the film. The ways in which the director, John Huston, organizes formal motifs, explores narrative alternatives and manipulations, and develops subtextual implications of foreign-ness and deviant sexuality to give that mystery and danger its specificity demon-strate the complexity and aesthetic value of *The Maltese Falcon*.

Early in the film we see a night shot of a half-open window with a slowly fluttering curtain before it. A telephone and a clock sit on a night table in the front of the frame. The phone rings. A hand reaches in from the right and pulls the telephone out of frame. The camera does not move. On the sound track, Spade's voice responds as he learns that his partner, Miles Archer (Jerome Cowan), has been killed. His hand returns the telephone into the frame. Only when the room light goes on do we see Spade's head, in silhouette, enter the frame as the camera moves slightly back. The curtain still flutters (fig. 1).

Spade leaves the apartment to view the scene of Archer's murder. When he returns, two police detectives arrive to tell him of another murder, that of Floyd Thursby, the man Archer had been following. When Detective Polhaus (Ward Bond) describes how Thursby was killed ("He was shot in the back four times with

Fig. 1

a .44 or .45 from across the street") Polhaus is framed by the same window, with the same fluttering curtain. That window and curtain become visual motifs increasingly associated with sinister events in and influences upon Spade's life.

Although Brigid O'Shaughnessy had first approached Spade concerning Thursby, Archer took the case because he was attracted to her. This leads to his death, which provides the film's first victim of O'Shaughnessy's relentless duplicity. She had originally given her name as "Wonderly" along with a false story designed to get Spade to take the case. When she contacts him after the two killings, she is living under the name "Le Blanc." Her names have changed, and her stories have changed, each change giving Spade a different perception of the situation. Although she has not told him the truth and repeatedly endangers him, she throws herself on his mercy, saying she has no one to turn to. She says she has no money and coyly asks, "What can I buy you with?" He kisses her.

When Spade first brings her to his apartment, she continues to deceive and coyly tantalize him. He catches her in her lies and she reclines on his sofa, saying she is tired of lying, of not knowing what is the truth and what is not. Clearly, part of Spade's attraction to her lies in the very blatancy of her evil, in the seductive

Fig. 2

danger she embodies. When she reclines, Spade's fluttering curtains are directly behind her, and he bends over to kiss her. Huston cuts to a close shot of her (fig. 2), then Spade's head descends into the frame (fig. 3). Suddenly he stops and looks at the curtains (fig. 4). The camera moves toward and into them (fig. 5), and we see through an opening at the center a sinister-looking man in the street below, watching (fig. 6).

This shot encapsulates major motifs in the film. The curtains have become associated with the dangers that surround Spade's involvement in the case; they evoke the often malignant world that so often intrudes upon him. He is in this scene physically closer to the curtains than at any other time in the film. The man outside is a murderer who has already killed at least one character and will kill more. At this point Spade does not know who this man is or why he is there, but he knows he is dangerous. Furthermore, at this point the danger comes not only from outside the curtains, as it did in the earlier instances, but also from inside them. O'Shaughnessy is within the apartment. She is sexually desirable and available to Spade. As with the man outside, Spade knows little about her, but he knows that she too is dangerous.

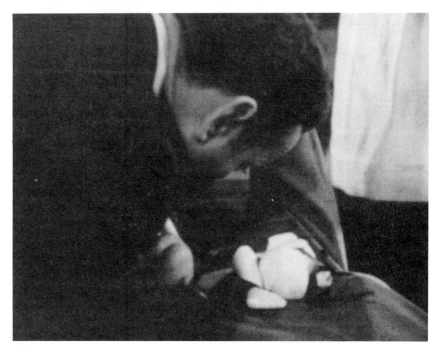

Fig. 3

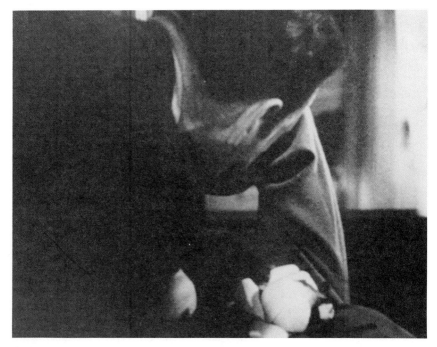

Fig. 4

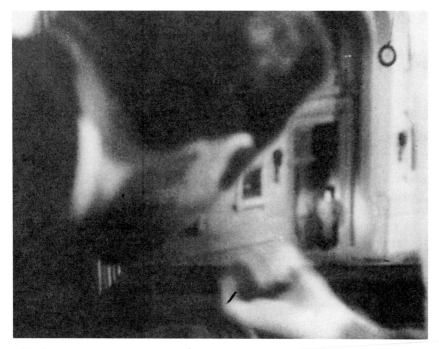

Fig. 5

Fig. 6

The narrative progression of this film is developed largely around befuddlement, around the trying out and discarding of one potential narrative linkage for another. Brigid O'Shaughnessy first came to Spade with a story about how Floyd Thursby ran off with her sister. She asked Archer to follow Thursby. Archer was killed and Thursby was killed and there was no sister. Spade had to return to square one. A bizarre, dandified foreigner, Joel Cairo (Peter Lorre), came to Spade's office and demanded the "black bird." Soon, both Cairo and O'Shaughnessy are terrified to learn that Gutman, "The Fat Man" (Sydney Greenstreet), is in town, and Spade learns that all seek the "bird," the fabled Maltese Falcon. From Brigid O'Shaughnessy's first story, apparent truths and continuities are replaced by other apparent truths and continuities: nothing is certain.

At the center of all of this is Samuel Spade, who is particularly suited to function in such an environment. One of his basic characteristics is a remarkable analytical intelligence. When O'Shaughnessy first comes to him, she gives him a complicated story. He says little; he watches. When Archer arrives, however, Spade fires off an elaborate and detailed summary of what has been said, showing that he had missed nothing, retained everything, and plotted out a course of action. When he visits the scene of Archer's death he says little, simply looking around for a few moments; but then he quickly tells the police precisely how the murder took place. Many shots in the film simply show him watching, taking it all in, with little indication of his response. The film carefully develops in the viewer the sense that Spade understands virtually everything in complex ways (fig. 7).

A reinforcing instance occurs the day after the first two killings when Spade goes to O'Shaughnessy's rooms. She admits that her initial story was false. He shows neither surprise nor annoyance but tells her that neither he nor Archer believed her story; what they did believe was the two hundred dollars she paid them. He says that they knew the money was more than she would have given had she been telling the truth, and they considered it "enough more" to make her lie all right with them. In going over whether or not she bears responsibility for Archer's death, he tells her no—"Of course you lied to us about your sister and all that, but that didn't count. We didn't believe you." This gives a further insight into what he knew but did not reveal the day before and indicates very untraditional notions of truth, truthfulness, and moral responsibility.

She throws herself on his mercy. She admits that she has been "bad," says she is all alone and in danger, and begs to be allowed to rely upon his strength. Utterly abject, she pleads, "Help me." She is appalled to find him not melting with compassion but smirking at her. He responds not to the abject situation she has described but rather critiques her performance in creating it. He says, "You won't need much of anybody's help. You're good. It's chiefly your eyes, I think, and that throb you get in your voice when you say things like, 'Be generous, Mr. Spade.'" In another scene in her room, after asking her a difficult question, he smiles and says, "You're not going to go around the room straightening things and poking the

Fig. 7

fire again, are you?" indicating his awareness of her ploys of nervous agitation, of diverting attention, of clever deception.

Spade is himself continually performing. In Gutman's rooms, dissatisfied at the slow pace of the negotiations, he loses control of himself, explodes, demands a deadline for a deal, and smashes a glass as he rages out of the room. Huston cuts to a long shot of him walking down a hallway toward the camera. He first appears to be storming in a rage, but as he gets closer to the camera it is obvious that he is smiling. It has all been an act.

When summoned before the district attorney, he apparently becomes enraged at the infringement on his rights and launches into a seemingly deeply felt tirade against the D.A.'s methods. He suddenly stops, looks at the stenographer, and asks, "You getting all this right, son, or am I going too fast for you?" When the stenographer says he is getting it, Spade says, "Good work," switches back to his tone of outrage, and continues the tirade. Once more he shows himself to be in command of and carefully orchestrating what initially appears to be a spontaneous emotional outburst.

Much of the film's forward narrative drive revolves around Spade's aggressive search for the truth and his processing of and acting upon each new piece of information he receives. He shows a strong awareness of impediments in his way, of people's ability to lie, both in the information they give and in their manner. Not only can he see through many of the deceptions of others but he is also himself able to link and interpret information so as to give the appearance of truth. When he gathers O'Shaughnessy and Cairo in his apartment for the first time, the police arrive and demand entrance. Spade refuses. Suddenly they hear a scream and a crash, and they enter. Cairo's face is bloodied and O'Shaughnessy is holding a gun on him. As the police prepare to arrest them all, Spade smiles and says, "Oh, don't be in a hurry, boys, everything can be explained." He then proceeds to concoct a story to "explain" the situation in a way that will divert the police from arresting them and also mollify the terrified Cairo. But no sooner has he finished with this story than he tells the police that both the violent incident and the story were a joke played upon them. He proceeds to tell an entirely different story using the same basic information but giving an entirely different narrative interpretation to the events. At the end of the second story, he provokes one of the police into hitting him, making the detective vulnerable to brutality charges should the incident become public. Finally the police leave and no one is arrested. O'Shaughnessy looks at Spade in astonishment and admiration and says, "You're absolutely the wildest, most unpredictable person I've ever known." He has, reflecting the narrative tactics of the film, given two entirely different and reasonably logical versions, both false, of a simple event. The next day he encounters the exhausted and suspicious Cairo, who tries to break off contact with Spade after telling him that he always has a smooth explanation for everything. Spade defends himself by saying that it worked and arrogantly asks, "What do you want me to do, learn to stutter?"

When the Falcon is delivered to his office by a dying man, Spade leaves with the statuette and advises his secretary to tell the police everything as it happened, only to leave out the arrival of the statuette and to say that he, and not she, received a call from O'Shaughnessy. We see him making very slight alterations in the truth to create a new truth—not true, but coherent enough to convince. The film is comprised of dozens of these small narratives and narrative adjustments.

One of Spade's prime antagonists is Gutman (fig. 8), whose activities also point to the existence of different realms of truth. When he first appears, approximately halfway through the film, he does not lie about his goals. He quickly clears up a number of cryptic references to the "black bird" by telling Spade the history of the coveted Maltese Falcon. He tells Spade, "These are facts, historical facts. Not school-book history, not Mr. Wells's history, but history nevertheless." He then gives the story, largely one of piracy and murder, of the Falcon. Here he provides not a false reorganization of present information, but facts not recorded in traditional histories. He gives an alternate truth—not a false one as those presented by O'Shaughnessy and Spade—but a repressed one associated with evil. He has devoted his life to it.

The trail of evil that the film explores comes mainly from the search for the Maltese Falcon—originally gold and bedecked with jewels but later covered with

Fig. 8

black enamel for concealment. The one that ultimately appears turns out to be a copy—an enamel-coated, lead statuette. Like most of the "truths" in the film, this is also a chimera; it is constructed to convince but is not real.

It is important that the statue is Maltese—foreign—because the notion of foreignness is central to the presentation of evil in the film. The film is set entirely in San Francisco and carefully associates things evil with things different from the position that Spade occupies—that of an American, hetero-sexual, Anglo-Saxon male. The notion of foreignness is introduced early on. O'Shaughnessy first claims Thursby had a wife and three children "in England." Spade instantly recognizes the gun that killed Archer as British. O'Shaughnessy later admits that she met Thursby, a killer, in "the Orient," and her clothes come from Hong Kong.

Before we even see Joel Cairo, Effie (Spade's secretary, played by Lee Patrick) hands Spade Cairo's scented card and with a knowing smirk says, "Gardenia," implying effeminacy. This introduces another aspect of foreignness, that of devi-ant sexuality. Cairo (fig. 9) is of unspecified origin, although he has at least three passports, and his name, if it is his, might suggest that he is Egyptian. But he is clearly coded as foreign, not American. The film also strongly implies that he is

Fig. 9

homosexual as perceived by codes of the 1940s; his effeminacy, dandification, "feminine" hysteria, at times mothering affection for Wilmer (Elisha Cook, Jr.), and apparent sexual rivalry with O'Shaughnessy over "that boy in Istanbul" all point to deviations from contemporary norms.

Associations of homosexuality are also given to Wilmer, Gutman's bodyguard and hired killer. While he shares none of Cairo's effeminate qualities and is in fact morosely pugnacious, he is constantly referred to as the "boy," and Spade refers to him as a "gunsel"—a term meaning gunman, but also meaning a boy used in pederasty. When Spade knocks him out near the end of the film, we see him unconscious on a sofa in a very curious shot that emphasizes his groin (fig. 10). Nothing is overt, but associations of homosexuality, of sexual otherness, are implied.

Gutman's nationality is not given, but he sounds and appears British. He shows a profound attraction to the Falcon, whose history is one of evil and betrayal in foreign places. His most recent encounter with it took place in Istanbul, where he also dealt with Cairo and O'Shaughnessy. When the false Falcon arrives, it has come from Hong Kong. When Gutman learns it is false, he prepares to return to Istanbul.

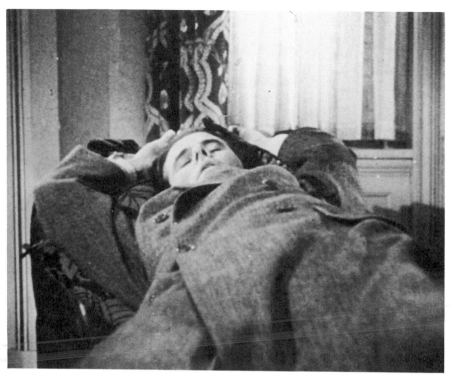

Fig. 10

Gutman's sexuality is questionable. He shows no interest in women. Wilmer and Cairo seem fiercely devoted to him. But his real obsession appears to be a fetishistic one with the Maltese Falcon. When Spade demands he betray Wilmer in order to get the Falcon, Gutman does so. By way of apology he tells Wilmer, "I couldn't be fonder of you if you were my own son but, well, if you lose a son, it's possible to get another. There's only one Maltese Falcon. When you're young you simply don't understand these things." When what he thinks is the Falcon arrives, he unwraps it in an almost orgiastic ecstasy.

The film opens with a number of shots of San Francisco. It and Spade become established as norms against which all else is measured. Virtually all danger and evil come from "somewhere else." The most immoral thing we see Spade involved in is heterosexual excess; he has been sleeping with Archer's wife. And Archer is killed largely as a result of his heterosexual lust for O'Shaughnessy. The film ends as Spade sends O'Shaughnessy off to jail for Archer's murder, a decision influenced by her sexual promiscuity. He knows she was Thursby's mistress and says, "I won't walk in Thursby's and I don't know how many other footsteps."

In many ways the film has two endings and two narratives cleverly blended. It seems to end after the Falcon is discovered to be false and Gutman and Cairo prepare to return to Istanbul to continue the hunt. Spade calls the police and reports them. All seems tied up. He has dealt definitively with the business of the Falcon, and he has saved O'Shaughnessy from the sinister crew, so the public and private spheres of the story seem resolved; but suddenly he turns on O'Shaughnessy and accuses her of Archer's murder. To this point it has seemed apparent that Thursby killed Archer, and all seem to accept this. Archer was following Thursby and was killed with Thursby's gun. Spade now shows O'Shaughnessy why this could not have happened, and she admits her guilt.

Now it is clear that what had first appeared to be the film's resolution was only a partial resolution. It is also apparent here that the story of O'Shaughnessy has very little to do with the story of the Maltese Falcon. It frames that story. That story really begins when Cairo enters Spade's office and ends when the statuette is found to be false. Within that story, O'Shaughnessy is little more than a pawn, an ally of Thursby, whom we never see. Even her intense sexual desirability serves her little good in that story, since that is the story of deviant sexuality, of Gutman's fetishistic obsession and his possibly homosexual acolytes in exotic, foreign places.

In San Francisco, however, her sexuality serves her much better, and the framing story, the one opening and closing the film, is of her and Spade. It is also one of heterosexual excess in which Spade is complicit. Spade desires her; so does Archer. She kills Archer to implicate her lover, Thursby. Spade is implicated in the killing because the police know he has been sleeping with Archer's wife, who was also suspiciously absent from her home on the night her husband was killed. Archer's wife at times implicates Spade, perhaps because Spade has lost interest in her after he has met O'Shaughnessy.

When Spade tells O'Shaughnessy he is going to turn her in to the police, he sits in his apartment with a sickened, dazed look on his face. It is the only time in the film that he appears to be genuinely speaking from his heart. He explains his confusion and his vestigial morality and the reasons he must turn her in. It is part of the only daylight sequence in his apartment, and he sits not in front of the curtains in the window but in front of their prominent shadow on the wall.

At this point, the Maltese Falcon has become irrelevant to the story, which now concerns only Spade, O'Shaughnessy, Archer, and Thursby. The curtains had earlier been significant in shots related to scenes of O'Shaughnessy's evil—when Spade learned of Archer's death, when Polhaus described Thursby's death, and when Spade was about to kiss O'Shaughnessy and paused as he spotted Wilmer through the curtains. At that point it appeared that Wilmer was the danger; we now know that in fact O'Shaughnessy was more dangerous. Her desirability masked her evil and almost entrapped Spade. It is likely that that kiss we never saw was only interrupted, not prevented by the sight through the curtains. The next time we see the two together they are much less formal, more affectionate; they call each other "Darling" and "Angel," and O'Shaughnessy tells Spade her apartment had been searched that morning, indicating that she may have spent the night with

Spade. Given the censorship codes of the time, these subtextual hints provide a strong indication that the two have slept together, thus making Spade more vulnerable to her machinations.

From that point to the final scene in Spade's apartment the curtains do not serve a significant formal function. Then, suddenly, when the Falcon story is cleared away, they again become central. O'Shaughnessy sits more or less in front of them, but most important, their shadow now frames Spade in daylight. Now that Spade understands everything they no longer appear ominous, but they serve as a muted reference to the dangers Spade encountered and tamed.

On the Trail of Dashiell Hammett (The Three Versions of *The Maltese Falcon*)

Jean-Loup Bourget (writing as Jacques Segond)

he Maltese Falcon/(Le Faucon maltais) of Dashiell Hammett has been adapted to the screen three times. The last version, the one directed by John Huston in 1941, is the most famous; it is so universally known and appreciated that its reputation outshines the preceding attempts: that of Roy Del Ruth, which came out ten years before and which is also entitled *Dangerous Female*, and that of William Dieterle in 1936, which is entitled *Satan Met a Lady*.[1]

A few words about *Dangerous Female*: Directed shortly after the publication of Dashiell Hammett's novel, the film is on the whole extremely faithful to it. It is here that the character of Rhea, Gutman's daughter, who plays only an insignificant role in the novel, already disappears. It is here also that, as William K. Everson (*The Detective in Film*) has remarked, the conclusion of the film conforms to that of the novel with Sam Spade denouncing to the police Miss Wonderly, who then finds herself back in prison even though it would have been easy (given the tolerance of the period, and the fact that the Hammett's novel had not yet become a classic) to invent a happy ending that would also have been relatively satisfying morally. The acting is excellent, with Ricardo Cortez (Sam Spade), Bebe Daniels (here christened Miss Wonderly from beginning to end, and not Brigid O'Shaughnessy), Dudley Diggs (as Gutman waving a fan, a visual motif which makes one think of the films of Sternberg and which foreshadows Sydney Greenstreet with his fly-swatters, not in the Huston version of *Falcon*, but in the *Casablanca* of Curtiz), Una Merkel (Effie, the secretary of Spade), etc. I limit myself to two remarks. First because the novel and the film are practically contemporaries, Roy Del Ruth brilliantly utilizes art deco, the style of 1925, in which the geometric contrasts are perfectly appropriate to the black and white film (the apartment of Miss Wonderly). On the other hand, Huston's version will do its best to make clear that the action takes place in 1940, the period of the shooting of the film.

Dangerous Female is, in another way, clearly anterior to the period of (self-) censorship instituted by the Hays Code. The dialogue is just as explicit as it is in Hammett's novel and this is not the case in the Huston version. In the novel Brigid O'Shaughnessy spends a night in the company of Sam Spade. Later when he suspects her of having pocketed a $1,000 bill, he undresses her completely.

---

1. A fourth version, a parody, has just been filmed with George Segal and Glenda Jackson.

From *Positif: Revue de cinéma* 171–172 (1975), 13–18. Translated by Connor Hartnett.

Nothing like this with Huston. But Del Ruth dots his *i*'s and crosses his *t*'s: Iva Archer (Thelma Todd), the widow of Miles Archer (the associate of Sam Spade), yells, in speaking of Miss Wonderly, "Who's that dame wearing my kimono?" It is then clear that Iva and Miss Wonderly have been the mistresses of Sam Spade.

In short, an adaptation of high quality, but without genius. I now come to the 1936 version, *Satan Met a Lady,* which does not enjoy a great reputation but which is, nevertheless, a pure delight. The adaptation was written by Brown Holmes, who had collaborated on the scenario of the preceding version. Great liberties are taken with the novel, as the credits indicate, which simply state that *Satan Met a Lady* was adapted from a novel by Dashiell Hammett. But these liberties are a constant source of invention and always successful. The dialogue is sparkling. The acting of Warren William (re-Christened "Ted Shane" = the role of Sam Spade) and of Bette Davis ("Valerie Purvis" = the role of Miss Wonderly, alias Brigid O'Shaughnessy) is dazzling, just as is that of the secretary of Shane, "Miss Murgatroyd" (Marie Wilson) and of the great Englishman in the role which corresponds to that of Joel Cairo, "Anthony Travers" (Arthur Treacher). *Satan Met a Lady* combines in a masterful way the detective story and the "screwball comedy." In its atmosphere the film is thus comparable, but also very much superior, to the *Thin Man* series (with William Powell and Myrna Loy; directed by Woody S. Van Dyke). The tone is established at the beginning: the scene is a train station in an American city on the Pacific coast; people board a train by threes; then Warren Williams is asked not to set foot again in the town in which he has created a scandal. A little later, Shane pushes open the door of the office of Ames (Archer), and Miss Murgatroyd, adorable blonde, falls from a ladder into his arms. Ames assures Shane that his wife, Astrid (who apparently married Ames when she could not get her hooks on Shane) has completely forgotten him; and so Astrid falls in her turn into the arms of Shane, kisses him full on the mouth, and asks him, "Is it really your birthday tomorrow?" Ames, who would like someone to remember his birthday, is hurt. The same evening, Shane takes Murgatroyd to a nightclub. An incorrigible seducer, he makes a date with the star dancer. After the murder of Ames and the man who shadowed Ames, Shane meets the dancer at the "Artists' exit." He stands at the foot of the stairs facing a detective who interrogates him because he suspects Shane of having avenged the death of his associate. One by one the dancers descend the stairs and Shane leaves only a minute space between himself and the detective in order to rub himself against the girls as they go by. A second detective, who also takes a bit of an advantage of this situation, indicates his approval as he watches the young beauties.

As to the Kasper Gutman–Joel Cairo–Wilmer Cook trio, it undergoes certain metamorphoses. Gutman becomes "Madame Barabbas" (Alison Skipworth); Joel Cairo, a big Englishman armed with a knife who searches in vain through Shane's apartment. On his return, they drink together: the Englishman, in keeping with his Englishness, asks for sherry, and ends up finding whatever it was that Shane had assured him he didn't have. Later the Englishman visits Shane at his office, a bouquet of flowers in hand, to make amends for having ransacked everything and for having locked Miss Murgatroyd in a closet. Wilmer Cook is now Kenneth (Maynard Holmes) with a beret pulled down over his big head and smoking bad cigars. . . . As to the Falcon, it is no longer a falcon, but . . . the horn Roland blew at Roncevalles.

There's the same sovereign cheeky manner in the scenes between Warren William and Bette Davis: in Valerie's apartment, it's Shane who begins to attack the chairs with a knife. She threatens him with her pistol; she orders an intimate supper for two. . . . Then Shane begins rummaging all over the place while dropping allusions to King Kong (for example, he hangs from the drapes like a big ape).

However, the real triumph is that of Marie Wilson, absolutely brilliant in the role of Miss Murgatroyd, with the insane charm of a featherbrain who does not know how to spell her own name, but who has an inimitable way of answering the telephone, and who at the end of the film (again on a train) finds herself alone with Shane. There is no doubt that their promise to really enjoy themselves together will be realized.

Curiously, this very free, even delirious, adaptation is faithful to Dashiell Hammett's novel at certain precise points. For example, when Shane learns that the gang is in search of Roland's horn, he conveniently remembers that Miss Murgatroyd has an archeologist uncle who could be consulted regarding the authenticity of this object. One is tempted to take this detail for one of the loony inventions of Brown Holmes and Dieterle. Nothing of the kind! In Dashiell Hammett's novel, Effie Perine has a historian uncle who confirms, in its general outline, the story of the Maltese Falcon told by Gutman. In addition, the personalities of the characters in *Satan Met a Lady* do not depart much from the indications given by Hammett. The novel defines in a number of instances Sam Spade as a "blond Satan" and Effie Perine as a "featherhead," and these are descriptions which apply wonderfully well to Warren William and Marie Wilson. If the Huston version is altogether remarkable thanks to Bogart, and above all to the Sydney Greenstreet-Peter Lorre-Elisha Cook, Jr., trio, it is more debatable in regard to its female characters: Bette Davis (in the Dieterle version) seems to me to be more convincing than Mary Astor, and a comparison puts in the shade Lee Patrick (Huston version), who is physically much too staid as Effie.

With his wide-brimmed hat and his pipe, Warren William sports certain exterior signs of Sherlock Holmes: *Satan Met a Lady* belongs to a tradition in which one can also place Billy Wilder's *The Private Life of Sherlock Holmes,* Robert Altman's *The Long Goodbye,* and Jean Renoir's *La Nuit du Carrefour.* These are films successful in the difficult fusion of a detective story plot and a bizarre or loony sense of humor that is so profound and omnipresent that it constitutes a personal vision of life.

The Huston version suffers, in the last analysis, by comparison: it is excellent, but appears labored and its atmosphere is a bit heavy. One has the impression of no longer drinking champagne but rather crème de menthe. We are now better able to judge the quality of the dialogue and the shots of this version, because one of the first titles of "Film Classic Library" (published in Great Britain by Macmillan, 1974) is, indeed, *The Maltese Falcon.* This is a very praiseworthy endeavor, but wrong in giving the impression (false, in my opinion) that the Huston version is practically the only one and in any case the best. Be that as it may, the book produced by Richard J. Anobile is an indispensable research tool,[2] reproducing scenes from the film shot by shot as well as the complete text of the film.[3] The music, for instance, which plays a very important role in the Huston film because it accentuates the somberness of the atmosphere—and it is absent, but also because Anobile proceeds, as a matter of fact, to vary both the dimensions and the form of the frame with each new shot. For example, the number of images per page is generally six, but varies from a minimum of two to a maximum of twelve, which has the effect of overemphasizing the close ups selected for the large illustrations and of underemphasizing the importance of master shots. One could imagine in this regard a "transcription" of the film which would be doubtlessly less clear and more monotonous, but also more neutral, or an entirely different transcription. In addition, something perhaps more disturbing, the format varies from cinemascope (cf. p. 19) to vertical band (cf. p. 75). The dialogue reproduced in Anobile's book permits us to verify that, as Huston himself has affirmed, it is taken word for word from Hammett's novel. The principal differences lay in the suppression already mentioned (the disappearance of Rhea Gutman; the night which Sam Spade and Brigid O'Shaughnessy spend together; downplaying the homosexual relationship between Joel Cairo and Wilmer Cook, and also on the affair between Sam Spade and Iva Archer). Additional matters are minimal. Let's cite, so as not to forget them, those related to the use of film rhetoric, such as "establishing shots" of San Francisco at the beginning of the film. Also the suggestion by Sam Spade that Cairo be left to the mercy of the police (rather than Wilmer) is an invention of Huston, which here adds to the apparent Machiavellianism of Sam Spade. The words at the end of the film (the detective Polhaus, taking the Falcon in his hands, asks Spade, "What is it?" "It's the stuff dreams are made of." Huh?") is indeed characteristic of Huston, in his rather pretentious explication of the beauty/vanity of the quest doomed to failure. (On the other hand, the Falcon is a forgery even in the Hammett novel, an element which fits in quite naturally with John Huston's thematics which is there, let's remember that, in the first staging.)

Minimal also, the variations. In the novel, Gutman is killed by Wilmer, but here survives in the film, and—we don't see his arrest—we have the strongest impression, a visual impression, of his new departure in search of the authentic Falcon.

2. On the other hand I point out in passing that the scenario of *Satan Met a Lady,* as is summarized in Gene Ringgold's *The Films of Bette Davis* (The Citadel Press, New York, 1966), is incorrect from beginning to end.

3. Of course, a book like this also belongs to a particular kind of discourse, not only because it can't account fully of the complete film text.

In a more important way (the detail has been pointed out by William K. Everson), the anger of Sam Spade during his first meeting with Gutman is a *sham* by Bogart in the Huston film, and that makes the character of the private eye more sympathetic, more intelligent and more of an "actor" also. For the rest, the work of the adaptation of Huston has not then essentially consisted of "rewriting" but in directing the actors (Sam Spade ought first to have been acted by George Raft who, one imagines, would have been closer to the Ricardo Cortez of *Dangerous Female*) and in the meticulous framing shots (for example, the low angle shots of Peter Lorre and Sydney Greenstreet; at the end of the film, the face of Mary Astor behind the grillwork of the elevator, a metaphor for the bars of the prison which awaits her, etc.). It must be noted that, curiously, *Satan Met a Lady* and *The Maltese Falcon,* so disparate in tone and atmosphere, were both photographed by Arthur Edeson. *The Maltese Falcon* of John Huston is archtypical of the 40s: Mary Astor has a sophistication that is in the end almost Victorian, prim, buttoned-up. It's not hard to think that the 30s had more style and real brio.

The Beam That Fell and Other Crises in *The Maltese Falcon*
Ilsa J. Bick

Mention *The Maltese Falcon,* and most will invariably assume you mean Huston's 1941 film version of Dashiell Hammett's 1929 novel, as if they were one and the same. What image is more indelibly etched into *noir* consciousness than the stark, harsh shadows of the elevator grate slanting across the worn, tearstained face of Ruth Wonderley (Mary Astor), the pretty bird confined to her cage, or the tragic, world-weary heroism embodied in Humphrey Bogart as his Sam Spade descends the staircase, clutching the scarred, counterfeit falcon, the stuff of which dreams are made? Yet two other films of the same book, *The Maltese Falcon* (Del Ruth, 1931; renamed *Dangerous Female*) and *Satan Met a Lady* (Dieterle, 1936), have not commanded this type of attention or recognition. One could argue that they are "inferior" films, their characters not as compelling, or their veracity to Hammett's original vision somehow submerged in a way that compromises their true potential. In a recently published interview, John Huston disingenuously asserted as much stating, "I tried to be as faithful to the dialogue he [Hammett] had written . . . I simply translated the novel into images."[1]

Perhaps. But particularly telling in all three versions are the omissions of two important parts of the novel. One is a fairly lengthy story Hammett's Spade tells Brigid early on in the story. In brief, Spade was hired earlier in his career to find a man named Flitcraft, who simply vanished one day, leaving behind a wife, two children, and a sizable estate. Spade eventually located Flitcraft living under an assumed name in another state, but leading a life almost identical to the one he left behind. When Spade questioned Flitcraft about his disappearance, Flitcraft related that, on the day he left, he passed by a construction site at just the moment that a heavy beam plummeted down some ten stories. Flitcraft escaped unhurt, save for a bit of concrete which nicked his cheek. At that moment, however, Flitcraft realized that "somebody had taken the lid off life and let him look at the works."

I wish to express my profound gratitude to Kevin Little at Turner Broadcasting for graciously and expediently providing me with a copy of *Satan Met a Lady;* to Kathy Lendech and Richard May at Turner Entertainment Company for doing the same with *Dangerous Female;* to William Luhr for several hours of thought-provoking conversations; and to Krin Gabbard for unfailing support, textual suggestions, and singlehandedly keeping Federal Express in business.
1. Rui Nogueira and Bertrand Tavernier, "Encounter with Rui Nogueira and Bertrand Tavernier (and interview with John Huston)," in *Reflections in a Male Eye: John Huston and the American Experience,* ed. Gaylyn Studlar and David Desser (Washington, D.C.: Smithsonian Institution Press, 1993), 220.

Life could be ended for him at random by a falling beam: he would change his life at random by simply going away. . . . I don't think he even knew he had settled back naturally into the same groove he had jumped out of. . . . He adjusted himself to beams falling, and then no more of them fell, and he adjusted himself to them not falling.[2]

This repetitive circularity to the living of one's life, of following along a given trajectory out of a compulsive repetition and replaying of one's life story rather than the fabrication of new narrative out of a series of seemingly random series of events to which one simply adjusts, is a central theme in Hammett's book. Just as Gutman, O'Shaughnessy, and Cairo all search for the elusive falcon and adjust, despite their most calculated plans, to random events and suffer repeated disappointments, so Spade himself is subject to the same type of circularity and endless repetition. The Spade of Hammett's novel is not the "embodiment of self-sufficient phallic potency"[3] of Huston's film. Hammett has Spade re-encountering his own Flitcraftian fate: After sending Brigid away with the police, he settles back into his office, only to find Iva Archer, his dead partner's widow and the woman with whom he has been engaged in a casual adultery, waiting for him. Like Flitcraft, Spade sinks into the random events of his life, unable to change them but merely accommodating as, with a shiver, he utters the last line of the novel, "Well, send her in."[4] For Hammett, the only sure release from such repetition is death, as when Gutman is murdered by Wilmer and Cairo is killed in a shootout with the police. Huston deviates from these conclusions, sending Gutman and Cairo on a jolly little romp before they are apprehended by the police. The Law prevails, and Huston propels Bogart's Spade on a linear trajectory away from repetition as, cognizant of what quests represent, Spade renounces the seductive and dangerous woman and aligns himself with the Law, turning his back upon the stuff of which dreams are made.

Huston's circumnavigation around Hammett's *noirish* fatalism begs for contextualization of not only his film, but also its two predecessors. All three films share with *film noir* and Hammett's novel an emphasis on seduction, whether it be expressed through the need to contain the seductive, dangerous woman or the dangers inherent in other temptations (such as wealth). When one compares the 1941 *Falcon* with its two predecessors, *Dangerous Female* and *Satan,* an interest-

2. Dashiell Hammett, *The Maltese Falcon* (1930; reprint, New York: Vintage, 1957), 63–64.
3. Frank Krutnik, *In a Lonely Street: Film Noir, Genre, Masculinity* (London: Routledge, 1993), 95.
4. Hammett, *Falcon,* 217. In addition, Hammett makes it clear that Effie Perrine is no longer Spade's "pal" nor the "good man"/"sister." Spade derides her "woman's intuition," pointing out that the instincts and obligations of the detective are far superior to (womanly) impressions. Disgusted by Spade's callousness and self-serving cynicism, Effie can only feel appalled that turning Brigid over to the police appeared to cost Spade very little.
Another interesting omission is Gutman's death. In the novel, Wilmer shoots Gutman just as the police catch up with them, presumably in revenge for Gutman's willingness to set up "the boy" as the fall guy.

ing historical progression emerges. Both the earlier films highlight Spade's unrestrained and adroit heterosexuality and his aggressive seduction of others: Spade's true "manliness." For example, in *Satan Met a Lady,* a version loosely based upon the novel,[5] Ted Shane (Warren William) is continually on the make, surrounded by a veritable bevy of women of every shape and description, the entire ensemble more than willing to share his company (and presumably his bed). Unhampered by Production Code restrictions, *Dangerous Female* went much further, showing Ruth Wonderley actually in Spade's bed, taking a bath, and needling Spade about his inability to handle all his women. Spade and Shane (in *Satan*) are ladies' men, from pointed remarks about shared kimonos, closeups of women's legs, and soulful kisses (*Dangerous Female*) to monkeylike antics and insinuating scratchings at bedroom doors (*Satan*).

By contrast, Huston's *Falcon* is more *re*strained and *con*strained, and most of its overt sexuality goes, almost literally, underground while being deflected into the dangers that seduction possesses in whatever form it may assume, and rechanneled into adroit maneuverings to avoid them. In the 1941 version, the number of women populating *Dangerous Female* and *Satan* is reduced to three; and of these, only two, Archer's wife, Iva, and Brigid O'Shaughnessy are threatening and in need of containment. Spade is constantly ushering Iva out and instructing her to go home, and references to Brigid's "badness" are wonderfully, almost brilliantly muted, yet more "dangerous."[6]

This analysis shall investigate the permutations these men and their women undergo as they appear in these three films. I will also explore sociocultural and historical events that might have influenced these characterizations. In the case of *The Maltese Falcon,* we have a history made to order in the appearance of the

---

5. In *Satan,* Spade is renamed Ted Shane; his partner is Milton Ames; Brigid O'Shaughnessy becomes Valerie Purvis (Bette Davis); Effie is transformed into Murgatroyd; Gutman is now a portly gut-woman, the criminal mastermind Madame Barabbas; and the Falcon is exchanged for the mythical ram's horn of Roland. Even the character Wilmer, now renamed "Kenny," is allowed his phallic moment in the sun when the film actually shows him shooting Captain Espinoza (a.k.a. Jacobi) on the pier.

Most telling, there is no Joel Cairo per se—the closest approximation this staunchly heterosexual film offers to the "effeminate," homosexual male is Travers, a prissy and foppish Englishman who nonetheless reaffirms his manliness by presenting flowers to Murgatroyd and having been "seduced" by Purvis.

6. In both Huston's *Falcon* and Del Ruth's *Dangerous,* Brigid tells essentially the same story about Floyd Thursby's sleeping habits. What distinguishes Huston's handling of the event from Del Ruth's is that while Brigid confesses that she is "bad" and has always been so, the smirking pride she takes in her badness, the way in which she casually makes reference to it, hints at the "dangerousness" Spade discerns in her. For example, when Spade questions her about Thursby's habits, Brigid casually remarks that Thursby "never went to sleep without crumpled newspapers around the bed" and so could never be taken by surprise. Of course, how else could she have known this if not through direct experience? By contrast, the impact of this same sequence in *Dangerous* is lessened by the way in which Wonderley (she never changes her name to O'Shaughnessy) delivers the lines and the fact that the emphasis shifts to an intense examination of her body, from the cleavage of her bosom to the sinuous length of her glistening white leg as she tucks money into an enormous roll hidden in her stocking. She is not bad so much as she is naughty.

novel and three radically disparate films based on this same novel in a relatively short, yet momentous period in American history (1929–1941, with a two years' interval between the publication of the novel and *Dangerous Female,* and five years each between *Dangerous Female* and *Satan* and *Satan* to *Falcon*). At the same time, identifiable generic shifts occurred in American cinema, from starkly drawn gangster serials and more "free and easy" films of the 1930s and early 1940s (especially the screwball comedies) to the more intricate and psychological *films noirs,* crime thrillers, and troubled women's films of the 1940s and 1950s (the latter "couched" in the spate of Hollywood's own particular brand of psycho-analytically informed and oriented films produced immediately following World War II).

Specifically, I am intrigued by what appears to be a shift, within the context of the three versions of *The Maltese Falcon,* in women's and men's characteriza-tions, from a sexuality that is raucous, bawdy, madcap, and unrestrained (yet nonetheless threatening) to one which is nefarious, duplicitous, secretive, mutedly erotic, and seductive, but substantially less central (yet nonetheless threatening). In *Dangerous Female,* the focus is primarily upon the ways in which the elusive woman is scrutinized, apprehended, and penetrated by the clearer sight of the male subject while at the same time the film suggests that such a "danger" is best contained by the all-encompassing umbrella of patriarchy and the Law. Unre-quited desire as pathos is preferable to fulfillment, tragic sacrifice valued above consummation. As is true with Huston's version, these lovers end up the prisoners behind bars of their own construction.

Satan represents a radical departure from this vision, positing its (anti)-hero as definitively outside such Law while engaging in ribald drolleries and grotesque-ries more characteristic of screwball comedies. Just as these comedies chafe at the limitations of institutions, so *Satan* declares that adherence to the Law is problem-atic at the least and noxious at most—the death of fun and romance, which, in their own ways, are no less repetitive.

Unlike its predecessors, Huston's film does not figure the woman as central to the plot. *The Maltese Falcon* is principally about men and men's dealings with other men. Huston's version emphasizes a crisis in masculine ideals and represen-tations close but not identical to Hammett's own, while reintegrating some of the formulations delineated in the original film. Huston focuses our attention upon a masculine sexuality no longer true, straight, and narrow but open to a myriad of possibilities, random events, and tiny seductions. The man becomes, suddenly, as vague, elusive, fractured, chimerical, and indistinct as the woman. In some ways, the narrative returns to the doubling apparent in the first film, yet this thematic tension results in a palpable narrative strain. Just as Hammett presents no compel-ling reason why Spade should be in love with Brigid (as opposed to succumbing to lust and opportunism), neither does Huston. In other words, rationality and logic no longer suffice as explanations. Instead the focus shifts to the irrational, the barely repressed and suppressed, the deviant, and the dangerously foreign. The "craziness" of the original *Dangerous Female* is no longer the isolated loss of control provoked by the sight of the woman but the dominator of the landscape of the film in the multiplicity of the men's visions. The woman is increasingly marginalized through this cycle of films and pushed to the periphery, yet para-doxically achieves a greater prominence precisely *because* she is more elusive, mysterious, and enigmatic, allowing of no precise and penetrating vision, the forerunner of the dark lady of *film noir.* This presents Huston with the perplexing dilemma of Spade's motivation; such "craziness" precludes logic; and Huston's Spade utters protestations that appear forced and stilted, continually undercut by ironic asides and less-than-heartfelt endearments. *The Maltese Falcon* struggles to reassure us that the Law and an essential internal ethic remain intact; that such adherence substitutes for a clear and penetrative sight; that while dodging beams, the dangerous female and pretty bird may still be vanquished by the purity, however shady, nefarious, blurred, or seducible, of one's moral vision.

Dangerous Female: I'm Crazy about You, Baby

Late in Del Ruth's version of *The Maltese Falcon,* the principal protagonists all sit idly around in Spade's apartment, waiting for the delivery of the promised statu-ette. Gutman is soaking his feet and swatting at flies; Cairo snoozes beneath a sheaf of newspapers; Wonderley (Bebe Daniels) plays solitaire (and cheats); and a weary Spade (Ricardo Cortez) amuses himself with a trick card. Set upon the face of the card is the back of a head and neck which is clearly an unfinished portrait of a woman; by contrast, the lines of the profile are not set but comprised of a shifting bit of string which, at the flick of the wrist, can be molded into any variety of monstrous and grotesque shapes. Flipping the card repeatedly, Spade tries to get the features to conform in some way to Wonderley's profile (an inference made explicit by the number of point-of-view shots of the card followed by a shot of Spade glancing toward Wonderley, and then his perspective on her profile). Try as he might, however, Spade is unable to achieve this, and just as Wonderley cheats at her own card game, the implication is, ultimately, that the woman is both a cheat and a chameleon, ephemeral as effluvia and just as fleetingly insubstantial.

Yet for a detective story about an elusive statuette, this lack of certainty is confined in this film specifically to the domain of the female. For this Spade, the viewer is left little doubt that there is almost nothing that cannot be known or resolved. Even the Falcon makes a brief appearance in Spade's offices where it is first delivered by the mortally wounded Captain Jacoby (unlike the other two films where the elusive prize is never shown until near the end). With the excep-tion of Wonderley, all the other characters are precisely what they seem, and indeed none of their actions is hidden from view. For example, in the Mickey Finn sequence, there is a cutaway to an exchange between Cairo and Gutman as they discuss how to get rid of Spade—in this case, to drug him. This is, of course, quite different from Huston's version where Spade's descent into unconsciousness is as surprising to the viewer as it is to him. Consistent with the more tongue-in-cheek quality of *Satan,* this lapse never occurs at all. But this type of laborious explanation of hidden motives and actions occurs repeatedly in *Dangerous Female.* Even Cairo, whose effeminacy in Hammett's novel and Huston's film is so beautifully and meticulously choreographed, is reduced in *Dangerous Female* merely to a modestly prim, somewhat "tight" little man with a gun and goatee. The homo-erotics of his characterization are not so subliminal as they are nonexistent. There is nothing more here than meets the eye.

Just as telling is the fact that Spade's point of view is never compromised in any fashion, not even when he slips into unconsciousness after downing his Mickey Finn—his gaze is consistently clear, true, smugly self-confident, and, for the most part, penetrating. Not only does he make Wonderley his lover, but as she sleeps in his bed, he steals her apartment key and, in a brilliantly executed sequence, systematically ransacks her apartment (alternating with crosscuts to the sleeping Wonderley), effectively penetrating the body/apartment of the woman. When Spade suspects that Wonderley may have palmed some money, he orders her to strip bare, and it is only the sight of her naked (phallisless?) body that reassures him that she does not have "it."[7]

Enhancing Spade's ability to penetrate the foreign is the fact that Spade speaks Chinese, marking him as both an outsider and one privy to mysterious, faintly exotic secrets (including the sight of the naked woman's body) at which the rest of us can only guess. Near the end of the film, the viewer learns that Spade produced a surprise witness at Wonderley's trial in the form of a Chinese merchant who witnessed the killing. During the scene following upon Archer's murder, Spade exchanges some brief conversation with a Chinese gentleman—in Chinese, of course. Evidently he has known the identity of Archer's murderer all along.

Just as *Satan* will underscore Shane's phallic prowess, so *Dangerous Female* leaves little doubt that this Spade not only enjoys his women but keeps a stable of them as well. Half-nude photographs and pictures of women dot his apartment and office; and the very first glimpse we have of Spade is his silhouette (echoing uncannily the sequence with the trick card), shifting and changing as his shadow merges with the head and arms of someone else. The next shot focuses upon a pair of women's legs prancing lightly in a flouncy print dress; the unnamed, unseen woman reaches down a hand to twitch up her stockings. Cut to Spade holding the woman's hand in his, giving it a long kiss, and then bidding his "darling" adieu; we see the legs prance out of the frame. Similar to *Satan,* Spade's adultery with Iva

---

7. On the other hand, women are depicted as just as shrewd, astute, and cunning. Effie is continually narrowing her eyes with a knowing nod or making insinuating remarks, a far cry from the "good man/sister" of Huston's film; and Iva's sight is as clear as Spade's, for she discerns almost immediately that Spade has another lover in his apartment. Catching a glimpse of Wonderley clad in a flowing silk kimono, Iva shrieks, "Who's that dame wearing *my* kimono?"

is known to Archer (although this is treated with more flippancy and as good, clean fun in *Satan*). An interesting point, however, is that whereas Archer and Spade are roughly contemporaries in *Falcon* and the disparity between Shane and Ames in *Satan* is primarily defined in terms of accomplishment, Archer is depicted as a much older, gruffer man in contrast with his blonde, buxom, youthful wife—old enough to be her father. It is almost as if the film alternatively attempts to condemn Spade for his duplicity yet to justify him as clearly the more palatable, virile, and worthy lover.

In keeping with this thematic shift, just as Spade's womanizing serves to exclude him from the "moral" circle of men and patriarchy (a motif repeated in *Satan*), so the task of *Dangerous Female*, at one level, appears to be to recuperate Spade back into the right and true way of (patriarchal) authority he has earlier betrayed—in a sense, to avoid the beam. Although the interiorization of moral or psychological struggles is lacking in this film, the closest approach rests in Spade's renunciation of Ruth Wonderley to the Law. Not only are there long conversations between Spade and Wonderley where he professes his "craziness" for her, but they share passionate, soulful kisses quite different from the flippant trysts and dalliances with other women depicted earlier in the film. Unlike *Satan* or even *Falcon,* this Spade is seen as condemned to a torment as brutal and lengthy as Wonderley is, because he has succumbed to passion just as Wonderley (and indeed all the other characters) search passionately and endlessly for the true riches they will never find. This may also have been a concession toward attempting a resolution closer to Hammett's vision of a man trapped within endless repetition. While having Spade continue his adultery with Iva may not have been acceptable, positing Spade as trapped in a misery of endless and unrequited love may have been an acceptable substitute. And in fact, in a curious, perverse twist, the film explicitly identifies the two as sharing this same "tragic" fate, of an imprisonment that is virtually eternal. The film extends the ending such that we learn of Wonderley's conviction; Spade, now chief district attorney, visits her in jail. It is clear that they both love one another, yet must remain apart (literally unable to touch—now more empowered by her refusal, Ruth declines to clasp Spade's hand). At the film's end, the bars close over Spade's face as he stares intently back at her cell. Clasping the bars in both hands, he insists that Wonderley receive everything she wishes while in prison. The film then closes with a jocular aside that the bill be sent to the district attorney's office.

There appears to be an uneasy reconciliation here between lust and law. On the one hand, what is implied in this sequence is not only the preservation of a moral order but also that resisting the allure of the "dangerous female" rewards one. Implied in *Falcon* and fleetingly glimpsed in *Satan, Dangerous Female* posits Spade now as "inside," the very incarnation of the (phallic) Law—as the chief district attorney, he has the ultimate authority to "penetrate." In so doing, however, the necessity for him to remain impervious and isolated from *women* would suggest that the vagaries of sexual capriciousness are to be avoided, trapped within himself and the frustration of desire. In the end, the sexual man retreats to the phallic narcissistic stance, untouched and untouchable, and the woman remains dangerous because she is enigmatic, penetrated but never truly known, a dame in one's bed from whom one is protected only when she is safely confined by the Law behind bars.

Satan Met a Lady and the Screwball Comedy

In marked contrast to the dame in the bed, Dieterle's *Satan* pays homage to the stereotypical gentleman sleuth and "lovable rake" films popular in American cinema of the 1930s as well as the hijinks and frenetic antics encoded in farcical encounters and close approximations to the machinations of screwball comedy (e.g., *The Thin Man* [Van Dyke, 1934] to which *Satan* bears the closest resemblance). While it would be difficult to "pigeonhole" *Satan* as "merely" or even predominantly screwball, the ways in which desire and the desiring subject are configured make this characterization particularly compelling.

David Shumway's analysis of screwball comedies specifies several conditions peculiar to the romantic structure of these "comedies of remarriage."[8] Specifically Shumway points out that "in romances, the narrative structure is actually represented by a triangular set of relationships between lovers, but the narrative structure is not identical with the love triangle, since other relationships, for example, father/daughter or king/court, may constitute the included pair."[9] Furthermore, "sutured into the point of exclusion,"[10] the viewer experiences the same desire to redress absence and lack in much the same way that the film's principal characters go through their paces, negotiating the (necessary) obstacles to romance. In other words, romances are narrative vehicles of (con)quest (regardless of genre, as this same narrative strategy was operative in *Dangerous Female*). In these comedies as well, Shumway contends that women are distinguished from their roles in other narrative forms by the fact that "the woman is never merely an item of exchange between two men, but is also presented as a desiring subject"[11] (although how this distinguishes woman's desire as subject and object from, say, a maternal melodrama, crime thriller, or *film noir* is problematic).

Other features also personify screwball comedies, including emphases upon the rich (i.e., as concrete manifestation of the rewards of romance), pointed bantering and verbal exchanges (including the *double entendre*), the (desirable) state of marriage as consummation of romantic encounters (and hence the death of ro-

8. David Shumway, "Screwball Comedies: Constructing Romance, Mystifying Marriage," *Cinema Journal* 30, no. 4 (Summer 1991), 7–23.
9. Ibid., 10.
10. Ibid., 10.
11. Ibid., 12.

mance), and the romantic project enacted in a pastoral, pristine, highly idealized "natural" sphere.[12]

These elements are played out in *Satan* from the beginning. Accompanied by jaunty, big band music,[13] the credits display not the sought-after ram's horn (instead of falcon) but highlight Valerie Purvis (Bette Davis) in the shadow cast by the spread cape of a Satanic-looking man replete with top hat, tails, and goatee, implying that the demonic woman is the object of the quest. The death of such romantic questing is figured in marriage, a theme to which the film will return at its end, as in the opening sequence where Shane (a dyslexic step away from "Shame") is being literally railroaded out of town by the local police amid a jubilant parade celebrating the birth of sextuplets. Reporters and photographers jostle one another for position, at first mistaking him for the object of their admiration. Shane then watches in wry amusement as the momentous question is posed of a top-hatted, upright gentleman—"Are you the father?" Standing barely noticed in the background, a rotund, beleaguered-appearing man asserts, outraged, "I am!"

Never without his pipe, tailored raincoat, ascot, rakishly cocked hat, and cane, Ted Shane is more an unscrupulous, suave, and roguish con man than private detective (intent upon convincing wealthy, older women that they require protection from thieves and then throwing that business to his barely competent partner, Milton Ames). Throughout the film, he succeeds in seducing (and thereby besting) virtually anything female while jousting in barbed witticisms with the "boys"/ police. His is an unrestrained phallic, mockingly paternal/Oedipal sexuality (he dubs himself several times as "Papa Shane"). *Satan*'s appropriation of some of screwball comedy's me-chanics is explicitly designed to valorize the avoidance of marriage as the death of (romantic) adventure and the preference for having fun over serious commitment.[14]

As the desired and desiring object, Purvis is visualized almost immediately during the opening sequences upon the train. Shane pays her a passing glance as she walks by, seating herself back-to-back with Shane. The film then focuses upon

12. The latter quality is quite interesting from a psychoanalytic perspective inasmuch as narrative exploits in "natural" surroundings, from latency-age stories to more "mature" adult fantasies, com-monly represent not only an escape from the more rigid and punitive strictures of Oedipal/superego authority and "descent" to more primitive, intensely affectively cathected object-and-drive-representa-tions but also a closer approximation to the reunion with the idealized maternal imago/ego ideal. Such a quest is perhaps the most circular—and romantically elusive—of all. See Ilsa J. Bick, "The Look Back in *E.T.*," *Cinema Journal* 31, no. 4 (Summer 1992), 25–41; Perry Nodelman, "Out There in Children's Science Fiction: Forward into the Past," *Science-Fiction Studies* 12 (1985), 285–296; and Ellen Handler Spitz, "Primary Art Objects: Psychoanalytic Reflections on Picturebooks for Children," *Psychoanalytic Study of the Child* 44 (1989), 351–368.

13. In contradistinction to the highly stylized choreography of Huston's *Falcon*, where there is no diegetic source music whatsoever, all of *Satan*'s music is diegetic in nature, restricted to two of Shane's scenes with Valerie Purvis (in her apartment and at a jazz hall) and another where Shane has taken Murgatroyd out on a date to a nightclub. The same is true of *Dangerous*.

14. One of Shane's most frequently repeated lines to every single woman he seduces—and the film's coda—is "When this is over, you and I are going to have a lot of fun."

a tight two-shot, with Purvis, properly mysterious and darkly bespectacled, listening intently to Shane as he babbles on, unaware, to an elderly, wealthy matron. Of course, audiences would have immediately recognized Bette Davis, first from the credits and then in this shot, and be searching for her next appearance. When she does resurface in the film, she is configured in a three-shot in the Ames Detective Agency offices, her back to the camera, exposed finally to the audience as the lady on the train. Thereafter most of Shane's dealings with Purvis are in searching or looking for her, and, as he puts it later in the film, "sticking pretty close" (as in the earlier *Dangerous Female,* sharing the illicit kisses Huston elides).

Just as Shane and the (sutured) viewer seek after the woman as the object of desire, so the women—particularly Purvis and Madame Barabbas—are figured as desiring subjects. All are desirous of having or renewing their liaisons with Shane; and again Shane's brand of sexuality is blatant, disruptive, and penetrative. Adultery is his accepted province as Ames's wife greets him in her bathrobe (with Ames present), gives him a long, soulful kiss, giggles about the "fun" she will now have with Shane around, and enthusiastically sends her husband out to tail Purvis. As trapped within marriage as the anonymous father in the beginning of the film, Ames is a chubby, emasculated, failed chump. As Shane quips upon seeing his partner's body (in *Satan,* the murder occurs in a graveyard), "Poor Ames. This is about the only time where he did something in the appropriate place."

The film settles into being a contest of wits between Shane and Purvis. When she is introduced, Purvis's desires are constrained within conventional boundaries—she is seeking the lover who jilted her in Baltimore. Indeed Shane assures Purvis that he and Ames will find her "betrayer." When Purvis's desires step outside patriarchal constraints, however, she becomes dangerous and the only (desiring) woman who disturbs Shane's dominance to any perceptible degree.[15] For example, when Shane breaks into her apartment intent upon searching for the horn of Roland, Purvis surprises him in her bedroom. (The comparable sequence is posited in *Dangerous Female* as brutal and secretive—Spade tears apart Wonderley's apartment as she sleeps.) Clad in an elegant dressing gown, she threatens Shane with a gun; he shrieks in terror and jumps up, grabbing hold of the doorjamb and swinging, apelike, to and fro. Cigarette in one hand and gun in the other, Purvis giggles and mockingly calls him, "King Kong." Still, Shane is worth seducing—they share a sumptuous and elegant dinner, and Valerie cloyingly asserts that they "could mean something to each other . . . *really.*" Yet, at the moment that Purvis indicates her willingness to be seduced, Shane snatches the gun away from her, instructing her, "Scratch your head, sweetheart, with both hands!" The tables are turned; and as soon as the woman betrays and follows what ought to be her *true* nature

---

15. Like other screwball comedies, their machinations take place in the world of the rich and privileged. Purvis's apartment is an elegant, lavish affair; Shane seems never to want for money or the means in which to spend it, dividing his time between nightclubs and jazz halls; and for an underemployed private investigator, even Milton Ames is not badly off. This is also similar to *Dangerous* where Spade lives in fairly lavish and unrestrained comfort.

(i.e., in succumbing to the attractions of a virile, potent, and irresistible male), then her (deviant) power is circumvented and returned to its proper, phallic owner (just as in *Dangerous Female,* she is penetrated *after* she sleeps with Spade). This is further reinforced when Shane turns her sarcasm to his advantage when he returns to scratch at her bedroom door, teasingly calling himself "King Kong."

Satan never leaves the viewer much doubt as to Spade's prowess or (putative) intelligence. This Spade is smart enough to sidestep Madame Barabbas's Mickey Finn and just as duplicitous, having slipped her a drugged cigarette. (The two wags cheerfully confess to one another.) Presumably the film's intention is never to allow for the possibility that Shane could possibly be bested by anyone, female or male.[16]

The ending of the film codifies woman's desire into the ultimate goal—marriage. Marriage is equated with the literal death of "fun" and "adventure" exemplified by Purvis's screaming out, as she is taken away by the police, "You'll always remember me—the one woman you couldn't take for both love and money; the one woman who handed you double-cross for double-cross right up to the end. . . . You'll find out that a woman can be as smart as you are, and someday you'll find one who'll be smarter. She'll marry you!" Here, the desired woman and woman as a desiring subject are neatly subsumed under the unifying and lawful rubric of matrimony. Valerie Purvis may desire an object—and this quest for the ram's horn (a displacement of a phallic signifier, if ever there was one)—forms the "other" relationship specified by Shumway as a necessary component to the screwball comedy (and for romantic quests in general). But Purvis's desire must ultimately be constrained by patriarchy. Left unfettered, this other relationship multiplies upon itself to fill the textual landscape with covetous couplings—Valerie desires the horn; Shane desires his partner's killer, the horn, *and* women; Barabbas is after the horn, Purvis, and Travers; and so on. Furthermore, having a pair of women— one, an older, matronly, and duplicitous "auntie" and the other a glamorously lethal, young blonde fighting for possession of the horn and Shane's loyalty can be seen as a reenactment of an almost Oedipal scenario (with the dangerously phallic maternal figure split, literally, in two). In the end, Shane reduces both women to "kittens," delivering them up to the police/paternal authority. While he evades direct competition with the Law (he works in concert with the police to hand over Valerie), he also neatly circumvents the restraints of *paternity* by eluding marriage, children, and family life, rescuing romance from matrimony, and dashing off with his dizzily daffy, blonde secretary Murgatroyd to have, presumably, "an awful lot of fun."[17]

16. For example, after Shane returns to discover that Travers has ravished his apartment, he sets Travers to straightening things up while recalling that he has to place his bet on that evening's fights. Shane mocks Travers's accent, pulls out a gun at the same moment Travers does, instantly recognizes Travers's money as counterfeit; and for his part, Travers asserts that, when he found Shane's address book, he copied down most of the numbers "including the marginal notes."

17. Reinforcing encoded patriarchal Law and authority is underscored by the fact that virtually nothing discursive that Purvis does remains "hidden" from the viewer, just as the viewer was similarly reassured and empowered in *Dangerous.*

The Beam That Fell

Thus far, I have considered seduction as the means through which *Dangerous Female* and *Satan* variously play out the temptations and random turns of fate. *Dangerous Female* offered a vision of the woman as, merely, a dame, a *femme fatale* whose ulterior motives are never hidden from the privileged sight of the male for very long, yet the film comes much closer to what might be supposed to be Hammett's vision of the circularity of tragedy and fate by having Spade long for the elusive and ultimately unapproachable woman even as it reassures its audience that Spade retains phallic prowess. In marked contrast, *Satan* takes these same seductions and random events and twists them into comedic and farcical mechanisms demonstrative of phallic prerogative. Shane's seducibility is more a character trait than a ploy—nevertheless, the perception that Shane may be seduced is the trick that he turns to his advantage to gather a confession from Purvis. Furthermore, *Satan* implies that the (successful) seduction of the man by a woman ends, fatally, in the confines and restraints of marriage (an interesting twist upon the tragedy of failed romance found in *Dangerous Female* but one in keeping with Shumway's premise that love survives only in romance)—and in any event, marriage is really all that women may hope to both desire and obtain.

Yet, in *The Maltese Falcon* we are confronted with the depiction of the man no longer in control of his sexuality, whose vision has become blurred by the passage of time. Among a proliferation of temptations and even in the face of a continually shifting and uncertain feminine presence, *Dangerous Female* reaffirms that Spade retains prowess in and out of bed; in *Satan,* women are continually clamoring for Shane's attentions. For the most part, sexuality is depicted along the straight and narrow.

By contrast, there is no such simple economy or division in *Falcon.* As other writers have pointed out, Spade's characterization fluctuates between dalliances in hetero- and homoerotic flirtations, promulgating the illusion that Spade is seducible.[18] To a certain extent, Spade appears to be in control of these flirtations as he towers over Cairo or manhandles Wilmer. But I would like to emphasize my profound disagreement with any assumption that Spade possesses an unassailed phallic potency or *truly* controls anything.[19] What some mistake as self-sufficiency

---

Lastly I think it significant that before the film's denouement, Purvis and Shane escape from the city together, headed on a train for some pastoral paradise—an escape to the natural for "romance." Indeed, even after Shane exposes Purvis as the murderess, she comes the closest to an avowal of love for Shane, stipulating that in spite of all that has happened, "everything will be all right now."

18. See Harvey Greenberg, "The Detective Film: *The Maltese Falcon,*" in *Screen Memories: Hollywood Cinema on the Psychoanalytic Couch* (New York: Columbia University Press, 1993), 67–92; also William Luhr, "Tracking *The Maltese Falcon:* Classical Hollywood Narration and Sam Spade," in *Close Viewings: Understanding Films,* ed. Peter Lehman (Gainesville: University Press of Florida, 1990).

19. Cf. Krutnik, *In a Lonely Street.*

appears more, if one looks at Spade from a characterological point of view, as a defense against emotional investment (something much closer to Hammett's vision of his detective). Film characters are not "people," however; they can not be neatly appended with character diagnoses.[20] Taken as a symbol or symptom of masculine concerns, Spade may best be characterized as a man whose control over his world is continually on the brink of slippage and disaster. Beams crash all around him. Not only does Spade have to juggle his trio of women in quick succession, but the extent of his control over these random elements is continually suspect. As Effie puts it early in the film, "Sam, you always think you know what you're doing, but you don't."

In Huston's film, there are many instances where Spade's most calculated maneuvers are outdone by the very people he is trying to seduce and outwit. A telling example occurs when he meets with Gutman for the first time. Spade breaks out into an uncharacteristically hysterical outburst; yet, as he leaves Gutman's hotel room, there is an enormous grin on his face. As William Luhr notes, his performance has been staged.[21] Spade teeters, however, on the brink between calculated performance and loss of control—his hand shakes as he waits for the elevator. Then as he enters the elevator, the camera pulls back to reveal Joel Cairo emerging from another elevator and heading for Gutman's rooms. The viewer is immediately privileged with knowledge Spade does not have, something which the first two films were at pains to reassure its viewers could *not* happen. The viewer's sight is clearer and briefly "superior" to Spade himself.[22]

Until the very last moment, Spade's fate is primarily a series of accidents and fortuitous discoveries. Indeed, as Brigid astutely points out to him, if the Falcon had been real, perhaps he might have shifted his allegiances yet again. Even when Spade believes he is in control of his second encounter with Gutman, he is not—and an interesting point is to note that Spade's *only* "blind" moment (and the viewer's as well), signified by a blurred image of Gutman from Spade's point of view, occurs as Gutman caresses his knee while exhorting Spade to consider how much the Falcon might be worth. Thereafter, it is only by happenstance that Spade discovers where Gutman and the others are heading, yet he arrives too late—*La Paloma* has been sacked. Jacobi stumbles into Spade's office rather than Spade's finding anything; and in fact when Spade believes he's finally "got" it (i.e., the Falcon), he and the viewer never see it, and Spade is immediately sent out on a

20. I take exception to Greenberg's "diagnosis" of Spade as schizoid or paranoid; certainly these elements are present, but facile diagnostic appellations add little and suffer from ad hoc reductionism and postulated motives.
21. William Luhr, "Tracking," 15.
22. This type of suture is also evident from the film's beginning. Although the Falcon appears under the credits, it then disappears from view until film's end, in much the same way that Valerie Purvis/Bette Davis in *Satan,* as the desired object, is "looked for" by the "sutured" desiring viewer-subject. The emphasis is consistently upon redressing lack, whether it be the lack of an object such as the Falcon or in the lack of knowledge as the viewer obtains momentary superiority over Spade.

wild "goose" chase in pursuit of the elusive bird/female Brigid (a sequence not in either of the other two films).

Related to this uncertainty in the male's "aim" and vision is the more intense scrutiny to which the male's sexuality is subjected in the form of homoerotic ploys and the vagaries of a man's sexuality. *This* Spade is conspicuously restrained in his sexuality—and if indeed something is "dangerous" here, it is that Spade's phallic-ness threatens to career out his control into shows of savage violence, or be done away with altogether when it *does* reveal itself. Only once in the entire film does Spade kiss Brigid, and he does so in a particularly brutal fashion, grabbing her by the face and digging his thumbs into her cheeks. Significantly it is following this that he stammers, becomes uncertain, and speaks openly about his inability to continue on without more confidence in her (something Hammett did not specify). But what *is* missing from this version of the film is the break-in at O'Shaugh-nessy's apartment, an episode that reaffirmed Spade's penetrating powers and his *sighted-ness* in *Dangerous Female* and Shane's phallic prowess in *Satan.* For a screenplay which Huston professes to be so close to the original novel, I find this elision intriguing because it makes Huston's meditation upon what constitutes masculine identity and power all the more nebulous. Specifically, the potential for a more overt homoeroticism is pointedly underscored in the graphic depiction given over to Joel Cairo's effeminacy (associated with an appropriate glissando of violins).[23] While the homoerotic ploy is also quite pointed in the Mickey Finn sequence with Gutman,[24] Joel Cairo's effeminacy and gardenia-scented handkerchiefs imply that such seductions are literally erupting around Spade, almost as if his adultery with Iva was mere prelude for more "deviant" polymorphisms boiling within him. For example, an interesting exchange occurs between Brigid and Joel in Spade's apartment where Brigid needles Joel about a "boy" in Istanbul who remained loyal to Cairo. In return, Cairo retorts that she was unable to turn the boy against him (presumably she was unsuccessful in seducing the boy). Brigid responds instantly by slapping Cairo, and the two engage in a catfight until Spade intervenes, wrests Cairo's gun away and then slaps Cairo who protests that this is the second time Spade has laid his hands upon him without permission. Smiling savagely, Spade beats Cairo again, stating, "When you're slapped, you'll take it and like it!" The implication is, of course, that Cairo is just as capable of seducing men as Brigid; and as with his women, Spade is intent upon proving his superior phallic authority. One might be tempted to imagine him saying the same to a woman he has casually beaten—when Iva tearfully asks him if he murdered Archer, Spade's face darkens with violence as he moves away from her and slams his fist into his hand, barking out, "Ha! You killed my husband, Sam, be kind to me."

On the other hand, Spade himself suffers from this type of (castrating) humiliation twice in the film—at the end of the scene just described, Lieutenant Dundy slaps Spade who is restrained by his friend, Tom (and there is really no threat that Spade will take on the lieutenant). Similarly Wilmer kicks Spade in the face, but only after Spade is rendered unconscious by a Mickey Finn. What is telling, however, is that this type of humiliation *never* befalls Spade in *Dangerous Female* or Shane in *Satan*.[25]

Can this masculine characterization be seen only as emblematic of Huston's peculiar auteurial vision? Certainly the answer to that question must be a resound-

23. As I have already pointed out, *Dangerous* offered a fairly restrained and prim, but definitely not effeminate Joel Cairo. *Satan* elides Cairo's questionable phallic prowess altogether by transposing him into the prim and prissy Englishman Travers (who nonetheless is signified as "phallic" and along the "straight and narrow"—his first sequence has him ransacking Shane's apartment with an enormous machete-like knife and later in the film he pays a visit to Shane's offices, offering a corsage to Murgatroyd to apologize for having had to lock her in the closet). Indeed Travers' "penetration" of Shane's apartment is prior to Shane's ransacking of Purvis's, and one can only wonder if this comic redress was meant in any way to reassure phallic potency to the one man who had been violated to any measurable degree.

24. I would agree with Luhr that Gutman's characterization is vaguely homoerotic; however, asexual seems more accurate. In the novel, Gutman has a daughter, something which not only reinforces the Oedipal byplays in the book but signals Gutman's heterosexuality and patriarchal prowess—he is a father. Thus his protestation that Wilmer is like a "son" fits nicely into this schema of the benevolent, patriarchal protector rather than hinting vaguely at the stable of "boys" of which Cairo and Wilmer may be only two.

25. And, as I noted earlier, the one humiliation to which Shane is subjected—having his apartment ransacked—is neatly turned on its head in the next sequence when in a seeming "identification with the aggressor," Shane does the same to Purvis.

ing "yes"; Huston's portrayal of men perched on the edge, and his use of Bogart in particular, is a large portion of his oeuvre.[26] Indeed, Bogart's importance in promoting *noirish* cinema is undisputed.[27] Beyond this appeal to a star persona, however, one must ask what might have favored the depiction of such sexual vagary, or rather how the manifest concerns of the society and culture for whom *The Maltese Falcon* was manufactured and later copied both enhanced and were reflected in the film's contextual themes. Vernet is quick to point out that historical events are not film events, and the usual disclaimers and explanations surrounding *film noir*'s inception, including the brooding danger overseas of World War II and the difficulty most in the United States would have in seeing the misery of their lives depicted so graphically during the Depression of the 1930s, do not convince him. Yet I would emphasize that there is ample *ante*cedent to hypothesize that national traumas, particularly those bound by denial, are not as easily digested and pronounced fit for the consumer as Vernet so blithely imagines. Contemporaneous images of the Vietnam War itself are notably lacking during the war years, even though there are a few films—*Getting Straight* (Rush, 1970), *Summertree* (Newley, 1971), *Taxi Driver* (Scorsese, 1976), and *Coming Home* (Ashby, 1978)—which deal either with the protest over the war, the ethical obligations in supporting American involvement, or its aftermath in terms of its effects and results (with the inevitable "crazed" and ultimately unsympathetic Vietnam veteran). Furthermore, *Coming Home* explicitly dealt with themes of healing and recuperation of a man paradoxically more phallic and sexual by virtue of his physical handicap and aided by the love of a good woman, not with the carnage or bestiality of the war itself (something embodied in the militaristic, emotionally handicapped character played by Bruce Dern),[28] in much the same way that *The Best Years of Our Lives* (Wyler, 1946) focuses not just upon the erotic appeal of the castrated male,[29] but essentially indicates that all a "damaged" man really has to do is pull himself together (with the unfailing maternal support of a good woman) and find a job in order to heal a war's wounds. Again, he needs to divest himself of a "bad," quasi-*femme fatale* along the way.

Although begun with *Apocalypse Now* (Coppola, 1979), it was not until *Some Kind of Hero* (Pressman, 1982), *Birdy* (Parker, 1984), *Platoon* (Stone, 1986), *Hamburger Hill* (Irvin, 1987), *Good Morning, Vietnam* (Levinson, 1987), *Born on the Fourth of July* (Stone, 1989) to name just a few, that commercially viable films

26. See Martin Rubin, "Hero, Antihero, Aheroci: John Huston and the Problematical Protagonist," *Reflections,* 137–156.
27. Jean Vernet, "*Film Noir:* On the Edge of Doom," in *Shades of Noir,* ed. Jean Copjec (London: Verso, 1933), 1–32.
28. Indeed the subtle condemnation and contempt afforded to Vietnam veterans—and the military in general—is even more pointed when the principal female protagonist (Jane Fonda) realizes that, war aside, her career military husband hasn't even been able to give her a decent orgasm.
29. See Kaja Silverman's discussion of this film in *Male Subjectivity at the Margin* (New York: Routledge, 1992).

concerning actual images of the war itself as well as its aftermath were produced—beginning a good seven years and more (to hit the cycle's stride) after the
war.[30] By contrast, not only were World War II films produced, they were highly
propagandized, officially sponsored enterprises, designed to foster support and
enthusiasm for a just and honorable war abroad.

But which trauma does *film noir* address or does it access multiple insults? On
the one hand, there are a paucity of grim depictions of American urban or rural life
during the height of the Depression years themselves. Films of the 1930s, especially the screwball comedies, predominantly highlight the exploits and follies of
the rich as, for example, *Satan* has Shane living amid an array of creature comforts
and Valerie Purvis never wants for money. Similarly, *Dangerous Female* makes no
mention of poverty or want. Yet *The Maltese Falcon* is unabashed in its seedi-
ness—Spade's apartment is cramped, unkempt, unglamorous, merely a place to
flop. Just as American cinema could not "deal" with the realities of the Vietnam
War and predictably applied a highly polished gloss lauding the daring exploits of
aviators in World War I and patriotic soldiers in World War II, so the misery of the
Depression would have hardly served as good, escapist entertainment.

An intriguing question, however, concerns why the times might have been
"ripe" for depictions of men overwhelmed by circumstance, torn by internal
conflict, possessed of a blurred vision, divided by constrained desires, and literally
split into disparate facets of "self" (as for example, the argument could be made in
Huston's *Falcon* that all the male characters serve, at some level, as doubles or
projected concerns of Spade as the principal protagonist, something which might
"explain" the extreme feminization of the Joel Cairo character). Beginning in the
middle and late 1930s (roughly contemporaneous with *The Maltese Falcon* and
recognizable *film noir*) and gaining in momentum by the mid-1940s and on into
the 1950s, more and more Hollywood films were addressing themselves to an
acculturated and adulterated popularization of psychoanalysis as that discipline
became more available to the public, and psychiatry gained in power, prestige, and
status, something Janet Walker catalogues in meticulous detail.[31] Psychiatry offered the promise of cure *and* explanation, a means of delving directly into the
spiritual essence of the self as Krin Gabbard and Glen O. Gabbard note, the word

---

30. On the other hand, Julian Smith makes a compelling argument for cinematic equivalents of Vietnam
imagery encoded by means of denial and displacement—or compromise formation—from the middle 1960s
throughout the 1970s. Smith sees films as diverse as *Major Dundee* (Peckinpah, 1965), *The Wild Bunch*
(Peckinpah, 1969), *Little Big Man* (Penn, 1970), *M*A*S*H* (Altman, 1970), *Tora! Tora! Tora!* (Fleischer,
1970), and *Slaughterhouse Five* (Hill, 1972) as symbolic equivalents and displacements for American
preoccupations about the war, all the way from overt condemnation (e.g., *Little Big Man*) to lauding the
virtues of American military preparedness (*Tora! Tora! Tora!*). Some of Smith's arguments stretch the
point; however, far from detracting from my hypothesis that American culture fosters a cinema of denial
(specifically referencing tremendous national traumas), Smith's acute observations lend credence to this
idea. See Julian Smith, *Looking Away: Hollywood and Vietnam* (New York: Scribner's, 1975).
31. Janet Walker, *Couching Resistance: Women, Film, and Psychoanalytic Psychiatry* (Minneapolis:
University of Minnesota Press, 1993), cf. specifically 1–22.

psychiatrist translates into "doctor of the soul." "The growth of psychiatry following World War II was partly related to its ability to explain behavior, such as malingering among soldiers, in a psychodynamic manner. Hence, what was previously condemned as immoral or evil behavior was now understood as psychopathological."[32]

Certainly, an explanation resting upon internal dynamics rather than external concerns was incorporated into film representations of men in *noir* cinema (cf. *Gilda* [Vidor, 1946]) that were earlier primarily relegated to the return of the repressed in the horror and "fantastic" cinema (as in *Frankenstein* [Whale, 1931]), film genres with stylistic and thematic compatibilities with *noir*.[33] This even allows us to make sense of Huston's allusion to dreams in *Falcon,* something not in the original novel, where Spade recognizes that his dreams and fantasies have encroached upon his waking life. The message is clear: *Falcon* has been a journey of self-discovery and exorcism, a way of avoiding repetition just as psycho-analysis's claims are to expose the traumas of the past and obliterate the compul-sive need to repeat. Suddenly Spade's vision is true and clear, his soul seized by a moral, authoritarian imperative he doesn't exactly understand. Confronted with the counterfeit bird—and it's all been just a dream—he now penetrates the enigma of the counterfeit woman and pieces together the riddle of Archer's death. His demon has assumed material form and may now safely be locked away in a literal descent back to the unconscious as Brigid is caged and lowered out of sight and Spade trudges down the stairs, Falcon in hand.

In similar fashion, Walker notes that psychiatry and psychoanalysis paid in-creasing attention to penetrating the female enigma, the dark, fathomless, un-discovered country Freud found so difficult to comprehend or "see," as more therapeutics, explanations, and investigatory modalities shifted from the war-neuroses to the inner conflicts of women—from the healing of men to the need to contain their troubled and troubling women. The ideological mindset of much of Hollywood (and popular American) psychoanalysis of the 1940s and 1950s strove to help the troubled woman make the necessary "adjustments" and discover fulfillment within the institutional hierarchies of marriage, with psychoanalysis itself critiquing "the neurotogenic properties of marriage as well as enforcing the institution."[34] My point here—and it is Walker's as well—is that troubled and divided *women* are entrusted to the care of the good psychiatrist who will curb women's deviant desires (or die trying, as in *Cat People* [Tournier, 1942]), unite their disparate selves, and deliver women back to patriarchy. On those few occasions where the psychiatrist is evil (as in the malevolent hypnotist of *Whirl-pool* [Preminger, 1949]), the woman is still rescued and recuperated into mar-

32. Krin Gabbard and Glen O. Gabbard, *Psychiatry and the Cinema* (Chicago: University of Chicago Press, 1987), 165–166.

33. Cf. Robin Wood, "Return of the Repressed," *Film Comment* 14, No. 4(1978), 25–32.

34. Walker, *Couching Resistance,* 55.

riage—in the case of Gene Tierney in *Whirlpool* by her psychiatrist husband, a "plot device that often enables psychiatry to collude with traditional marriage."[35]

In marked contradistinction to women who are shepherded and healed by men, the male antiheroes of *film noir,* while just as internally divided and conflicted as their female counterparts, are provoked by their women and then rampage unchecked, usually with fatal consequences. These men's obsessions and conflicts characteristically revolve around infatuations and dalliances with dangerous women who pose a threat to their putative phallic authority while, at the same time, serving as their nightmarish doppelgangers. These men can not "deliver" themselves into the care either of other men (as this might be too blatantly homoerotic, given the contemporaneous patriarchal thrust of the psychiatrically informed films) *or* women (with only rare exceptions, and the women analysts must *pro forma* fall in love with their male patients in order to help them). Thus these men's conflicts become exteriorized, projected, external and *active* into a paranoid universe demonstrably similar to the paranoid and darkly *noir*—yet *passive*—perspectives of the "troubled woman" film.

Could it be that this inculcation of psychoanalytic thought, along with the conflation of other variables—among them those which Vernet highlights as well as a delayed reaction to the social trauma and upheaval of the Depression and the growing paranoia and concern over events in Europe in the early 1940s[36]—found their cinematic equivalents in *film noir*-ish depictions of psychologically divided and tormented men, men whose sight of the darkly elusive woman is increasingly compromised and uncertain? The conditions existing in the United States in the early 1940s might have been ripe for a more extended and extensive investigation of unconscious motivations, doubts, and vagaries, if only because demands were being made upon the populace both internally and externally. But more important of all, the *language* of psychiatry and psychoanalysis now existed where it never had before in more popularized, authoritative, and institutional modalities. Suddenly there were answers begging for questions.

All these suggestions are necessarily speculative and conjectural—and probably just as open to the crush of a random beam as others before them—yet they are hypotheses worthy of our consideration. And perhaps there is a certain poetry to the fact that a film genre cycle so elusive, ill-defined, and contested as *film noir,* a Flitcraftian device developed around and accommodating to any number of falling beams, a "collector's idea that, for the moment, can only be found in books,"[37] should claim as its father a film manifestly concerned in the search for the stuff dreams are made of.

---

35. Ibid., 53.
36. Note, for example, that the "foreign" quality of Gutman and Cairo is all the more pointed in Huston's *Falcon* than in either of the two previous films, particularly since it is clear that Cairo is German and Gutman is decidedly English (an allusion to varying bids and claims for American loyalty?).
37. Vernet, *"Film Noir,"* 26.

Filmography and Bibliography

Huston Filmography, 1931–1987

This filmography includes films both directed and written by Huston. All entries include production, screenplay, and source information as well as the initial release date. For those films written but not directed by Huston, the director's name is given. For more detailed information on these films, as well as Huston's acting, narrational, and television work, see *Reflections in a Male Eye: John Huston and the American Experience,* edited by Gaylyn Studlar and David Desser (Washington, D.C.: Smithsonian Institution Press, 1993), 279–306.

Films Directed by John Huston

1941   *The Maltese Falcon*
Production: Warner Brothers
Script: John Huston, from the novel by Dashiell Hammett

1942   *In This Our Life*
Production: Warner Brothers
Script: Howard Koch (and John Huston, uncredited), from the novel by Ellen Glasgow

1942   *Across the Pacific*
Production: Warner Brothers
Script: Richard Macaulay, from the *Saturday Evening Post* serial, "Aloha Means Goodbye," by Robert Carson

1943   *Report from the Aleutians*
(documentary)
Production: Army Pictorial Service,
Signal Corps, U.S. War Department
Script: John Huston

1945   *(The Battle of) San Pietro*
(documentary)
Production: Army Pictorial Service,
Signal Corps, U.S. War Department
Script: John Huston

1946   *Let There Be Light* (documentary)
Production: Army Pictorial Service,
Signal Corps, U.S. War Department
Script: Charles Kaufman, John Huston

1948   *The Treasure of the Sierra Madre*
Production: Warner Brothers
Script: John Huston, from the novel by B. Traven

1948   *Key Largo*
Production: Warner Brothers
Script: John Huston and Richard

Brooks, from the play by Maxwell Anderson

1949   *We Were Strangers*
Production: a Horizon Production released by Columbia Pictures
Script: John Huston, Peter Viertel, from a segment in *Rough Sketch,* by Robert Sylvester

1950   *The Asphalt Jungle*
Production: Metro-Goldwyn-Mayer
Script: John Huston and Ben Maddow, from the novel by W. R. Burnett

1951   *The Red Badge of Courage*
Production: Metro-Goldwyn-Mayer
Script: John Huston, from the novel by Stephen Crane

1951   *The African Queen*
Production: Horizon-Romulus in association with S. P. Eagle for United Artists release
Script: John Huston and James Agee, from the novel by C. S. Forester; additional dialogue by Peter Viertel

1952   *Moulin Rouge*
Production: a Romulus Production for United Artists release
Script: Anthony Veiller, John Huston, from the book by Pierre de La Mure

1954   *Beat the Devil*
Production: a Romulus-Santana Production for United Artists release
Script: John Huston, Truman Capote, from the novel by James Helvick; Anthony Veiller, Peter Viertel (uncredited)

1956   *Moby Dick*
Production: a Moulin Picture released by Warner Brothers
Script: John Huston, Ray Bradbury, from the novel by Herman Melville

1957   *Heaven Knows, Mr. Allison*
Production: Twentieth Century–Fox Film Corp.
Script: John Huston, John Lee Mahin, from the novel by Charles Shaw

1958   *The Barbarian and the Geisha*
Production: Twentieth Century–Fox Film Corp.
Script: Charles Grayson, from a story by Ellis St. Joseph

1958   *The Roots of Heaven*
Production: Twentieth Century–Fox Film Corp.
Script: Romain Gary, Patrick Leigh-Fermor, from the novel by Romain Gary

1960   *The Unforgiven*
Production: Continental Hecht/Hill/Lancaster; released by United Artists
Script: Ben Maddow, from the novel by Alan LeMay

1961   *The Misfits*
Production: Seven Arts Productions; distributed by United Artists
Script: Arthur Miller, from his novella published in *Esquire* in 1957

1962   *Freud (The Secret Passion)*
Production: a John Huston Production for Universal International Pictures
Script: Wolfgang Reinhardt, Charles Kaufman

1963   *The List of Adrian Messenger*
Production: Universal Pictures;
distributed by Joel
Productions–Universal Pictures
Script: Anthony Veiller, from the
novel by Phillip MacDonald

1964   *The Night of the Iguana*
Production: a John Huston-Ray
Stark Production for Seven Arts;
released through Metro-Goldwyn-
Mayer
Script: John Huston, Anthony
Veiller, from the play by Tennessee
Williams

1966   *The Bible . . . In the Beginning*
Production: De Laurentiis
Cinematografica; distributed by
Twentieth Century–Fox Film Corp.,
Seven Arts Pictures
Script: Christopher Fry

1967   *Casino Royale*
Production: Famous Artists
Productions; a Columbia Pictures
release
Directors: John Huston, Ken
Hughes, Val Guest, Robert Parrish,
Joseph McGrath
Script: Wolf Mankowitz, John Law,
Michael Sayers, suggested by the
novel by Ian Fleming; additional
writing by Billy Wilder, Ben Hecht,
John Huston, Val Guest, Joseph
Heller, Terry Southern

1967   *Reflections in a Golden Eye*
Production: John Huston-Ray Stark
Production; a Warner Brothers–
Seven Arts International release
Script: Chapman Mortimer, Gladys
Hill, based on the novel by Carson
McCullers

1969   *Sinful Davey*
Production: John Huston-Walter
Mirisch Production; distributed by
United Artists
Script: James R. Webb, based on
the book *The Life of David
Haggart,* by David Haggart

1969   *A Walk with Love and Death*
Production: a John Huston-Carter
DeHaven III Production; Twentieth
Century–Fox Film Corp.
Script: Dale Wasserman; adapted
by Hans Konigsberger from his
novel

1970   *The Kremlin Letter*
Production: a John Huston-Carter
De Haven III Production; Twentieth
Century–Fox Film Corp.
Script: John Huston, Gladys Hill,
from the novel by Noel Behn

1972   *Fat City*
Production: a John Huston-Rastar
Production; Columbia Pictures
release
Script: Leonard Gardner, from his
novel

1972   *The Life and Times of Judge
Roy Bean*
Production: National General
Script: John Milius

1973   *The Mackintosh Man*
Production: Warner Brothers
Script: Walter Hill, from *The
Freedom Trap,* by Desmond Bagley

1975   *The Man Who Would Be King*
Production: Associated Artists;
released by Columbia Pictures
Script: Gladys Hill, John Huston,
from the story by Rudyard Kipling

1976 *Independence*
Production: National Park Service
and Twentieth Century–Fox
Script: Joyce Ritter, Lloyd Ritter,
Thomas McGrath

1979 *Wiseblood*
Production: Ithaca-Anthea; released
through New Line Cinema
Script: Benedict Fitzgerald, from
the novel by Flannery O'Connor

1980 *Phobia*
Production: Spiegel-Bergman Films
Script: Ronald Shusett, Gary
Sherman, Lew Lehman, James
Sangster, Peter Bellwood

1981 *Victory*
Production: Lorimar; a Paramount
release
Script: Evan Jones, Yabo Yablonsky,
from a story by Yablonsky, Djordje
Milicevic, Jeff Macquire

1982 *Annie*
Production: Rastar; a Columbia
Pictures release
Script: Carol Sobieski, from the
stage play by Thomas Meehan,
based on the comic strip created by
Harold Gray

1984 *Under the Volcano*
Production: Ithaca-Conacine; a
Universal release
Script: Guy Gallo, based on the
novel by Malcolm Lowry

1985 *Prizzi's Honor*
Production: an ABC Motion
Pictures Presentation; released by
Twentieth Century–Fox Film Corp.
Script: Richard Condon, Janet
Roach, based on the novel by
Richard Condon

1987 *The Dead*
Production: Liffey Films; released
by Vestron Pictures
Script: Tony Huston, based on the
short story from *Dubliners,* by
James Joyce

Films Written but Not Directed by Huston

1931 *A House Divided*
Production: Universal
Director: William Wyler
Script: John B. Clymer and Dale
Van Every, from the novel *Hearts
and Hands,* by Olive Edens;
additional dialogue by John Huston

1932 *Murders in the Rue Morgue*
Production: Universal
Director: Robert Florey
Script: Robert Florey, Tom Reed,
and Dale Van Every, from the short
story by Edgar Allan Poe;
additional dialogue by John Huston

1932 *Law and Order*
Production: Universal
Director: Edward L. Cahn
Script: Tom Reed, from the novel
Saint Johnson, by W. R. Burnett;
additional dialogue by John Huston

1938 *Jezebel*
Production: Warner Brothers
Director: William Wyler
Script: Clements Ripley, Abem
Finkel, and John Huston, from the
play by Owen Davis

1938 *The Amazing Dr. Clitterhouse*
Production: Warner Brothers
Director: Anatole Litvak
Script: John Huston and John

Wexley, from the play by Barre
Lyndon

1939 *Juarez*
Production: Warner Brothers
Director: William Dieterle
Script: John Huston, Wolfgang
Reinhardt, Aeneas Mackenzie,
based on *Maxmilian and Carlotta,*
by Franz Werfel, and *The Phantom
Crown,* by Bertita Harding

1940 *Dr. Ehrlich's Magic Bullet*
Production: Warner Brothers
Director: William Dieterle
Script: John Huston, Heinz Herald,
Norman Burnside, from an idea by
Burnside, developed from letters
and notes held by Mrs. Ehrlich

1941 *High Sierra*
Production: Warner Brothers
Director: Raoul Walsh
Script: John Huston and W. R.
Burnett, from the novel by Burnett

1941 *Sergeant York*
Production: Warner Brothers
Director: Howard Hawks

Script: Abem Finkel, Harry
Chandler, John Huston, and Howard
Koch, from *War Diary of Sergeant
York* by Sam K. Cowan; *Sergeant
York and His People,* by Sam K.
Cowan; *Sergeant York: Last of the
Long Hunters,* by Tom Skeyhill

1946 *The Killers*
Production: Universal
Director: Robert Siodmak
Script: Anthony Veiller and John
Huston (Huston was not credited)

1946 *The Stranger*
Production: RKO, International
Pictures
Director: Orson Welles
Script: Anthony Veiller, from a
story by Victor Trivas and Decla
Dunning; John Huston and Orson
Welles (uncredited)

1946 *Three Strangers*
Production: Warner Brothers
Director: Jean Negulesco
Script: John Huston, Howard Koch,
from a 1936 story by Huston

Selected Bibliography

Abramson, Leslie H. "Two Birds of a Feather: Hammett's and Huston's *The Maltese Falcon.*" *Literature/Film Quarterly* 16 (1988), 112–118.

Agee, James. "Undirectable Director." *Life,* September 18, 1950. In this volume.

Anobile, Richard J., *The Maltese Falcon.* New York: Universe Books, 1974.

Archer, Eugene. "John Huston—The Hemingway Tradition in American Film." *Film Culture* 19 (1959): 66–101.

Bachmann, Gideon. "How I Make Films." (An interview with John Huston.) *Film Quarterly* (Fall 1965), 3–13.

———. "Watching Huston." *Film Comment* (January-February 1976), 21–22.

Behlmer, Rudy. "'The Stuff That Dreams Are Made Of': *The Maltese Falcon.*" In *Behind the Scenes: The Making of . . .* Hollywood: Samuel French Trade. Also in *America's Favorite Movies: Behind the Scenes.* New York: Frederick Unger Publishing Company, 1982. In this volume.

Benayoun, Robert. *John Huston.* Paris: Editions Seghers, 1966.

Bick, Ilsa J. "The Beam That Fell And Other Crises in *The Maltese Falcon.*" In this volume.

Bourget, Jean-Loup (writing as Jacques Segond). "On the Trail of Dashiell Hammett (The Three Versions of *The Maltese Falcon*)." Trans. Connor Hartnett. *Positif* 171–172 (1975), 13–18. In this volume.

Buache, Freddy. "John Huston." *Premier Plan* (June 1966), 5–30.

Frank, Nino. "A New Kind of Detective Story." Trans. Connor Hartnett. *L'Écrán Français,* no. 61 (August 28, 1946), 8–9, 14. In this volume.

Goode, James. *The Making of the "The Misfits."* New York: Bobbs-Merrill, 1963.

Gow, Gordon. "Pursuit of the Falcon." *Films and Filming* 20 (March 1974), 56–58.

Greenberg, Harvey Roy. *Screen Memories: Hollywood Cinema on the Psychoanalytic Couch.* New York: Columbia University Press, 1993.

Grobel, Lawrence. *The Hustons*. New York: Charles Scribner's Sons, 1989.

Hammen, Scott. *John Huston*. Boston: Twayne, 1985.

Hammett, Dashiell. *The Maltese Falcon*. New York: Knopf, 1930.

Huston, John. *An Open Book*. New York: Knopf, 1980.

John Huston. [Washington, D.C.: American Film Institute], 1983.

Kaminsky, Stuart. *John Huston: Maker of Magic*. Boston: Houghton Mifflin, 1978.

Krutnik, Frank. *In a Lonely Street: Film Noir, Genre, Masculinity*. London and New York: Routledge, 1991.

Luhr, William. "Tracking *The Maltese Falcon:* Classical Hollywood Narration and Sam Spade." In *Close Viewings: Understanding Films,* ed. Peter Lehman. Gainesville: University Press of Florida, 1990. In this volume.

McCarthy, John. *The Films of John Huston*. Secaucus, N.J.: Citadel, 1987.

Madson, Axel. *John Huston*. Garden City, N.Y.: Doubleday., 1978.

Naremore, James. "John Huston and *The Maltese Falcon*" *Literature/Film Quarterly* 1, no. 3 (1973), 239–249. In this volume.

Nolan, William F. *John Huston: King Rebel*. Los Angeles: Sherbourne Press, 1965.

Phillips, Gene D. "Talking with John Huston." *Film Comment* (May 1973), 15–19.

Pratley, Gerald. *The Cinema of John Huston*. South Brunswick, N.J.: A. S. Barnes, 1977.

Ross, Lillian. *Picture*. New York: Rinehart & Co., 1952.

Sklar, Robert. *City Boys: Cagney, Bogart, Garfield*. Princeton, N.J.: Princeton University Press, 1992.

Studlar, Gaylyn and David Desser, eds. *Reflections in a Male Eye: John Huston and the American Experience*. Washington, D.C.: Smithsonian Institution Press, 1993.

Tomasulo, Frank. "The Maltese Phallcon: The Oedipal Trajectory of Classical Hollywood Cinema." Paper delivered at the 1993 Florida State University Film and Literature Conference.

Viertel, Peter. *White Hunter, Black Heart*. Garden City, N.Y.: Doubleday, 1953.

———. *Dangerous Friends: At Large with Hemingway and Huston in the Fifties*. Garden City, N.Y.: Doubleday, 1992.

Wexman, Virginia Wright. *Creating the Couple: Love, Marriage, and Hollywood Performance*. Princeton, N.J.: Princeton University Press, 1993.

DUE DATE

	201-6503		Printed in USA